NEUE BRITISCHE ARCHITEKTUR IN DEUTSCHLAND
NEW BRITISH ARCHITECTURE IN GERMANY

**NEUE BRITISCHE ARCHITEKTUR
IN DEUTSCHLAND
NEW BRITISH ARCHITECTURE
IN GERMANY**

MICHAEL JENNER

Prestel   Munich · London · New York

© 2000 Prestel Verlag,
München · London · New York

Umschlagbild vorne:
Photonikzentrum, Berlin,
von Sauerbruch Hutton Architekten, Berlin
(Bitter + Bredt Fotografie, siehe Seite 90)
Abbildung auf der Banderole:
Britische Botschaft, Berlin,
von Michael Wilford and Partners, London
(Peter Cook)

Die Abbildungsvorlagen für die vorgestellten
Projekte wurden dem Verlag von den jeweili-
gen Autoren bzw. Architekten zur Verfügung
gestellt. Angaben dazu siehe im Abbildungs-
nachweis auf Seite 160. Die Namen der
Urheberrechtsinhaber wurden dem Verlag von
den Architekten genannt. Für etwaige
Ungenauigkeiten können weder die Britische
Botschaft in Berlin noch der Prestel Verlag die
Verantwortung übernehmen.

Die Deutsche Bibliothek –
CIP-Einheitsaufnahme

Jenner, Michael:
Neue Britische Architektur in Deutschland =
New British architecture in Germany / Michael
Jenner. – München : Prestel, 2000
 ISBN 3-7913-2297-4

Prestel Verlag
Mandlstraße 26
D-80802 München
Telefon: (089) 381709-0
Fax: (089) 381709-35

Lektorat:
Elisabeth Rochau
Übersetzung aus dem Englischen:
Christiane Court
Gestaltung und Satz:
Thomas Manss und Caterina Krumrey
Herstellung:
Maja Kluy, Berlin
Reproduktionen:
LVD, Berlin
Druck und Bindung:
Westermann Druck, Zwickau
Gedruckt auf chlorfrei gebleichtem Papier

Printed in Germany

ISBN 3-7913-2297-4

© Copyright 2000 Prestel Verlag,
Munich · London · New York

Jacket image:
Photonics Centre, Berlin,
Sauerbruch Hutton Architekten, Berlin
(Bitter + Bredt Fotografie) (see p. 90)
Bellyband image:
The British Embassy, Berlin,
Michael Wilford and Partners, London
(Peter Cook)

All projects illustrations have been made
available to the publisher by the respective
authors and architects. Names of copyright
holders of the project material used have
been supplied by the architects themselves.
Neither the British Embassy, Berlin nor
Prestel Verlag shall be held responsible for
any omissions or inaccuracies. Photographic
acknowledgements can be found in the list
of picture credits on page 160.

Library of Congress
Card Number: 99-069136

Prestel
4 Bloomsbury Place
London
WC1A 2QA
Tel.: (020) 7323 5004
Fax: (020) 7636 8004

175 Fifth Avenue
New York
NY 10010
Tel.: (212) 627-9090
Fax: (212) 627-9511

Prestel books are available worldwide. Please
contact your nearest bookseller or any of the
above addresses for information concerning
your local distributor.

Editorial direction by
Philippa Hurd
Translation from German by
John W. Gabriel
Designed and typeset by
Thomas Manss and Caterina Krumrey
Production by
Maja Kluy, Berlin
Colour separations by
LDV, Berlin
Printed and bound by
Westermann Druck, Zwickau

Printed in Germany on acid-free paper

ISBN: 3-7913-2297-4

INHALT
CONTENTS

Regierung und Kultur
Government and Culture

Haus und Wohnen
Housing

Industrie
Industry

Handel und Verwaltung
Commerce and Administration

8 **VORWORT DES AUTORS**
FOREWORD
Michael Jenner

9 **VORWORT**
PREFACE
Meinhard von Gerkan

10 **EINE LANGE TRADITION**
A LONG TRADITION
Michael Jenner

32 **DER REICHSTAG – NEUER DEUTSCHER BUNDESTAG**
THE REICHSTAG – NEW GERMAN PARLIAMENT
Foster and Partners
Berlin

42 **STAATSGALERIE STUTTGART**
STAATSGALERIE STUTTGART
James Stirling, Michael Wilford and Associates
Stuttgart

48 **MUSIKHOCHSCHULE**
MUSIC SCHOOL
James Stirling, Michael Wilford and Associates
Stuttgart

52 **LANDESGARTENSCHAU**
REGIONAL GARDEN SHOW
Zaha M. Hadid with Schumacher, Mayer, Bährle
Weil am Rhein

58 **WISSENSCHAFTSZENTRUM FÜR SOZIALFORSCHUNG**
SOCIAL SCIENCE RESEARCH CENTRE
James Stirling, Michael Wilford and Associates
Berlin

64 **STAATSARCHIV**
STATE ARCHIVES
Alsop & Störmer
Hamburg

68 **BRITISCHE BOTSCHAFT**
BRITISH EMBASSY
Michael Wilford and Partners
Berlin

76 **WOHNUNGEN DAIMLER CHRYSLER POTSDAMER PLATZ**
DAIMLER CHRYSLER APARTMENTS, POTSDAMER PLATZ
Richard Rogers Partnership
Berlin

82 **WOHNHAUS**
PRIVATE HOUSE
Foster and Partners

86 **WOHNHAUS**
PRIVATE HOUSE
David Chipperfield Architects

90 **PHOTONIKZENTRUM**
PHOTONICS CENTRE
Sauerbruch Hutton Architects
Berlin

96 **BRAUN ZENTRALE**
BRAUN HEADQUARTERS
James Stirling, Michael Wilford and Associates in association with Walter Nägeli
Melsungen

100 **MABEG ZENTRALE**
MABEG HEADQUARTERS
Nicholas Grimshaw & Partners
Soest

104 **VITRA FEUERWACHE**
VITRA FIRE STATION
Zaha M. Hadid
Weil am Rhein

110 **STO ZENTRALE**
STO HEADQUARTERS
Michael Wilford and Partners
Weizen

114 **VITRA MÖBELFABRIK**
VITRA FURNITURE FACTORY
Nicholas Grimshaw & Partners
Weil am Rhein

118 **KREUZFAHRTTERMINAL UND BÜRO-CENTER FISCHEREIHAFEN**
CRUISESHIP TERMINAL AND OFFICES, HAMBURG HARBOUR
Alsop & Störmer
Hamburg

122 **LUDWIG-ERHARD-HAUS**
LUDWIG ERHARD HOUSE
Nicholas Grimshaw & Partners
Berlin

130 **KAISTRASSE**
KAISTRASSE
David Chipperfield Architects
Düsseldorf

134 **BÜROGEBÄUDE DAIMLER CHRYSLER POTSDAMER PLATZ**
DAIMLER CHRYSLER OFFICES, POTSDAMER PLATZ
Richard Rogers Partnership
Berlin

140 **COMMERZBANK**
COMMERZBANK
Foster and Partners
Frankfurt

146 **GLASHALLE NEUE LEIPZIGER MESSE**
GLASS HALL, NEW LEIPZIG TRADE FAIR
Architects von Gerkan, Marg und Partner in cooperation with Ian Ritchie Architects
Leipzig

152 **GSW HAUPTVERWALTUNG**
GSW HEADQUARTERS
Sauerbruch Hutton Architects
Berlin

156 **AGIPLAN ZENTRALSTELLE**
AGIPLAN HEADQUARTERS
Foster and Partners
Mühlheim

160 **ABBILDUNGSNACHWEIS**
PHOTOGRAPHIC ACKNOWLEDGEMENTS

VORWORT DES AUTORS
PREFACE

Die Anregung zu diesem Buch ist der Britischen Botschaft in Bonn (jetzt Berlin) zu verdanken, die sich vergeblich bemüht hatte, ein fundiertes Werk zum Thema ›Britische Architektur in Deutschland‹ aufzutun. Unterstützt von der Botschaft machte ich mich daran, herauszufinden, ob genügend Material vorhanden war, um ein solches Buch zu rechtfertigen. Ich stellte sehr schnell fest, daß es daran keinen Zweifel geben konnte und machte mich ernsthaft an die Arbeit. In der Folge wurde eine Studienreise geplant, die viele der wichtigsten, neuen britischen Bauten in Deutschland, darunter die damals im Bau befindliche Britische Botschaft, umfaßte. Zwischenzeitlich hatten die beteiligten britischen Architekten ihre volle Unterstützung zugesagt und stellten Pläne und Zeichnungen sowie ausgewähltes Bildmaterial ihrer eigenen Fotografen zur Verfügung, denen unser besonderer Dank gilt. Aber es fehlte noch Einiges, ehe aus der Idee Wirklichkeit werden konnte. Das Projekt kam entscheidend voran, als der namhafte Designer Thomas Manss bereitwillig seine Mitarbeit zusagte. Ihm und seiner Kollegin Caterina Krumrey hat die vorliegende Publikation viel zu verdanken. Als schließlich der Prestel Verlag diesen Titel in sein renommiertes Architekturprogramm aufnahm, war die letzte Hürde genommen. Mein Dank gilt Urban Meister bei Prestel in München und Philippa Hurd im Büro von Prestel in London für das persönliche Engagement, mit der sie die Arbeit begleiteten und zu einem erfolgreichen Abschluß führten. Besonderer Dank gilt dem herausragenden deutschen Architekten Meinhard von Gerkan, der freundlicherweise das Vorwort beigesteuert hat. Abschließend sollte erwähnt werden, daß die in diesem Buch vorgestellten Bauten dem engagierten Einsatz und fachlichen Können zahlreicher englischer wie deutscher Architekten, Ingenieure und technischer Berater zu verdanken sind, die leider aufgrund ihrer großen Zahl nicht einzeln genannt werden können.

Michael Jenner, London, Juli 2000

The inspiration for this book came out of an idea from the British Embassy in Bonn (now Berlin), who had looked for and failed to find a substantial work on British architecture in Germany. With the Embassy's encouragement I embarked on finding out whether there was sufficient material to justify such a book. I very soon discovered this was indeed the case and so I pursued the idea in earnest. Subsequently, a study trip taking in many of the most prominent of the new British buildings in Germany, including the new British Embassy, then under construction, was arranged. Meanwhile, the British architects involved pledged full co-operation with the supply of plans and drawings as well as selected images by their own photographers, to whom special thanks are also due. But there were still some elements missing in order to turn idea into reality. It was a great step forward when the noted designer Thomas Manss readily agreed to apply his skills to the project. The present publication owes much to him and to his colleague Caterina Krumrey. The final piece fell into place when Prestel Publishing accepted this title on their highly regarded architecture list. I would like to express my gratitude to Urban Meister of Prestel in Munich and Philippa Hurd from the new Prestel office in London for their personal commitment in seeing things through to a successful conclusion. A special word of thanks goes to the distinguished German architect Meinhard von Gerkan, who kindly agreed to contribute the Foreword. Finally, it should be noted that the buildings featured in this book owe much to the dedicated professionalism of a host of architects, engineers and technical consultants in both Britain and Germany who are too numerous to mention individually.

Michael Jenner, London, July 2000

VORWORT
FOREWORD

Meinhard von Gerkan

Unter den vielen, teils hervorragenden ausländischen Architekten, die in Deutschland schon seit eh und je – also weit vor Einführung der Europanormen – etliche ihrer Hauptwerke realisieren konnten – man denke an Alvar Aalto, Arne Jacobsen, Hans Hollein, Gustav Peichl oder Ernst Gisel – dominieren in den letzten Jahren die Briten. Die geringere sprachliche Barriere gegenüber allen anderen europäischen Sprachen, die der Tatsache zu danken ist, daß Englisch zur Weltsprache avanciert und selbst im Umgang mit Spaniern, Holländern oder Dänen als Verständigungsebene dient, mag einer der Gründe sein, aber gewiß nicht der ausschlaggebende.

Ich meine vielmehr, daß hier eine sehr ausgeprägte Affinität in der deutschen Mentalität gegenüber allem Britischen zu sehen ist. Wenn ich mich selbst frage, warum ich seit Jahrzehnten britische Autos fahre, stoße ich auf Erkenntnisse, Wahrnehmungen und Gefühle, die auch der britischen Architektur und den britischen Architekten entgegenkommen. Es ist eine im höchsten Grade sympathische Symbiose aus Distinguiertheit, Coolness und Ironie, Kleverness und Irrationalität, Pragmatismus und künstlerischem Anspruch, Geschäftstüchtigkeit und entwaffnend freundlicher Verbindlichkeit.

Ich hatte Gelegenheit, jedem der in diesem Buch gefeierten britischen Architekten – bis auf einen – ein oder mehrere Male zu begegnen. Ausnahmslos verfügen alle über eine unverwechselbare und sehr starke persönliche Ausstrahlung, die ein hohes Maß glaubwürdiger Autorität mit offener, herzlicher Freundlichkeit vereint.

Alle in diesem Buch gezeigten Bauten sind von ausdrucksstarkem Charakter. Nicht jede der baulichen Charaktereigenschaften findet meine ungeteilte Sympathie. Ich schätze das Distinguierte und schätze das Ironische, ich bekunde anerkennende Hochachtung vor der konsequenten Stimmigkeit vieler Konzepte und deren gelungener Umsetzung. Gegenüber der einen oder anderen formalen Attitüde oder selbstgefälligen Überstrapazierung regen sich distanzierende Zweifel.

Entscheidend ist jedoch, daß dieses Buch ausschließlich charaktervolle Bauten dokumentiert – und starke Charaktere bieten immer Angriffsflächen – zumal unser heutiges Bauen nach wie vor von einer Überzahl beliebiger und charakterloser Bauten beherrscht wird. In diesem Sinne begrüße ich den aktiven Beitrag britischer Architekten zum Dialog in der Architektur und zur gebauten Umwelt in Deutschland sehr und freue mich, daß dieser Beitrag hier anschaulich und nachvollziehbar wird.

An dieser Stelle drängt sich aber eigentlich auch die Frage nach einem möglichen Buch mit dem Titel ›Neue deutsche Architektur in Großbritannien‹ auf. Aber ein solches Buch würde mit leeren Seiten erscheinen. Denn in der Nachkriegsepoche konnte kein deutscher Architekt auch nur einen einzigen bekannten Bau auf der Insel errichten. Meine persönliche Sicht dieser konträren Sachlage kommt im folgenden Kapitel ›Eine lange Tradition‹ zum Ausdruck. Es bleibt der Wunsch an die Briten, daß sie in Großbritannien auch deutschen Kollegen Gelegenheit geben, ihren architektonischen Charakter zu zeigen.

Among the many, often outstanding, foreign architects who, long before the introduction of the European Union directives, were able to realise major projects in Germany – one thinks of Alvar Aalto, Arne Jacobsen, Hans Hollein, Gustav Peichl or Ernst Gisel – the British have in recent years held a predominant position. The English language poses few problems to the rest of Europe, since English has become the international lingua franca and forms the basis of communication even among Germans and Spaniards, Dutchmen and Danes; this may be one of the reasons for the situation, but it is certainly not the salient one.

In my opinion, what is at work here is a very marked affinity between the German mentality and everything British. When I ask myself why I have been driving British cars for decades, I respond with a series of insights, perceptions and feelings which apply just as well to the country's architecture and architects. They strike me as possessing a highly appealing symbiosis of distinction, coolness and irony, cleverness and irrationality, pragmatism and aesthetic audacity, business acumen and disarmingly friendly sincerity.

I have had the good fortune to personally meet all but one of the British architects represented in this book, some of them several times. All of them, without exception, possess a unique and very strong personal charisma in which a high degree of convincing authority is allied with candid cordiality.

All of the buildings illustrated in this volume are highly expressive in character. Still, I must admit that not every architectural trait they evince finds my undivided approval. Their distinguished and ironic aspects appeal to me, and I greatly admire the logic of many of the concepts and their successful realisation. Doubts only begin to arise in the face of the occasional formalistic gesture or self-indulgent flourish.

Be this as it may, the present volume is devoted solely to buildings of strong character – and strong personalities always invite criticism, especially in a day and age in which arbitrary and characterless structures still dominate the architectural scene. In this regard one can only welcome the active contribution made by British architects to the architectural dialogue and the built environment in Germany, and greet the publication of the present volume and its illustration of the extent and quality of this contribution.

At this juncture one cannot help wondering if a book with the title *New German Architecture in Britain* might be possible. If it were published tomorrow, however, its pages would be empty. Since the last war, to my knowledge, not a single German architect has been able to erect a single significant building in the British Isles. My personal views on this unequal state of affairs are expressed in the following essay, *A Long Tradition*. In conclusion, I would only express the wish that the British might provide the opportunity for their German colleagues also to show their architectural mettle.

EINE LANGE TRADITION
A LONG TRADITION

»Es wird nur einen Reichstag geben. Es wird nur ein Parlament geben, das durch die Wiedervereinigung Deutschlands entstand, durch den Umzug von Bonn nach Berlin. Es ist ein einmaliges Ereignis im Leben.« Dies sind die Worte von Norman Foster in einer weiteren, aufwendigen Fernsehdokumentation über seine Arbeit.[1] In Fosters Erklärung klingt jedoch keine Spur von Triumph an. Statt dessen handelte es sich um die nüchterne Bestätigung der großen Verantwortung, mit der man ihn betraut hatte. Selbst für den weltweit produktivsten Architekten unserer Tage bedeutete der Auftrag zum Umbau des Deutschen Parlaments eine einzigartige, beachtliche Herausforderung. An der symbolischen Bedeutung des Reichstags, dieses kühnen Wahrzeichens in der Berliner Stadtlandschaft, kann es keinen Zweifel geben; er ist ebenso Dreh-und Angelpunkt der demokratischen Hoffnungen für das neue Jahrtausend wie Erinnerung an die dunkelsten Tage einer gar nicht so fernen Vergangenheit.

Ganz unabhängig von sämtlichen Medienkommentaren zu den technischen und künstlerischen Aspekten von Fosters Entwurf, wurde viel über den bemerkenswerten Umstand gesprochen, daß ein britischer Architekt in Deutschland so große Anerkennung findet. Der in London erscheinende Daily Telegraph bemerkte: »Es entbehrt nicht einer gewissen Ironie, daß es sich beim führenden Architekten des wiedervereinigten Deutschland tatsächlich um den aus Manchester stammenden Sir Norman Foster handelt.«[2] Diese Feststellung scheint jedoch einen wichtigen Aspekt des modernen Architekturbetriebes zu übersehen, dessen Weltsicht in hohem Maße internationalistisch ausgerichtet ist.

Die britische Beteiligung an einem derart herausragenden Projekt wie dem Reichstag erscheint schon weit weniger überraschend, wenn man sie im Zusammenhang mit der von Deutschland konsequent betriebenen Umwerbung auswärtiger Architekten sieht. Am deutlichsten tritt dies bei der seit dem Fall der Mauer in Gang gekommenen, dynamischen Wiedergeburt Berlins zutage. Die Neubebauung des früheren Niemandslandes am Potsdamer Platz lud einige der international führenden Architekten dazu ein, der einstigen und künftigen deutschen Hauptstadt ihren Stempel aufzudrücken. José Rafael Moneo aus Spanien, Arata Isozaki aus Japan, Richard Rogers aus England und Renzo Piano aus Italien zählen ebenso wie Christoph Kohlbecker, Hans Kollhoff und Lauber & Wöhr aus Deutschland zur Schar der in Berlin tätigen Architekten. Bei der neuen Metropole Berlin, die im Begriff ist, sich aus der allgemein so bezeichneten größten Baustelle der Welt zu erheben, handelt es sich um ein wahrhaft globales Unterfangen. Fosters Reichstag erscheint auch dann weniger ungewöhnlich, wenn man ihn im Kontext des unglaublich vielfältigen Wirkens betrachtet, das englische Architekten in jüngster Zeit in Deutschland entfalteten. James Stirlings Ende der siebziger Jahre entstandener, spektakulärer, postmoderner Erweiterungsbau der Staatsgalerie Stuttgart hat anscheinend die Schleusen geöffnet. Seither übernahmen praktisch sämtliche anderen großen Namen des englischen Architekturbetriebs in allen Teilen Deutschlands bedeutende Aufträge, und zwar sowohl von privater als auch öffentlicher Seite.

Aber selbst das ist nichts eigentlich Neues. Bereits im neunzehnten Jahrhundert betrachteten zahlreiche britische Architekten Deutschland als natürliches Betätigungsfeld, wo sie ihre fachlichen Kenntnisse zur Anwendung bringen konnten. Tatsächlich ist denkbar, daß schon der ursprüngliche Reichstag von einem englischen Architekten erbaut worden wäre. George Gilbert Scott, Architekt des Außenministeriums in London, und W. Emerson gehörten zu einer Gruppe von Engländern, die zum ersten Reichstagswettbewerb des Jahres 1872 Beiträge einreichten. Edward Godwin wurde mit dem zweiten Preis bedacht, obgleich im letzten Stadium nur deutschsprachigen Architekten die Teilnahme gestattet war.[3]

Scotts Entwurf, mit dem er im Jahre 1855 den Wettbewerb für das Hamburger Rathaus gewonnen hatte, wurde ein ähnliches Schicksal zuteil. Die Umstände ergaben, daß der Plan nicht ausgeführt wurde. Unbeschadet der Tatsache, daß er vom nachfolgenden Wettbewerb ausgeschlossen war, veröffentlichte Scott im Jahre 1876 mehrere Entwürfe, einen davon im neogotischen, einen anderen im Stil der deutschen Renaissance. Scotts Beharrlichkeit läßt sich mit der Ermutigung erklären, die er einem früheren Erfolg in Deutschland verdankte, als er sich nämlich im Jahre 1844 den Auftrag zum Bau der Sankt Nikolaikirche in Hamburg sichern konnte.

Dieser Auftrag stellte einen bedeutenden Meilenstein in Scotts Architektenlaufbahn dar. Um seine Vorstellungen des Projekts verdeutlichen zu können, trat er eine zweimonatige Reise auf den Kontinent an, die ihn durch Belgien nach Deutschland führte. Seine detaillierten Studien des Kölner Doms überzeugten ihn von der einzigartigen Eignung des gotischen Stils für den Kirchenbau. Zu dieser Zeit hielt Scott Deutschland für das Ursprungsland der Gotik – die wahre Heimat der Gotik entdeckte er erst im Jahre 1847 auf einer nachfolgenden Reise nach Frankreich – und machte folglich in seinem Beitrag der Jury gegenüber viel Aufhebens von diesem »Nationalstil«. Später erinnerte er: »Da sie in dem alten Irrtum befangen waren, die Gotik sei ein deutscher Stil, wurden ihre patriotischen Gefühle aufs wunderbarste entfacht.«[4]

George Gilbert Scott, Entwurf, Reichstag, Berlin, 1872.

George Gilbert Scott, design for the Reichstag, Berlin, 1872.

›Die Nikolaikirche in Hamburg‹,
Holzstich, 1864 nach einer
Zeichnung von R. Koch.

The Nikolaikirche in Hamburg,
1864, wood engraving
after a drawing by R. Koch.

'There will only be one Reichstag. There will only be one parliament, which is created through the reunification of Germany, the move from Bonn to Berlin. It is a once-in-a-lifetime event.' These were the words of Norman Foster in yet another lavish TV documentary[1] about his work. But there was nothing remotely triumphalistic about Foster's statement. Rather, it was a sober acknowledgement of the great responsibility with which he had been entrusted. Even for the world's most prolific contemporary architect the commission for the rebuilding of the German Parliament represented a unique and awesome challenge. For no one can doubt the symbolic importance of the Reichstag, a bold landmark on the Berlin skyline and a focal point for the democratic hopes of the new millennium as well as a reminder of the darkest days of the not-so-distant past.

Quite apart from all the media comment about the technical and artistic aspects of Foster's scheme, there has also been much talk concerning the remarkable fact that a British architect had achieved so much success in Germany. A London newspaper, *The Daily Telegraph*,[2] commented: 'The irony is that the leading architect of a reunified Germany is actually a Mancunian: Sir Norman Foster'. That, however, seems to overlook a crucial point about the modern business of architecture, which is essentially internationalist in outlook.

British involvement in such a high-profile project as the Reichstag also looks far less surprising when placed in the context of Germany's consistent policy of courting foreign architects. This is most evident in the case of Berlin's dynamic rebirth since the Wall came down. The redevelopment of Potsdamer Platz on former no-man's-land invited some of the leading international architects to leave their mark on the once and future capital of Germany. The names of José Rafael Moneo from Spain, Arata Isozaki from Japan, Richard Rogers from Britain and Renzo Piano from Italy stand proudly together with those of Christoph Kohlbecker, Hans Kollhoff and Lauber & Wöhr from Germany. The new metropolis of Berlin, emerging from what was popularly billed as the world's largest building site, has been a real global undertaking.

Foster's Reichstag also looks less of an anomaly when seen alongside a phenomenal outpouring of British architectural talent in Germany in recent years. James Stirling's spectacular post-modern extension to the Staatsgalerie in Stuttgart in the late 1970s appears to have opened the floodgates. Since then, virtually all the other big names of British architecture have built prominent commissions both private and public in town and country the length and breadth of Germany.

But even this is not entirely new. In the nineteenth century many British architects regarded Germany as a natural field of operation, where they might expect to deploy their professional skills. In fact, the original Reichstag might just conceivably have been built by a British architect. George Gilbert Scott, architect of the Foreign Office in London, and W. Emerson were among several Britons who submitted designs in the first Reichstag competition of 1872. Edward Godwin was actually awarded second prize, although in the final stage only German-speaking architects were permitted to enter.[3]

A similar fate had befallen Scott's design, which in 1855 won the competition for the Hamburg Town Hall. As it happened, the scheme was not carried out. Then, in 1876, albeit excluded from the subsequent competition, Scott published a couple of designs anyway, one in Gothic Revival and another in German Renaissance style. Scott's persistence may be explained by the encouragement he could draw from an earlier success in Germany, when in 1844 he had secured the commission for the Sankt Nikolaikirche in Hamburg.

This was an important milestone in Scott's architectural career. In order to clarify his ideas for the project, he embarked on a two-month journey to the Continent, which took him via Belgium to Germany. His detailed study of Cologne Cathedral convinced him of the unique qualities of Gothic style for church building. At this time Scott was under the impression that Gothic originated in Germany – he only discovered the true home of Gothic on a subsequent trip to France in 1847 – and as a result he made much of this 'national style' in his submission to the jury. He later recalled: 'As they were labouring under the old error that Gothic was German style, their feelings of patriotism were stirred up in a wonderful manner'.[4]

Scott also thought it appropriate to apologise to the jury for having the temerity as a foreigner to participate even while thanking them for their liberal attitude in allowing other nationalities to compete. Although Scott's design arrived in Hamburg three weeks too late on account of the ice at Cuxhaven and only achieved third place, his ideas found an enthusiastic reception. Soon a powerful Scott bandwagon was rolling that eventually carried the day. Scott's project was begun in 1845 and finally completed in 1882, four years after the death of the architect in 1878. By a sad irony, the Sankt Nikolaikirche, once rated one of the finest Gothic Revival churches in Germany, is now no more

---

Tatsächlich ist denkbar, daß schon der ursprüngliche Reichstag von einem englischen Architekten erbaut worden wäre.

In fact, the original Reichstag might just conceivably have been built by a British architect.

Karl Friedrich Schinkel,
Altes Museum,
Berlin, 1823–29.

Scott hielt es darüber hinaus für angemessen, bei der Jury für seine Kühnheit, sich als Ausländer zu beteiligen, um Verzeihung zu bitten, während er ihr gleichzeitig für ihre liberale Haltung dankte, die anderen Nationalitäten die Teilnahme am Wettbewerb gestattete. Obwohl Scotts Entwurf wegen des Eisgangs bei Cuxhaven erst mit dreiwöchiger Verspätung in Hamburg eintraf und nur den dritten Platz belegte, stießen seine Ideen auf begeisterte Zustimmung. Bald formierte sich eine mächtige Bewegung zugunsten Scotts, die letztlich den Sieg davontrug. Der Bau von Scotts Projekt begann im Jahre 1845 und wurde 1882 vollendet, vier Jahre nach dem Tod des Architekten im Jahre 1878. Die traurige Ironie des Schicksals fügte es, daß von der einst als beste neugotische Kirche Deutschlands gepriesenen Nikolaikirche nach den Bombenangriffen, die Scotts Landsmänner im Zweiten Weltkrieg flogen, heute nurmehr der Turm übrig ist.

In Hamburg überdauerten bleibendere Andenken Englands. Nach dem großen Brand von Hamburg im Jahre 1842 mußte ungefähr ein Drittel der Stadt neu erbaut werden, und der britische Bauingenieur William Lindley war zum raschen Handeln bereit. Seine Anwesenheit vor Ort war nicht gänzlich zufällig, da er damals mit dem Bau der Hamburg-Bergedorfer Eisenbahnstrecke befaßt war. Lindleys Gesamtplan für Hamburg, den er im März 1843, nach rascher Konsultation mit Edwin Chadwick in London, unterbreitete, sah ein vollständig neues Abwassersystem vor. Der Plan, der wegen der damit verbundenen hohen Kosten auf wenig Gegenliebe stieß, wurde schließlich vom Hamburger Senat angenommen und zehn Jahre später fertiggestellt. Als Folge davon steht die Hamburger Innenstadt heute noch auf einem ausgedehnten Netz von Abwasserkanälen britischer Provenienz. Im Anschluß an diese Leistung erdachte Lindley ein neues System der Wasserversorgung für Hamburg. Unterstützt von seinem umtriebigen Assistenten Joseph Gordon, konnte Lindley sein Fachwissen auf dem Gebiet der Stadthygiene in anderen deutschen Städten wie Düsseldorf, Chemnitz, Krefeld und Frankfurt zum Einsatz bringen. Lindleys Ruf in Deutschland gründet sich jedoch vor allem auf Hamburg, wo vor kurzem ihm zu Ehren im Hafen eine Statue errichtet wurde.

Im Hinblick auf Architektur reicht das deutsche Interesse an Großbritannien sogar noch weiter zurück. Die Reise nach England und Schottland, die Karl Friedrich Schinkel, Preußens Geheimer Oberbaurat im Staatsbauamt, im Jahre 1826 unternahm, war ursprünglich von dem Wunsch veranlaßt, in London das damals im Bau befindliche British Museum zu studieren, um festzustellen, welche Lehren für den bevorstehenden Bau des Alten Museums in Berlin daraus zu ziehen wären. In diesem Fall jedoch war die augenfälligste Ähnlichkeit zwischen den beiden Gebäuden, die kolossale, ionische Säulenhalle, vermutlich von Durands veröffentlichter Darstellung eines idealen Museums angeregt.[5] Mit dem angeblichen englischen Einfluß auf Schinkels Friedrich-Werdersche Kirche in Berlin verhält es sich ähnlich. Einigen Reiseführern zufolge entstand diese neogotische Kirche als Reaktion auf Eindrücke, die Schinkel bei seinem Aufenthalt in England gewann. Tatsächlich aber war dieser Entwurf schon einige Jahre zuvor auf Geheiß Friedrich Wilhelms III. von Preußen und des Kronprinzen ausgearbeitet worden. Es überrascht nicht, daß Schinkel selbst einen klassizistischen Tempel mit korinthischen Säulen bevorzugt hätte. Nachdem er aber verpflichtet war, sich der Gotik zu bedienen[6], erfüllte Schinkel das Bauwerk mit seiner eigenen Raumvision. Er hielt es für »zweckmäßig, dem Gebäude mehr den Charakter der englischen Chapels zu geben, worin einige große Verhältnisse wirken und das Ganze sich eng zusammenschließt.«[7] So entstand eine von entschieden klassizistischer Zweckmäßigkeit bestimmte Neogotik. Eine eher durchschnittliche Ausprägung englischer Kirchenarchitektur des neunzehnten Jahrhunderts stellen die anglikanischen Kirchen dar, die in Orten wie Baden-Baden, Dresden und Stuttgart für die dortigen britischen Gemeinden entstanden und die in keinem viktorianischen Vorort von Birmingham oder Manchester auffielen.

Als Deutschlands überragender Architekt, der sich im Zenit seiner Laufbahn befand, war Schinkel der Meinung, es gäbe in rein architektonischer Hinsicht wenig, was er von England lernen könnte. Im großen und ganzen tat er vieles von dem, was er in England sah, als unbedeutend ab. So erhielt beispielsweise Bath eine schlechte Besprechung: »Die Architectur von Bath wird in England sehr gerühmt, ist aber langweilig und ganz in den englischen Kleinlichkeiten.« In London erteilte er der 1819–22 im Greek-Revival-Stil erbauten St. Pancras New Church von William und Henry William Inwood widerstrebend Lob: »Ohne Turm recht schön.«[8] Dieses erstaunliche Bauwerk verfügt über zwei Portalvorbauten mit Karyatiden, die denen des Erechteion nachempfunden sind. Es wird allerdings behauptet, der Grundriß der Kirche habe auf Schinkels nachfolgende Werke einigen Einfluß gehabt.[9]

Auch von der Greek-Revival-Architektur in Edinburgh, dem vielgerühmten »Athen des Nordens«, zeigte sich Schinkel wenig beeindruckt, wenngleich er die Planung von Edinburghs New Town für lobenswert erachtete und »Pracht, Eleganz und Heiterkeit der neuen Straßen« erwähnte. In Glasgow entdeckte er einiges, an dem er Gefallen fand: »Die Architectur der Wohnhäuser ist reiner als in Edinburgh.« Es wäre interessant, Vermutungen darüber anzustellen, was Schinkel von Harvey

Carl-Friedrich Schmid,
Porträt von Karl
Friedrich Schinkel, 1832,
Öl auf Leinwand.

Von Schinkel besucht:
Das ›British Museum‹
von Robert Smirke
London, 1823–47.

Visited by Schinkel:
Robert Smirke's
British Museum,
London, 1823–47.

than a ruined stump as a result of the bombing raids on Hamburg conducted by Scott's compatriots during World War II.

Hamburg has retained more enduring relics of Britain. After the fire of 1842 about a third of the city had to be rebuilt, and the British civil engineer William Lindley sprang swiftly into action. His presence on the spot was not entirely fortuitous since he was then building the Hamburg to Bergedorf railway line. Lindley's masterplan for Hamburg, submitted in March 1843 after rapid consultation with Edwin Chadwick in London, proposed a completely new sanitation system. Overcoming fierce opposition on account of the high cost, the Hamburg Senate accepted Lindley's scheme, which was completed ten years later. As a result, Hamburg's inner city still stands on an extensive network of British-designed sewers. Lindley followed up this achievement by devising a new water-supply system for Hamburg. Later, through his industrious assistant Joseph Gordon, Lindley applied his expertise in urban sanitation in other German cities such as Düsseldorf, Chemnitz, Krefeld and Frankfurt. But Lindley's reputation in Germany is most closely associated with Hamburg where a statue in his honour has recently been erected on the waterfront.

In terms of architecture, Germany's interest in Britain goes back even further. The journey to England and Scotland in 1826 of Karl Friedrich Schinkel, Prussia's Privy Councillor for Public Works, was prompted initially by a desire to study the British Museum in London, then under construction, in order to see what lessons might be learned for his forthcoming project, the Altes Museum in Berlin. In the event, however, the most obvious similarity between the two buildings, namely the colossal Ionic order of the colonnade, was probably inspired by Durand's published scheme for an ideal museum.[5]

It is a similar story with regard to the alleged English influence on Schinkel's Friedrichwerdersche Kirche in Berlin. Some guidebooks claim this Gothic Revival church to be the result of impressions gained by Schinkel during his stay in England. However, the design had actually been elaborated several years earlier at the behest of Friedrich Wilhelm III of Prussia and the Crown Prince. Schinkel's own preference, not surprisingly, was for a neo-classical temple with Corinthian columns. But having been obliged to embrace Gothic,[6] Schinkel infused the building with his own spatial vision. He considered it 'appropriate to give the building the character of English chapels, in which a few dominant relationships create a strongly unified whole'.[7] The finished result is Gothic Revival but with a decidedly neo-classical clarity of purpose. A more run-of-the-mill brand of nineteenth-century English ecclesiastical architecture may be seen in Anglican churches built for the expatriate communities in places such as Baden-Baden, Dresden and Stuttgart that would look entirely at home in a Victorian suburb of Birmingham or Manchester.

As Germany's pre-eminent architect poised in mid-career and at the very height of his powers, Schinkel felt he had little to learn from Britain in a strictly architectural sense. In the main, Schinkel was rather dismissive about much of what he saw in England. Bath, for example, received a poor review: 'The architecture of Bath is very well thought of in England, but is rather boring and wholly in the mean English style'. In London, he noted the neo-Grecian creation of St Pancras New Church by William and Henry William Inwood in 1819–22 with grudging approval: 'Quite good except the tower'.[8] This amazing edifice comes complete with two porches replicating the Erechtheum caryatids. It has been argued, however, that the plan of the church did exert some influence on Schinkel's subsequent work.[9]

Nor was Schinkel over-impressed with some of the Greek Revival in Edinburgh, the much vaunted 'Athens of the North', though he did find merit in the urbanism of Edinburgh's New Town, remarking on 'the magnificence, elegance and airiness of the new streets'. He found things more to his liking in Glasgow: 'The architecture of the ordinary houses is purer than in Edinburgh'. It is interesting to speculate what Schinkel would have thought of St George's Hall in Liverpool by Harvey Lonsdale Elmes, but this outstanding neo-classical temple structure had not yet been built. Elmes, on the other hand, did make a study of German architecture in the course of his 1840 trip to Munich.

In reality, Schinkel used his stay in Britain to carry out an extensive technological fact-finding tour of the country. The new constructional possibilities of iron absorbed his attention. His notebooks show him to be most fascinated by railway stations, market halls, docks, warehouses and factories. Above all, he admired the bridges and aqueducts of the great British engineers. Two of Schinkel's fine panoramic sketches are devoted to Thomas Telford's newly constructed Conway Suspension Bridge and Menai Straits Bridge in north Wales; and he described the latter in glowing terms as 'a wonderful, daring work'.

As for the castellated reconstruction of Windsor Castle, it was 'an impressive sight in the distance', but Schinkel remained unmoved by the interior: 'Details all indifferent, passage with coffering, heavy and irregular'. Windsor Castle, however, along with a variety of English country houses, was to come

Als Deutschlands überragender Architekt, der sich im Zenit seiner Laufbahn befand, war Schinkel der Meinung, es gäbe in rein architektonischer Hinsicht wenig, was er von England lernen könnte.

As Germany's pre-eminent architect poised in mid-career and at the very height of his powers, Schinkel felt he had little to learn from Britain in a strictly architectural sense.

In Nachahmung von Schloß Windsor: Schloß Babelsberg bei Potsdam, Stahlstich, um 1850, von G. Hess nach F. A. Borchel.

Echoes of Windsor: Schloß Babelsberg, Potsdam. Steel engraving, c. 1850, G. Hess after F. A. Borchel.

Lonsdale Elmes' St. George's Hall in Liverpool gehalten hätte, aber dieser hervorragende, einem klassizistischen Tempel nachempfundene Bau entstand erst wenig später. Elmes hingegen befaßte sich, im Zuge seiner 1840 unternommenen Reise nach München, mit deutscher Architektur.

In Wirklichkeit nutzte Schinkel seinen Aufenthalt in England zu einer ausgedehnten Suche nach technischen Errungenschaften. Die neuen konstruktiven Möglichkeiten des Eisens nahmen seine Aufmerksamkeit in Anspruch. Seine Aufzeichnungen verraten, daß ihn Bahnhöfe, Markthallen, Hafenanlagen, Lagerhäuser und Fabriken am meisten faszinierten. Vor allem bewunderte er die Brücken und Aquädukte der berühmten englischen Ingenieure. Auf zwei von Schinkels schönen Panoramaskizzen sind Thomas Telfords neu errichtete Conway Suspension Bridge und Menai Straits Bridge in Nordwales zu sehen; letztere beschreibt er in begeisterten Worten als »ein bewunderungswürdiges, kühnes Werk«.

Was die zinnenbekränzte Rekonstruktion von Windsor Castle anging, so bot sie »in der Ferne einen schönen Anblick«, aber die Innenräume ließen Schinkel unbeeindruckt: »Die Details alle mittelmäßig, Corridore mit Cassetten, schwer und unregelmäßig.« Neben einigen englischen Landhäusern sollte sich jedoch Windsor Castle später als Vorbild für Schloß Babelsberg in Potsdam, das Schinkel für Prinz Wilhelm und Prinzessin Augusta entwarf, Bruder und Schwägerin von Friedrich Wilhelm IV., als nützlich erweisen. Auch als in Potsdam zwischen 1913 und 1917 Schloß Cecilienhof entstand, erfreute sich das englische Mittelalter noch großer Beliebtheit. Es mag erstaunen, daß die Hohenzollern auch nach Ausbruch des Ersten Weltkriegs noch den Landhausstil der englischen Aristokratie nachahmten; allerdings gingen Mode und Politik kaum je Hand in Hand.

Vor dem Hintergrund des kulturellen Kontexts des vorausgehenden Jahrhunderts betrachtet, erscheint dieses Paradoxon weniger überraschend. Entwicklungen im englischen Wohnhausbau wurden vielerorts in Deutschland nachvollzogen. Die Gegenwart von Prinzessin Victoria, älteste Tochter Queen Victorias, am preußischen Hof, bot Gewähr für Bekanntheit und Einfluß englischer Lebensart. Die Arts-and-Crafts-Bewegung wurde aufmerksam verfolgt, und selbst um 1900 fanden die ästhetischen Schriften von John Ruskin und William Morris noch eine interessierte deutsche Leserschaft. Das Interesse an sämtlichen englischen Dingen war um diese Zeit so ausgeprägt, daß die deutsche Botschaft in London mit Hermann Muthesius eigens einen Architekturattaché beschäftigte, dessen besonderer Auftrag darin bestand, Berichte über die jüngsten Neuerungen nach Berlin zu erstatten.[10]

Die Ergebnisse von Muthesius' harter Arbeit können noch heute in Form zweier eindrucksvoller Publikationen bewundert werden: *Die englische Baukunst der Gegenwart* aus dem Jahr 1900 und *Das englische Haus*, erschienen 1904. In diesen großformatigen Bänden entfaltet sich, dank Muthesius' photographischer Begabung, eine einzigartige Dokumentation der englischen Architektur um die Jahrhundertwende. Als Maßstab der Bedeutung, die der englischen Wohnhausarchitektur damals in der deutschsprachigen Welt zukam, ist es erwähnenswert, daß zwei Publikationen ähnlichen Namens schon Jahrzehnte zuvor erschienen waren.[11]

Man sollte jedoch nicht daraus schließen, daß man es hier mit einer Einbahnstraße zu tun hat, auf der Deutschland eifrig die neuesten Moden aus England einführte. Tatsächlich läßt sich im Laufe des achtzehnten Jahrhunderts in England ein beherrschenderer deutscher Einfluß feststellen, in dem Sinn, daß die Könige aus dem Hause Hannover, die in ethnischer, wenn nicht kultureller Hinsicht vollständig deutsch blieben, ihre königliche Schirmherrschaft für zahlreiche bedeutende architektonische, städtische und gärtnerische Projekte einsetzten.

Eine deutsche Prinzessin, Caroline von Ansbach, die durch die Heirat mit George II. zur Königin wurde, trug zur Schaffung der »Serpentine« bei, eines idyllischen Sees im Hyde Park, der, in Einklang mit der zeitgenössischen Vorliebe für künstlich angelegte, pseudo-natürliche Effekte, den gewundenen Lauf eines Flusses nachahmt. Ein verschwiegenes Denkmal am östlichen Ende der Serpentine erinnert an Carolines Beitrag zu diesem berühmten Londoner Park. Zur selben Zeit gewann die Theorie des englischen Landschaftsgartens in Deutschland zunehmend die Oberhand über die konventionelleren Barockgärten, wie sich an den Änderungen an der italienisierenden Anlage des Parks von Wilhelmshöhe in Kassel ablesen läßt. Wohl das bekannteste Beispiel dieses Typus' stellt der Englische Garten in München dar, für dessen Anlage der in Amerika gebürtige Benjamin Thompson verantwortlich zeichnet, der als Minister der bayerischen Regierung unter Kurfürst Karl Theodor angehörte.

Von sämtlichen Hannoveranern hinterließ George IV. sowohl als Prinzregent wie als König in England das dauerhafteste Vermächtnis. Sein visionärer Weitblick ermöglichte John Nash, im Londoner Westend die Elemente eines »Grand Design« umzusetzen. Nashs an den Regents Park angrenzende, palastartige Häuserzeilen bieten noch heute einen prächtigen Anblick. Vom partnerschaftlichen Zusammenwirken George IV. und John Nashs zeugt darüber hinaus die stilistische Extravaganz des Royal Pavilion in Brighton, einem Bauwerk, das sogar Schinkel Bewunderung abnötigte.

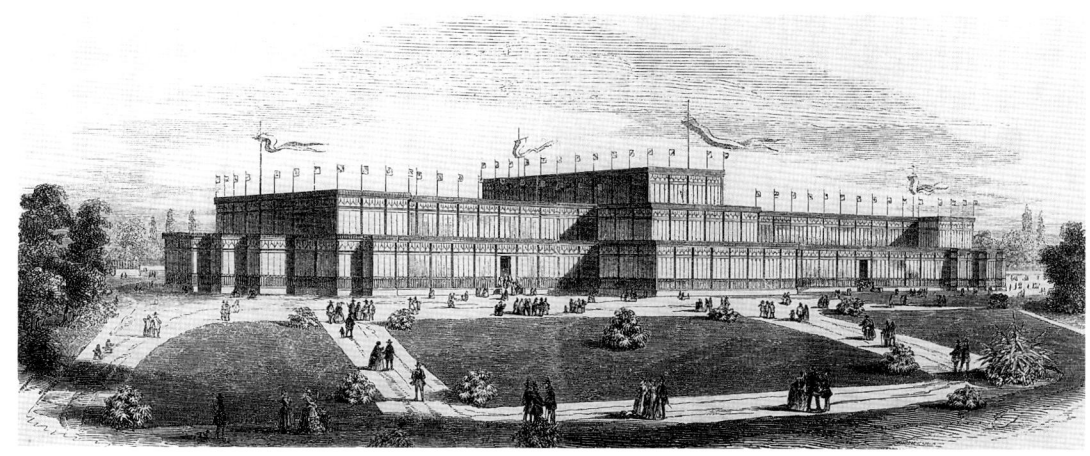

Glaspalast München, Holzstich, 1854.

The Glaspalast, Munich, wood engraving, 1854.

in useful later as a model for Schloß Babelsberg in Potsdam which Schinkel designed for Prince Wilhelm and Princess Augusta (brother and sister-in-law of Friedrich Wilhelm IV). English medievalism was still in vogue when Schloß Cecilienhof was built in Potsdam between 1913 and 1917. It may seem amazing for the Hohenzollerns to be aping the country house lifestyle of the British aristocracy even while World War I was raging; but fashion and politics never did go hand in hand.

This paradox is less surprising when viewed in the cultural context of the preceding century. Developments in English domestic architecture were widely followed in Germany. The presence of Princess Victoria, daughter of Queen Victoria, at the Prussian Court ensured that English ways were highly visible and very influential. The Arts and Crafts movement was keenly followed, and even around 1900 there was still an avid German readership for the aesthetic writings of John Ruskin and William Morris. Indeed, so great was the interest in all matters English at this time that the German Embassy in London even employed an architectural attaché in the person of Hermann Muthesius, whose particular mission it was to report back to Berlin on the most recent productions.[10]

The results of the hard work by Muthesius may still be admired in the shape of two formidable publications: *Die englische Baukunst der Gegenwart* of 1900 and *Das englische Haus* of 1904. In these large-format volumes the photographic skills of Muthesius provide a unique record of turn-of-the-century British architecture. As a measure of the importance then ascribed in the German-speaking world to English domestic architecture it is worth noting that two publications of the same name had previously been published decades earlier.[11]

But it should not be concluded that it was simply a one-way street with Germany avidly lapping up the latest fashions from England. Indeed, a more pervasive Germanic influence may be perceived to have been at work in Britain during the eighteenth century in the sense that the Hanoverian kings, who remained ethnically if not culturally fully German, applied their royal patronage to many significant architectural, urban and landscape projects.

A German princess, Caroline of Ansbach, as Queen to George II, was instrumental from 1727 to 1731 in creating the Serpentine, a scenic lake in Hyde Park which imitated the sinuous curve of a river in line with the contemporary taste for artificially contrived, pseudo-natural effects. A discreet memorial at the eastern end of the Serpentine commemorates Caroline's contribution to this famous London park. At the same time, English landscape-garden theory increasingly held sway in Germany over the more formal approach of the Baroque gardens, as may be seen in alterations to the Italianate layout of the Wilhelmshöhe near Kassel. Arguably the best-known example of this type is the Englischer Garten in Munich created by the American-born Benjamin Thompson, who served as a minister in the Bavarian government under Elector Carl Theodor.

Of all the Hanoverians, George IV, both as Prince Regent and as King, left behind the most lasting architectural legacy in Britain. His vision enabled John Nash to impose the elements of a 'Grand Design' for the West End of London. Nash's palatial terraces bordering Regent's Park still form a noble vista. The George IV – John Nash partnership is also evidenced by the stylistic extravaganza of Brighton's Royal Pavilion, a building that drew admiration even from Schinkel.

In terms of direct and lasting German influence on Britain, no one can match the record of Queen Victoria's incomparable consort, Prince Albert of Saxe-Coburg-Gotha, who between 1837 and 1861 brought German values to many areas of British life. His solid promotion of *Kultur* in the widest sense is best demonstrated by his masterminding of the Great Exhibition of 1851 in which Joseph Paxton's spectacular Crystal Palace provided a showcase for glass-and-iron construction. This epoch-making structure was promptly imitated in Munich by the Glaspalast of 1853–54, an industrial exhibition hall for the second German Industrial Exhibition. Neither Munich's smaller Glaspalast nor its British parent have survived. The former burnt down in 1931 while the latter, having been dismantled immediately after the Great Exhibition and re-erected in an enlarged version in South London, eventually met a similar fate when it was destroyed by fire in 1936.

There is one small but fascinating relic in central London of the Great Exhibition in the Prince Consort's Model Lodge which was designed by Henry Roberts for the Society for the Improvement of the Condition of the Labouring Classes of which Albert was President. Originally sited in Hyde Park, the dwellings were rebuilt in 1852 in Kennington Park and bear an inscription that reads: 'Model houses for families erected by HRH Prince Albert'. The 'Albert' design was later applied in Cowley Gardens, Stepney and Fenelon Place, Kensington.

Of more enduring significance was the financial legacy of the Great Exhibition.

In bezug auf unmittelbaren, dauerhaften deutschen Einfluß in England kann es keiner mit Prinz Albert von Sachsen-Coburg-Gotha aufnehmen, Queen Victorias unvergleichlichem Gemahl.
In terms of direct and lasting German influence on Britain, no one can match the record of Queen Victoria's incomparable consort, Prince Albert of Saxe-Coburg-Gotha.

Alfred Waterhouse,
Rundbogenstil am Natural
History Museum,
London, 1873–81.

Alfred Waterhouse,
Rundbogenstil at the
Natural History Museum,
London, 1873–81.

In bezug auf unmittelbaren, dauerhaften deutschen Einfluß in England kann es keiner mit Prinz Albert von Sachsen-Coburg-Gotha aufnehmen, Queen Victorias unvergleichlichem Gemahl, der zwischen 1837 und 1861 deutsche Werte in viele Bereiche des englischen Alltags einbrachte. Seine dauerhafte Förderung von Kultur im weitesten Sinne zeigt sich am deutlichsten an der führenden Rolle, die er bei der Weltausstellung des Jahres 1851 spielte, auf der Joseph Paxtons aufsehenerregender ›Kristallpalast‹ als Demonstrationsobjekt des Bauens mit Glas und Eisen fungierte. Dieses epochale Bauwerk wurde in München in Form des 1853/54 entstandenen Glaspalastes, der auf der Zweiten Deutschen Industrieschau als Ausstellungshalle diente, unverzüglich nachgeahmt. Der Münchner Glaspalast und das Londoner Original haben beide nicht überlebt: Der erste brannte 1931 ab, während letzterer sofort nach der Weltausstellung abmontiert und im Süden von London größer wieder aufgebaut wurde. Den Londoner Glaspalast ereilte aber letztlich das gleiche Schicksal, als er 1936 den Flammen zum Opfer fiel.

Es gibt im Herzen von London ein kleines, aber faszinierendes Überbleibsel der Weltausstellung in Form des Modellhauses, das von Henry Roberts für die Society for the Improvement of the Conditions of the Labouring Classes (Gesellschaft zur Verbesserung der Lebensbedingungen der Arbeiterklasse), deren Vorsitzender Prinz Albert war, entworfen wurde. Die ursprünglich im Hyde Park stehenden Wohnungen wurden 1852 im Kennington Park wieder aufgebaut und tragen folgende Inschrift: »Model houses for families erected by HRH Prince Albert«. Der ›Albert‹-Entwurf kam später in Cowley Gardens, Stepney und Fenelon Place, Kensington, zur Anwendung.

Als von dauerhafter Bedeutung erwies sich der finanzielle Nachlaß der Weltausstellung. Mit dem Erlös von £ 186.000 initiierte Albert den Erwerb eines Gebietes in South Kensington zum Bau einer Fülle kultureller Einrichtungen, darunter Museen, eine Konzerthalle sowie Lehrinstitute. Albert verstarb zu früh, um die Vollendung seiner ›Albertopolis‹ zu erleben, aber Imperial College, Science Museum, Royal Albert Hall, Victoria & Albert Museum und andere zeugen allerorten von seiner weitreichenden Vision. Selbst im Rundbogenstil von Alfred Waterhouses Natural History Museum ist ein gewisser deutscher Einfluß zu erkennen.

Das inzwischen von English Heritage zu früherer Pracht wiederhergestellte Albert Memorial kann sich ebenfalls auf deutsche Bezüge berufen, da sein Architekt, George Gilbert Scott, Rauchs Standbild von Friedrich dem Großen in Berlin oder Schinkels Bühnenbilder für die Oper ›Undine‹ gekannt haben könnte, die sich durch ein ähnlich gestaltetes, gotisches Bauwerk auszeichnen.[12]

Das Royal Mausoleum in Frogmore, in dem sowohl Queen Victoria als auch Prince Albert bestattet sind, wurde von Professor Ludwig Grüner aus Dresden entworfen. Alberts posthumer Einfluß reichte sogar in seine bayerische Heimat zurück, indem das Victoria & Albert Museum teilweise dafür verantwortlich ist, daß Oskar von Miller im Jahre 1906 mit dem Deutschen Museum in München eine vergleichbare Einrichtung begründete.[13]

Etwa zu dieser Zeit wurde das kühne, neue Konzept der Gartenstadt – im Jahre 1898 von Ebenezer Howard in seinem Buch *Tomorrow: a Peaceful Path to Real Reform* vorgestellt und 1902 unter dem Titel *Garden Cities of Tomorrow* [dt.: *Gartenstädte in Sicht*, Jena 1907] neu aufgelegt – in Deutschland rasch und begeistert aufgenommen. Die deutsche Gartenstadtgesellschaft von 1902 war die erste, die außerhalb Englands gegründet wurde. Tatsächlich kam Howards erstem Buch zwei Jahre früher eine deutsche Publikation ähnlichen Inhalts mit dem Titel *Die Stadt der Zukunft* von Theodor Fritsch zuvor. Dieses richtungsweisende Werk hatte jedoch weniger Einfluß auf die deutsche Gartenstadtbewegung als Howards Schrift.

Bei der deutschen Gartenstadt handelte es sich jedoch keineswegs um eine sklavische Nachahmung des englischen Vorbildes. Anstatt Gartenstädte in weiter Entfernung vom, nach Meinung Howards, üblen Einfluß der Großstädte zu errichten, entschied man sich in Deutschland vernünftigerweise für den Bau von Gartenvorstädten, die, wie Hellerau bei Dresden, mit vorhandenen Städten verbunden waren. Außerdem wurden die frühen deutschen Gartenvorstädte von einem stärker ausgeprägten Idealismus getragen, der von den kooperativen Vorstellungen des Deutschen Werkbundes durchdrungen war. Im Gegensatz dazu wird Howard, seines vorrangigen Interesses an Fragen des Landbesitzes und seiner praktisch orientierten Begeisterung für Stadtplanung wegen, von der angesehenen deutschen Autorin Kristiana Hartmann als »trockener Pragmatiker« eingestuft.[14]

Nachdem die Nationalsozialisten im Jahre 1933 das Bauhaus in Dessau geschlossen hatten, kamen führende deutsche Architekten mit ihren neuen Ideen und Vorstellungen nach England. Die architektonische Moderne war in England bis dato praktisch nicht vorhanden.[15] Der Hauptexponent der neuen deutschen Architektur war der große Walter Gropius, der zusammen mit dem Engländer Maxwell Fry in der 66 Old Church Street, Chelsea ein Privathaus und in Impington bei Cambridge eine Dorfschule baute. Diese zwar kurzzeitige, aber gleichwohl bemerkenswerte anglo-deutsche Zusammenarbeit schuf die Grundlage für die britische Moderne der Nachkriegszeit.[16] Durch eine seltsame Wendung des Schicksals

George Gilbert Scott,
Albert Memorial,
London, 1863–72.

George Gilbert Scott,
Albert Memorial,
London, 1863–72.

Nachdem die Nationalsozialisten im Jahre 1933 das Bauhaus in Dessau geschlossen hatten, kamen führende deutsche Architekten mit ihren neuen Ideen und Vorstellungen nach England.

In the 1930s, Britain received a vital infusion of leading German architectural talent following the Nazi closure in 1933 of the Bauhaus in Dessau.

With the profits of £186,000 Albert instigated the purchase of a tract of land in South Kensington for the construction of a galaxy of cultural establishments comprising museums, a concert hall and institutes of learning. Albert died too young to witness the completion of his 'Albertopolis'; but Imperial College, the Science Museum, Royal Albert Hall, Victoria & Albert Museum et al., offer ample proof of his powerful vision. One may even detect some Germanic influence in the *Rundbogenstil* of Alfred Waterhouse's Natural History Museum.

The Albert Memorial, now restored to its former glory by English Heritage, can also claim Germanic associations since its architect, George Gilbert Scott, may have been familiar with Rauch's statue of Frederick the Great in Berlin or Schinkel's stage sets for the opera *Undine*, which featured a Gothic structure of similar style.[12]

The Royal Mausoleum at Frogmore, where both Queen Victoria and Prince Albert are entombed, was designed by Professor Ludwig Grüner of Dresden. Albert's posthumous influence even spread back to his native Bavaria in that the Victoria & Albert Museum provided part of the inspiration for Oskar von Miller in 1906 to establish a similar institution in Munich with the Deutsches Museum.[13]

Around this time, the brave new concept of the garden city elaborated in 1898 by Ebenezer Howard in his book *Tomorrow: a Peaceful Path to Real Reform*, republished in 1902 as *Garden Cities of Tomorrow*, was speedily and enthusiastically taken up in Germany. The German *Gartenstadtgesellschaft* of 1902 was the first to be founded outside Britain. In fact, Howard's first book had been preceded two years earlier by a German publication on similar lines called *Die Stadt der Zukunft* by Theodor Fritsch. However, this pioneering work had less impact on the German garden city movement than Howard's.

But the German *Gartenstadt* was no slavish imitation of the British model. Rather than build garden cities far removed from what Howard perceived as the evil influence of the big towns, Germany opted quite sensibly for garden suburbs that were related to existing cities such as Hellerau near Dresden. There was also a stronger dose of idealism in the early German garden suburbs, which had been infused with the co-operative notions of the Deutscher Werkbund. By contrast Howard, with his overriding concerns for land ownership and his practical zeal for urban management, rates as 'a dry pragmatist' according to one respected German writer.[14]

In the 1930s, Britain received a vital infusion of leading German architectural talent following the Nazi closure in 1933 of the Bauhaus in Dessau. Modernism was then virtually unrepresented in Britain.[15] The main exponent of the new German architecture was the great Walter Gropius, who in partnership with England's Maxwell Fry built a private house at 66 Old Church Street, Chelsea, and a village school at Impington near Cambridge. This notable Anglo-German collaboration, although short-lived, laid the foundations for British Modernism of the post-war period.[16] By a curious twist of fate, the eminent name of Gropius later attached itself as an architectural consultant to an unremarkable London building (at 45 Park Lane) better known as the Playboy Club. Another leading German Modernist to come to Britain was Erich Mendelsohn who in 1935 designed, with the Russian Serge Chermayeff, the De la Warr Pavilion at Bexhill-on-Sea, Sussex and a house at 64 Old Church Street, Chelsea, next to Gropius and Maxwell Fry's building. But, like Gropius, Mendelsohn soon resumed his journey of exile and eventually settled in America.

No less remarkable was the achievement of German architectural historian Nikolaus Pevsner, a native of Leipzig forced to flee Hitler's Germany in 1934. During World War II Pevsner found himself helping to clear away rubble from the streets of London while writing his masterful *Outline of European Architecture*. But it was Pevsner's scholarly work as author of *The Buildings of England* series of books that made his name famous throughout the land. It is no exaggeration to say that Nikolaus Pevsner opened the eyes of the English to their own architectural heritage. His 1955 Reith Lectures on *The Englishness of English Art* marked a milestone in public awareness. But Pevsner was not one to insist overmuch on national boundaries when it came to culture, for he placed his perceptive studies of British architecture firmly within the wider context of Europe.

Indeed, ideas know no frontiers. Sometimes a cultural interaction has occurred in unexpected ways. How many Britons finding peace and contentment in their suburban vegetable patches have realised that the spiritual father of the modern allotment idea was a Dr Daniel Gottlieb Moritz Schreber of Leipzig who first promoted small garden plots for social recreation in the early nineteenth century?

In the immediate post-war period Britain left many a physical mark on the German landscape with installations from barracks and Nissen huts to command posts and housing estates that were transplanted direct to Germany

Die deutsche Gartenstadtgesellschaft von 1902 war die erste, die außerhalb Englands gegründet wurde.

The German Gartenstadtgesellschaft of 1902 was the first to be founded outside Britain.

James Stirling und der Erweiterungsbau der Staatsgalerie Stuttgart.

James Stirling and the extension to the Staatsgalerie Stuttgart.

wurde der berühmte Name von Walter Gropius später als architektonischer Berater mit einem eher belanglosen Londoner Gebäude in der Park Lane 45, besser bekannt als Playboy Club, in Verbindung gebracht. Als weiterer führender Vertreter der deutschen Moderne kam Erich Mendelsohn nach England, der 1935 zusammen mit dem Russen Serge Chermayeff in Bexhill-on-Sea, Sussex, den De la Warr Pavilion entwarf; des weiteren ein Haus in der Old Church Street 64 in Chelsea, das neben dem Gebäude von Gropius und Fry zu stehen kam. Ebenso wie Gropius setzte Mendelsohn jedoch bald seine Reise ins Exil fort und ließ sich schließlich in Amerika nieder.

Gleichermaßen bemerkenswert war die Leistung des deutschen Architekturhistorikers Nikolaus Pevsner, einem gebürtigen Leipziger, der sich 1934 gezwungen sah, Hitlerdeutschland zu verlassen. Während des Zweiten Weltkriegs half Pevsner beim Räumen des Schutts von Londons Straßen und schrieb zugleich an seinem Meisterwerk *An Outline of European Architecture* [dt.: *Europäische Architektur. Von den Anfängen bis zur Gegenwart*]. Es war jedoch Pevsners wissenschaftliche Arbeit als Autor der Buchreihe *The Buildings of England*, die seinem Namen zu landesweiter Bekanntheit verhalf. Man übertreibt nicht mit der Behauptung, Nikolaus Pevsner habe den Engländern die Augen für das eigene architektonische Erbe geöffnet. Seine 1955 gehaltenen Reith Lectures über *The Englishness of English Art* bedeuten einen Meilenstein im öffentlichen Bewußtsein. Wenn es um Kultur ging, war Pevsner jedoch nicht übermäßig an nationalen Grenzen interessiert, sondern verankerte seine weitsichtigen Studien zur englischen Architektur im größeren europäischen Kontext.

In der Tat nehmen Ideen keine Rücksicht auf Grenzen. Bisweilen geschieht kulturelle Interaktion auf unvermutete Weise. Wie vielen Briten, die in ihren vorstädtischen Gemüsegärtchen Frieden und Erfüllung finden, ist bekannt, daß der geistige Vater der modernen Gartenparzelle ein gewisser Dr. Daniel Gottlieb Moritz Schreber aus Leipzig war, der zu Beginn des neunzehnten Jahrhunderts als Erster kleine Gartengrundstücke zur gemeinschaftlichen Erholung empfahl?

In der Zeit unmittelbar nach dem Krieg hinterließ England zahlreiche sichtbare Spuren in der deutschen Landschaft, angefangen bei Kasernenbauten und Wellblechbaracken bis zu Gefechtsständen und Wohnsiedlungen, die direkt von den Zeichentischen des Verteidigungsministeriums in London nach Deutschland übertragen wurden. Ob vieles davon rechtmäßig als Architektur bezeichnet werden kann, ist fraglich, aber dieses umfangreiche bauliche Erbe belegt Englands gestaltgebende Rolle in der Frühzeit der Bundesrepublik.

Man kann sagen, daß britische Architektur in der vollen Bedeutung des Wortes im Jahre 1977 in Deutschland Einzug hielt, als das Londoner Büro von Stirling & Wilford den Wettbewerb zur Erweiterung der Staatsgalerie in Stuttgart gewann. Dieses Ereignis sollte sich als entscheidender Moment in der jüngsten Architekturgeschichte erweisen. Neben einem würdigen, klassizistischen Institut an Stuttgarts imposanter Kulturmeile erschien ein das Auge verwirrendes, postmodernes Bauwerk. Den gängigen Architektur- und Stilvorstellungen eine höchst ironische Nase drehend, stahl dieser freche Sprößling, als der er damals von einigen verstanden wurde, dem Mutterbau, als dessen Erweiterung er dienen sollte, komplett die Schau.

Der Entwurf machte Furore. Eine Gruppe deutscher Architekten zettelte eine lautstarke Kampagne gegen ein Bauwerk an, das lokale Empfindlichkeiten gleich in mehreren Punkten verletzte. Seine Monumentalität und der kompromißlose Gebrauch symbolischen Ornaments rief Erinnerungen an den nationalsozialistischen Baustil wach, etwas, das deutsche Architekten nach Kräften zu vermeiden suchten, indem sie sich einer zurückhaltenden, gewagte Aussagen ablehnenden Manier befleißigten. Michael Wilford erinnert sich an die damals herrschende Stimmung: »Das Gebäude wirkte provozierend, aber zum Glück wurden wir nicht nur von der Wettbewerbsjury unterstützt, sondern auch von den örtlichen Politikern, die der Meinung waren, für das Gebäude spräche sehr viel mehr, als nur diese Konnotationen.«

Es drängt sich ferner der Verdacht auf, es könne mancher bezweifelt haben, daß es sich hier um ein wirklich ernstzunehmendes Bauwerk handele. In jedem Fall waren die öffentlichen Vertreter Baden-Württembergs hinreichend mutig und überzeugt, um an dem von ihnen gewählten Architekten festzuhalten. Sie mußten für ihre Entscheidung geradestehen, während James Stirling sein spielerisch-postmodernes Wirken auf der ganzen Welt fortsetzte und dabei seine typischen lilafarbenen Socken vor dem von ihm bevorzugten grün-orangefarbenen Dekor zur Schau stellte.

Die Wogen der erregten Debatte haben sich längst geglättet, und jeglicher Zweifel an der Ernsthaftigkeit des Erweiterungsbaues der Staatsgalerie ist zerstreut. Der Bau wurde rasch zum geschätzten lokalen Wahrzeichen und zum Kultursymbol, durch das Stuttgart ins Gespräch kam. Im Laufe der Zeit leistete die Staatsgalerie einen bedeutenden Beitrag zum Wirtschaftsleben Stuttgarts, indem sie von nah und fern große Besucherscharen anzieht. Darüber hinaus fungierte sie als entscheidendes Sprungbrett für weitere Aufträge des Büros Stirling & Wilford, wie das Wissenschaftszentrum in Berlin und die Musikhochschule in Stuttgart.

Die Wogen der erregten Debatte haben sich längst geglättet, und jeglicher Zweifel an der Ernsthaftigkeit des Erweiterungsbaues der Staatsgalerie ist zerstreut.

The dust has long since settled on the heated debate and any doubt about the underlying seriousness of the Staatsgalerie extension has been dispelled.

---

from Ministry of Defence drawing-boards in London. Whether much of this can properly be considered as architecture is debatable, but this sizeable building legacy bears witness to Britain's formative role during the early years of the Bundesrepublik.

British architecture in the fullest sense of the term may be said to have arrived in Germany in 1977 when the London partnership of Stirling & Wilford won the competition for the extension to the Staatsgalerie in Stuttgart. This event turned out to be a defining moment in recent architectural history. An eye-dazzling, post-modern building appeared alongside a worthy neo-classical establishment on Stuttgart's stately cultural mile. Cocking a highly ironic snook at current architectural attitudes and notions of style, this cheeky offspring (as it was then perceived by some) completely upstaged the parent structure to which it was intended to serve as an extension.

The design caused a furore. A group of German architects launched a vociferous campaign to oppose a building that offended local sensitivities on several counts. Its monumentality and uncompromising use of symbolic ornament aroused memories of fascist style, something German architects took great pains to avoid by espousing a self-effacing manner that denied bold statement. Michael Wilford recalls the mood at the time: 'The building was provocative, but fortunately we were supported not only by the competition jury but also by the local politicians who felt that the building had a lot more going for it than just these connotations'.

One suspects also that some may have doubted whether this could be considered a really serious building. At any rate, the public representatives of Baden-Württemberg had the courage and conviction to stand by their chosen architects. They faced the critical music while James Stirling continued his playful post-modern dance across the world stage displaying his trademark purple socks against his favourite décor of green and orange.

The dust has long since settled on the heated debate and any doubt about the underlying seriousness of the Staatsgalerie extension has been dispelled. The building quickly became a cherished local landmark as well as a cultural icon that has put Stuttgart on the map. In the process, the Staatsgalerie has made a significant impact on the economic life of Stuttgart, attracting large numbers of visitors from far and wide. The building also provided the essential launchpad for subsequent Stirling & Wilford productions in Germany such as the Social Science Research Centre in Berlin and the Music School in Stuttgart.

Perhaps it may be claiming too much importance for a single building, but the Staatsgalerie seems to have ushered in an era of unprecedented success for British architects in Germany. The closing decades of the twentieth century have seen a wealth of exciting buildings from virtually all the leading and many of the less well-known London practices. All over the country, from the Swiss border up to the North Sea, as well as in big cities such as Berlin, Cologne, Düsseldorf, Frankfurt and Hamburg, German clients both public and private have entrusted some of their most significant projects to British architects.

Norman Foster, in addition to the Reichstag in Berlin, has also designed other major projects such as the Micro-Electronic Centre, Telematic Centre and Business Promotion Centre in Duisburg, the revamped Design Museum Zollverein in a former pit in Essen, and the Commerzbank headquarters in Frankfurt, which tops out as the tallest building in Europe, just two metres higher than Frankfurt's Messeturm.

Richard Rogers came to Germany rather late in his career, but he is the author of three major projects in Berlin. These consist of one residential and two office buildings in the Daimler Chrysler sector of the Potsdamer Platz development. The three Richard Rogers buildings occupy neighbouring sites and form an urban ensemble that creates one of the most cohesive views of the new Berlin.

Nicholas Grimshaw has left his mark most dramatically on Berlin with the distinctive armadillo shape of the Ludwig Erhard House. The same practice has designed some memorable and highly functional factories for companies such as Igus in Cologne, Vitra in Weil am Rhein and Pfeiffer Vakuum at Aßlar near Gießen. Grimshaw's headquarters for Mabeg at Soest shows how architecture can make a corporate statement through clever design rather than outright size; and his 'Spine House' for one of his satisfied industrial clients shows what dramatic results can be obtained with small-scale private commissions.

David Chipperfield has worked on a number of German projects that range from a private residence in the country to a stylish commercial building on Düsseldorf's Kaistraße. His understated architecture has stylistic affinities with the minimalist Modernist tradition, historically much stronger in Germany than in Britain. Chipperfield's German connections have become closer as a result of his part-time teaching in Stuttgart where he has recently accepted a full-time professorship.

Ian Ritchie has had similar teaching offers but he has opted, for the time

Norman Foster, Haus der Wirtschaftsförderung, Duisburg.

Norman Foster, Business Promotion Centre, Duisburg.

Vielleicht weist die folgende Behauptung einem einzelnen Gebäude zuviel Bedeutung zu, aber die Staatsgalerie scheint in Deutschland eine Ära beispiellosen Erfolges britischer Architekten eingeleitet zu haben. In den letzten Dekaden des zwanzigsten Jahrhunderts entstand eine Fülle interessanter Bauten von nahezu allen führenden und zahlreichen weniger bekannten Londoner Büros. Im ganzen Land, von der Schweizer Grenze bis zur Nordseeküste und ebenso in Großstädten wie Berlin, Köln, Düsseldorf, Frankfurt und Hamburg, vertrauten öffentliche wie private Auftraggeber einige ihrer bedeutendsten Projekte britischen Architekten an.

Neben dem Reichstag in Berlin hat Norman Foster auch andere Großprojekte entworfen, wie das Mikroelektronikzentrum, das Telematikzentrum und das Haus der Wirtschaftsförderung in Duisburg, das neu gestaltete Design-Museum in der ehemaligen Zeche Zollverein in Essen und die Zentrale der Commerzbank in Frankfurt, bei Fertigstellung Europas höchstes Gebäude und gerade zwei Meter höher als Frankfurts Messeturm.

Richard Rogers kam erst relativ spät in seiner Laufbahn nach Deutschland, zeichnet aber jetzt für drei Großprojekte in Berlin verantwortlich. Es handelt sich dabei um ein Wohn- und zwei Bürogebäude im Daimler-Chrysler-Sektor des Potsdamer Platzes. Die drei Bauten von Rogers stehen auf nebeneinanderliegenden Grundstücken und bilden ein urbanes Ensemble, das zu den geschlossensten Ansichten im neuen Berlin zählt.

Mit der prägnanten, zoomorphen Form des Ludwig-Erhard-Hauses hat Nicholas Grimshaw in Berlin ein dramatisches Zeichen gesetzt. Von demselben Büro stammt der Entwurf einiger bemerkenswerter, höchst funktioneller Fabrikgebäude für Firmen wie Igus in Köln, Vitra in Weil am Rhein und Pfeiffer Vakuum in Aßlar bei Gießen. Grimshaws Zentrale für Mabeg in Soest demonstriert, wie Architektur durch geschicktes Design anstatt schierer Größe für eine Firma identitätsstiftend wirken kann. Das für einen zufriedenen, industriellen Auftraggeber entstandene ›Spine House‹ zeigt, welch dramatische Ergebnisse sich mit eher klein dimensionierten, privaten Aufträgen erzielen lassen.

David Chipperfield ist an einer Reihe deutscher Projekte beteiligt, deren Bandbreite von Privathäusern auf dem Land zu einem eleganten Geschäftshaus in der Düsseldorfer Kaistraße reicht. Seine zurückhaltende Architektur weist stilistische Bezüge zur minimalistischen Tradition der Moderne auf, die in Deutschland historisch weit stärker vertreten ist als in England. Chipperfields Beziehungen zu Deutschland gestalteten sich aufgrund seines Lehrauftrags in Stuttgart enger, wo er vor kurzem eine volle Professur angenommen hat.

Ian Ritchie erhielt ähnliche Lehrangebote, will sich aber derzeit auf die Leitung seines Büros konzentrieren. Am Anfang stand das Angebot von Volkwin Marg, gemeinsam die Stahl-Glas-Strukturen für die Eingangshalle der Leipziger Messe von gmp – von Gerkan, Marg und Partner bis zur Baureife zu entwickeln, die das Symbol für Leipzigs Bestreben sein sollte, an seinen früheren Glanz als Messestandort und die große Zeit der Kristallpaläste anzuknüpfen. Ian Ritchie schlug Modifikationen der geplanten Glasstrukturen vor, die ebenso einfach wie attraktiv waren.

Der Stellenwert der Glashalle als kulturelle Ikone läßt sich an der Tatsache ermessen, daß sie auf einer deutschen Briefmarke aus Anlaß des fünfhundertjährigen Bestehens der Leipziger Messe abgebildet ist.

Michael Wilford, der seit James Stirlings Tod im Jahre 1992 unter eigenem Namen tätig ist, ist für mehrere prägnante Geschäftskomplexe verantwortlich, insbesondere den für die Sto AG in Weizen. Wilfords Entwurf für die neue Britische Botschaft in Berlin schließt den Kreis der Geschichte, da sie die Fortsetzung diplomatischer Beziehungen zwischen England und Deutschland an eben dem Ort gestattet, wo sie 1939 durch den Ausbruch des Krieges unterbrochen wurden. Überdies schlägt Wilfords Bau Brücken zwischen den Kulturen, indem er die traditionelle urbane Struktur der Gegend um Wilhelmstraße und Pariser Platz berücksichtigt, aber dennoch einige kühne, moderne Gestaltungselemente einfügt.

In der Laufbahn von Zaha Hadid, der aus Bagdad stammenden, in London ansässigen Architektin, war es Deutschland, das das unerläßliche Vertrauen aufbrachte, um ihren phantastischen, futuristischen Entwürfen den entscheidenden Schritt aus dem Reich der Phantasie in die steinerne Realität wirklicher Gebäude zu ermöglichen. Zaha Hadid, deren Bemühungen, in Großbritannien etwas zu bauen, bislang enttäuscht wurden, konnte in Deutschland zwei Projekte fertigstellen, die Vitra Feuerwache und einen Pavillon auf der Landesgartenschau in Weil am Rhein. In beiden Fällen wurde der künstlerische Wert ihrer visionären Entwürfe von sachkundigen deutschen Kreisen ausführlich gewürdigt.

Die nationalen Grenzen zwischen britischer und deutscher Architektur verwischen sich im Falle des anglo-deutschen Büros Alsop & Störmer, das eine Vielzahl von Projekten verwirklichen konnte, angefangen bei einem eindrucksvollen Bürogebäude an der Stresemannstraße in Berlin bis hin zum Handelshaus Neuer Wall, dem Staatsarchiv sowie einem Fährenterminal in Hamburg. Louisa Hutton und Matthias Sauerbruch, eine weitere deutsch-englische Architektengemeinschaft, die ihr Büro zwischen London und Berlin betreiben, konnten unlängst ihr

Die alte Britische Botschaft an der Wilhelmstraße, Berlin.

The old British Embassy on the Wilhelmstrasse, Berlin.

Wilfords Entwurf für die neue Britische Botschaft in Berlin schließt den Kreis der Geschichte, da sie die Fortsetzung diplomatischer Beziehungen zwischen England und Deutschland an eben dem Ort gestattet, wo sie 1939 durch den Ausbruch des Krieges unterbrochen wurden.

Wilford's new British Embassy in Berlin brings history full circle, allowing diplomatic relations between Britain and Germany to resume on the very site where they were interrupted by the outbreak of war in 1939.

being at least, to concentrate on running a successful practice. Ritchie was invited by Volkwin Marg to collaborate on the technical development of gmp's (von Gerkan, Marg und Partner) steel and glass structure for the entrance hall to the Leipziger Messe. This exhibition complex was to be the symbol of Leipzig's ambition to regain its former glory as a trade fair and a link to the era of glass construction. Ritchie's suggested modifications to the designs for the glass structure were both simple and attractive. The status of the Glashalle as a cultural icon may be judged from the fact that it has featured on a German postage stamp to mark the five-hundreth anniversary of the Leipziger Messe.

Michael Wilford, now working under his own name since the death of James Stirling in 1992, has several distinctive commercial projects to his credit, most notably for Sto at Weizen. Wilford's new British Embassy in Berlin brings history full circle, allowing diplomatic relations between Britain and Germany to resume on the very site where they were interrupted by the outbreak of war in 1939. This Wilford building also bridges cultures by paying respect to the traditional urban context of Wilhelmstrasse and Pariser Platz while injecting some dashingly modern elements of design.

In the career of Zaha Hadid, the Baghdad-born, London-based architect, it is Germany which has taken the essential leap of faith necessary for her stunning futuristic designs to make the decisive move out of the realm of fantasy into the concrete reality of actual buildings. Disappointed so far in her attempts to build something in Britain, Zaha Hadid has now completed two projects in Germany, the Vitra Fire Station and a pavilion for the Landesgartenschau in Weil am Rhein. In both instances, the artistic merits of Zaha Hadid's visionary schemes have been acclaimed by informed German opinion.

National boundaries between British and German architecture are blurred in the instance of the Anglo-German partnership Alsop & Störmer which has realised a diversity of projects, from an imposing office block on Stresemannstraße in Berlin to the Handelshaus Neuer Wall, Staatsarchiv and a ferry terminal in Hamburg. In the case of the Sauerbruch Hutton practice, which straddles London and Berlin, Louisa Hutton and Matthias Sauerbruch have recently completed the eye-catching Photonics Centre and the new headquarters in Berlin for GSW, the Gemeinnützige Siedlungs- und Wohnungsbaugesellschaft.

Among other British architectural projects in Germany by names not so much in the public domain are the Adam Opel House, Rüsselsheim by Building Design Partnership; Jenoptik Galleria, Jena by DEGW; a factory for Siemens in Treptow, Berlin by Stiff & Trevillion; the new Frankfurt Hilton and golf clubhouse at Seddiner See near Potsdam by John Seifert Architects. Househam Henderson have built restaurants, hotels and industrial buildings throughout the country; Dawe & Geddes designed the Mannheim Hi-Tech Park, various fast-food outlets and many hotel renovations in the former East Germany.

British architects and planners have also been active on the wider stage of urbanism. Norman Foster has devised masterplans for Duisburg and Neu-Isenberg. John Seifert Architects are working on the Westhafen redevelopment in Frankfurt. David Chipperfield has a real chance to achieve something on an urban scale since he has been entrusted with masterplanning the Museum Island in Berlin.

Richard Rogers was invited by private investors to draw up a masterplan for Potsdamer Platz. His scheme would have left cars outside the development and taken full advantage of the excellent public transportation, as Rogers explains: 'We wanted to reestablish the centre where it used to be in the Potsdamer Platz and make it a People's Square. In a sense the city planners felt it should really go back to being a place for cars and therefore left Renzo Piano with having to find a little square at the back and at the side. I thought Renzo's plan was very good, but it was a bit like asking someone to fight in a boxing match with one hand tied behind his back, but that is what he had to do'. Rogers still regrets the rejection of his scheme as 'a massive missed opportunity', and continues to disagree on this point with the Berlin planners: 'I believe that what could have been a wonderful integrated scheme has ended up with some very good buildings on a questionable nineteenth-century plan'.

Elsewhere in Berlin, British architects have been involved in some interesting initiatives that seek to remedy past and present divisions of the city. John Thompson & Partners, organised in August 1996 an International Community Planning Weekend in Ludwigsfelde under the banner 'Our Centre – Our Future'. The aim was to involve local people in devising a strategy for the regeneration of a marginalised neighbourhood that had been divided by the Berliner Ring orbital motorway. The same process of participatory planning had previously been applied by the same firm to the problems of Cecilienplatz in Berlin-Hellersdorf where the challenge was to breathe new life into a run-down, system-built, high-rise settlement, constructed in the former eastern sector of Berlin shortly before the fall of the Wall.

Most recently, John Thompson & Partners, on behalf of the Prince of Wales

Building Design Partnership, Adam-Opel-Haus, Rüsselsheim.

Building Design Partnership, Adam Opel House, Rüsselsheim.

Das deutsche Beharren auf höchsten ökologischen Baunormen hat die Findigkeit britischer Architekten herausgefordert.
German insistence on the highest ecological building standards has stretched the ingenuity of British architects.

aufsehenerregendes Photonikzentrum sowie die Zentrale der GSW, der Gemeinnützigen Siedlungs- und Wohnungsbaugesellschaft, in Berlin fertigstellen.

Zu anderen, von englischen Architekten mit nicht ganz so bekannten Namen betriebenen Projekten zählen das Adam-Opel-Haus in Rüsselsheim von Building Design Partnership, die Jenoptik Galleria, Jena, von DEGW, ein Fabrikgebäude für Siemens in Treptow, Berlin von Stiff & Trevillion, das neue Frankfurter Hilton und ein Golfclubhaus am Seddiner See bei Potsdam von John Seifert Architects. Househam Henderson errichteten landesweit Restaurants, Hotels und Industriebauten; Dawe & Geddes entwarfen den Mannheimer High-Tech-Park, verschiedene Verkaufsstellen für Fast-Food sowie zahlreiche Hotelrenovierungen im ehemaligen Ostdeutschland.

Britische Architekten und Planer waren darüber hinaus auch auf dem Gebiet der Stadtplanung tätig. Norman Foster konzipierte Gesamtpläne für Duisburg und Neu-Isenburg. John Seifert Architects arbeiten an der Sanierung des Westhafens in Frankfurt. David Chipperfield bietet sich die reale Chance, einen Beitrag zur Neugestaltung der Hauptstadt zu leisten, da man ihn mit der Gesamtplanung der Museumsinsel in Berlin betraut hat.

Richard Rogers wurde von den privaten Investoren aufgefordert, einen Gesamtplan für den Potsdamer Platz vorzulegen. Diese Planung sah keinen Autoverkehr für das Gebiet vor und hätte sich die hervorragenden öffentlichen Verkehrsverbindungen zunutze gemacht. Rogers erläutert: »Wir wollten das Zentrum wieder da errichten, wo der Potsdamer Platz einst war und ihn zu einem von Menschen bevölkerten Platz, einem ›People's Square‹, machen. Die Stadtplaner waren der Ansicht, es sollte eigentlich wieder ein Platz mit Autoverkehr daraus werden und überließen es Renzo Piano, auf der Rückseite und an der Seite ein Plätzchen zu finden. Ich fand Renzos Plan sehr gut, aber es war irgendwie so, als würde man jemanden auffordern, sich mit einer hinter dem Rücken festgebundenen Hand an einem Boxkampf zu beteiligen. Genau das mußte er tun.« Rogers trauert seinem abgelehnten Plan noch immer als »gewaltiger verpaßter Gelegenheit« nach und ist in diesem Punkt weiterhin anderer Meinung als die Berliner Stadtplaner. »Ich glaube, etwas, aus dem eine wunderbare ausgewogene Anlage hätte werden können, läuft letztlich hinaus auf einige sehr gute Bauten auf einem fragwürdigen Neunzehntes-Jahrhundert-Plan.«

Andernorts in Berlin sind britische Architekten an interessanten Initiativen beteiligt, die versuchen, den ehemaligen und auch heute noch präsenten Teilungsfolgen der Stadt abzuhelfen. Im August 1996 organisierten John Thompson & Partners in Ludwigsfelde unter dem Leitmotiv »Unser Zentrum – Unsere Zukunft« ein ›International Community Planning Weekend‹. Das Ziel war, dort ansässige Menschen an der Entwicklung einer Strategie zur Umgestaltung ihres randständigen, durch den Berliner Ring zerschnittenen, Wohnviertels zu beteiligen. Das nämliche Procedere der Planungsbeteiligung war zuvor vom selben Architekturbüro bei den Problemen des Cecilienplatzes in Berlin-Hellersdorf angewandt worden, wo die Aufgabe darin bestand, einem heruntergekommenen, systemkonformen Hochhausviertel, das kurz vor dem Fall der Mauer im früheren Ostberlin errichtet worden war, neues Leben einzuhauchen.

In jüngster Zeit wurden John Thompson & Partners im Auftrag der ›Prince of Wales Urban Design Task Force‹ eingeladen, sich bei der Abstimmung radikal gegensätzlicher Vorstellungen für den Schloßplatz einzuschalten, eines ausgedehnten, offenen Platzes im Herzen von Berlin, an dessen einer Seite sich als ödes, umstrittenes Memento an die schlechten, alten Zeiten der DDR, der Palast der Republik erhebt. Die Vorteile derartiger Interventionen werden sich erst im Nachhinein beurteilen lassen, aber schon das Vorhandensein solch internationaler Beratung ist Beleg für die neuen Kräfte, die Deutschlands städtisches Umfeld prägen. Die Stadtväter setzen nicht länger einfach ihre Ansichten durch, sondern es greift ein weit offenerer und demokratischerer Prozeß, aus dem andere Länder wertvolle Erkenntnisse gewinnen können.

Das neue Jahrtausend wird weitere Proben englischer Architektur auf deutschem Boden mit sich bringen, darunter Norman Fosters Arag Zentrale in Düsseldorf, David Chipperfields Landeszentralbank in Gera, das von ihm umgebaute Neue Museum in Berlin, einen Erweiterungsbau zum Grassi Museum in Leipzig sowie eine neue Zentrale für ein Unternehmen des Bekleidungseinzelhandels in Coesfeld-Lette. Richard Rogers plant in Frankfurt ein Projekt mit Wohnungen, Läden und Büros; Michael Wilford, der mit mehreren Aufträgen aus der Wirtschaft befaßt ist, wurde darüber hinaus aufgefordert, die Arbeit an Baden-Württembergs seit langem erwarteten ›Haus der Geschichte‹, einem Geschichtsmuseum in Stuttgart, fortzusetzen. Das Büro Sauerbruch-Hutton arbeitet an einem Niedrigenergie-Wohnungsbauprojekt in Berlin-Pankow, am Bundesamt des Bundesumweltministeriums in Dessau, einer experimentellen Fabrik in Magdeburg sowie einem neuen Haus für das British Council in Berlin. Ian Ritchie entwarf einen Bahnhof für ›Ferropolis‹, einem spannenden Projekt zur Umnutzung von Industriebrachen bei Bitterfeld. Nicholas Grimshaw baut derzeit eine neue Halle für die Frankfurter Messe mit einer spektakulären, 165 m langen vollverglasten Fassade.

Nick Grimshaw (links) mit Mabeg-Geschäftsführer Rainer Kranz (rechts), Projektleiter Michael Pross (Mitte) und Mitglieder des Architektenteams.

Nicholas Grimshaw (left) with Mabeg CEO Rainer Kranz (right), Project Director Michael Pross (centre) and members of the architectural team.

Briefmarke zum 500jährigen Messejubiläum mit der in Kooperation mit Ian Ritchie entwickelten Glashalle in der Neuen Leipziger Messe der Architekten gmp.

Stamp to mark 500 years of the Leipzig Fair featuring Ian Ritchie's glass construction in gmp's New Leipzig Trade Fair.

Urban Design Task Force, were invited to intervene to help resolve radically opposed visions for Schloßplatz, a vast open space in the heart of Berlin flanked by the Palace of the Republic, a stark and controversial reminder of the bad old days of the GDR. Only time will judge the benefits of such interventions, but the very existence of such international consultation shows new forces shaping Germany's urban environment. No longer are the city fathers simply imposing their views, but a much more open and democratic process is at work, from which other countries may learn valuable lessons.

The new millennium will see yet more examples of British architecture on German soil: among them Norman Foster's Arag HQ in Düsseldorf, David Chipperfield's Landeszentralbank in Gera, a revamped Neues Museum in Berlin, an extension to the Grassi Museum in Leipzig and a new headquarters for a clothing retailer at Coesfeld-Lette. Richard Rogers has a scheme of housing, shops and offices in Frankfurt. Michael Wilford, in addition to several commercial commissions, has been asked to proceed with Baden-Württemberg's long-awaited Haus der Geschichte, a history museum in Stuttgart. Sauerbruch Hutton has a low-energy housing project in Berlin-Pankow, the Federal Office in Dessau for the Ministry of the Environment and an experimental factory in Magdeburg, as well as a new base for the British Council in Berlin. Ian Ritchie has designed a railway station for Ferropolis, an exciting industrial heritage project near Bitterfeld. Nicholas Grimshaw is currently building a new hall for the Frankfurt Trade Fair that presents a spectacular 165-metre-long fully-glazed elevation.

All this amounts to a massive investment in British talent, a remarkable phenomenon that also raises some questions. First of all, on a practical level: how do British architects cope with German bureaucracy? David Chipperfield: 'On our first project we struggled with German building codes. It takes a while to understand the particular criteria from Germany which are very precise, not very open to interpretation'.

But, as Chipperfield discovered, there are usually good reasons: 'Building through a Berlin winter you start to realise why. It gets unbelievably cold and frozen, then very warm in summer, so thermal transmission is a much bigger issue than in London where it never gets that cold and is not such a big problem'. German insistence on the highest ecological building standards has stretched the ingenuity of British architects.

There are also a few linguistic challenges. Ian Ritchie has some knowledge of German: 'I understand maybe sixty per cent of it, but the Germans automatically assume they will speak English with the architect. That is, until the last five per cent where it gets deadly serious about contractual matters or decisions and then they switch to German. So I've always got to have a German with me for that last five minutes to make sure I don't misunderstand anything'.

Sometimes, different working methods become apparent in less obvious ways. Ian Ritchie went away from one meeting at the site of the Leipziger Messe charged to work out a specific technical solution: 'When I came back with an answer not based on what had been agreed, but an even better answer that would save another two million Deutschmarks, I was politely shown the meeting notes saying I would go away and do this and that would be the answer, and we are not interested in the alternatives, Mr Ritchie, otherwise we'll never get the building finished. So there is that time discipline in Germany, whereas the English will prevaricate. We are always looking at slightly better ways of doings things, and so things drift on and people end up not quite sure what is happening'.

But if the German system is more disciplined, this does not mean that its aspirations are restricted. David Chipperfield: 'I think systemization comes naturally to the Germans, but there is also a sort of respect for bigger things. From that position they then look romantically towards other visions, whereas in a strange way I think the English are much more capable of visions'. Ian Ritchie: 'In a general way there is an Anglo-Saxon way of thinking and a Cartesian way of thinking which is more functional, more rational; so there is a synergy between Britain and the German-speaking countries'.

Indeed, there seems to be a distinctively German attitude that appeals very much to British architects. Nicholas Grimshaw: 'I rather like the whole German industrial approach. They still make things in Germany very beautifully and they believe if they have a good product they should have a good building and that everyone should believe in it and there's a feeling of doing things properly'. Michael Wilford: 'Germany for us remains one of the best places in the world to work, and for several reasons. One is that the clients in Germany still realise the benefits of investing in the initial building costs, in other words of buying quality materials and quality construction'.

There is another factor at work, something to do with the cultural climate. Louisa Hutton: 'In Germany, people are more positive about modern buildings. The man in the street, Joe Public – whatever he is called in German – is more aware of architecture as part of a wider culture. Virtually any taxi-driver I

»Ich mag eigentlich diese Einstellung der deutschen Industrie zum Bauen. Es werden in Deutschland immer noch ausgesprochen schöne Dinge hergestellt, und sie glauben, wenn sie ein gutes Produkt haben, sollten sie auch ein gutes Gebäude haben und daß jeder daran glauben sollte, und man schätzt es, Dinge richtig zu tun.« Nicholas Grimshaw

'I rather like the whole German industrial approach. They still make things in Germany very beautifully and they believe if they have a good product they should have a good building and that everyone should believe in it and there's a feeling of doing things properly.' Nicholas Grimshaw

Michael Wilford in seinem Londoner Büro.

Michael Wilford at his London practice.

All dies läuft auf eine gewaltige Investition in englische Begabung hinaus, ein bemerkenswertes Phänomen, das einige Fragen aufwirft. Zum einen in praktischer Hinsicht: Wie kommen englische Architekten mit der deutschen Bürokratie zurecht? David Chipperfield: »Bei unserem ersten Projekt kämpften wir mit den deutschen Bauvorschriften. Man braucht Zeit, um die besonderen deutschen Kriterien zu verstehen; sie sind sehr präzise und lassen sich nicht unterschiedlich auslegen.« Wie Chipperfield feststellte, gibt es jedoch in der Regel gute Gründe: »Beim Bauen in einem Berliner Winter beginnt man zu begreifen, warum das so ist. Es wird dort unglaublich kalt und eisig, dann, im Sommer, sehr warm, also spielt die Wärmeableitung eine weit größere Rolle als in London, wo es nie so kalt wird und das kein solches Problem darstellt.« Das deutsche Beharren auf höchsten ökologischen Baunormen hat die Findigkeit britischer Architekten herausgefordert.

Es gibt auch einige linguistische Probleme. Ian Ritchie spricht etwas Deutsch: »Ich verstehe etwa sechzig Prozent, aber die Deutschen nehmen automatisch an, daß sie mit dem Architekten Englisch sprechen. Das heißt, bis auf die letzten fünf Prozent, wo es todernst wird und um vertragliche Dinge und Entscheidungen geht, dann gehen sie zu Deutsch über. Ich muß also für die letzten fünf Minuten immer einen Deutschen dabeihaben, um sicherzustellen, daß ich nichts mißverstehe.«

Bisweilen machen sich unterschiedliche Arbeitsweisen in weniger augenfälliger Weise bemerkbar. Ian Ritchie verließ ein Treffen auf der Leipziger-Messe-Baustelle mit dem Auftrag, eine spezifische technische Lösung auszuarbeiten: »Als ich mit einer Antwort zurückkam, die nicht auf den Beschlüssen beruhte, sondern mit einer noch besseren Antwort, die weitere zwei Millionen Mark gespart hätte, wurde ich vom Baumanagement höflich auf die Sitzungsprotokolle hingewiesen, in denen stand, ich würde hingehen und dies und jenes käme dabei heraus, und wir sind nicht an Alternativen interessiert, Mr. Ritchie, sonst wird das Gebäude nie fertig. Es gibt also in Deutschland diese Termindisziplin, während Engländer sich nicht festlegen. Wir sind immer auf der Suche nach der etwas besseren Methode, und so treiben die Dinge weiter, und die Leute wissen letztlich nicht genau, was los ist.« Auch wenn das deutsche System disziplinierter ist, bedeutet jedoch nicht, daß seine Ambitionen beschränkt sind.

David Chipperfield: »Ich glaube, daß Systematisierung der deutschen Natur entspricht, aber es gibt da auch eine Art Respekt vor größeren Dingen. Aus dieser Position schauen sie dann romantisch auf andere Visionen, wobei ich glaube, daß Engländer auf merkwürdige Weise weit fähiger zu Visionen sind.« Ian Ritchie: »Allgemein gesprochen gibt es eine angelsächsische Denkweise und eine kartesianische Denkweise, die praktischer und rationaler ist; es gibt also eine Synergie zwischen englischsprachigen und deutschsprachigen Ländern.«

Tatsächlich scheint es eine typisch deutsche Haltung zu geben, die britischen Architekten sehr zusagt. Nicholas Grimshaw: »Ich mag eigentlich diese Einstellung der deutschen Industrie zum Bauen. Es werden in Deutschland immer noch ausgesprochen schöne Dinge hergestellt, und sie glauben, wenn sie ein gutes Produkt haben, sollten sie auch ein gutes Gebäude haben, und daß jeder daran glauben sollte, und man schätzt es, Dinge richtig zu tun.« Michael Wilford: »Deutschland ist weiterhin für uns einer der weltbesten Arbeitsplätze, und zwar aus mehreren Gründen. Einer davon ist, daß Bauherren in Deutschland noch wissen, daß es vorteilhaft ist, anfänglich in die Baukosten zu investieren, mit anderen Worten, in erstklassige Materialien und erstklassige Baumethoden.«

Es spielt da noch ein weiteres Moment mit, das etwas mit dem kulturellen Klima zu tun hat. Louisa Hutton: »In Deutschland stehen die Leute modernen Bauten aufgeschlossener gegenüber. Der Normalbürger nimmt Architektur bewußter als Teil eines weiter gefaßten Kulturbegriffs wahr. Praktisch jeder Taxifahrer, mit dem ich in Berlin ins Gespräch komme, interessiert sich für die neuen Bauten. Die Berliner haben für einzelne Gebäude Spitznamen, und ich verstehe die meisten davon als eher freundlich.« Michael Wilford: »In England taucht Architektur in der Presse nur auf, um in irgendeiner Weise verhöhnt zu werden, weil alles zu teuer ist oder weil es reinregnet oder es irgendeine Art von Skandal gibt. In Deutschland dagegen wird von sachkundigen Leuten regelmäßig und umfassend darüber berichtet, und sie wird deshalb von der Allgemeinheit eher verstanden und geschätzt.«

David Chipperfield: »Ich glaube, wir sind fähig, sehr kraftvolle, aufregende und innovative Ideen zu produzieren. Aber wir sind nicht sehr gut, wenn es darum geht, sie mit Struktur zu vereinen, und das hat mir den meisten Spaß gemacht an der Zusammenarbeit mit Leuten und Organisationen in Deutschland, die interessiert daran sind, die beiden Dinge zusammenzuhalten.« Ian Ritchie: »In der deutschsprachigen Welt ist der Architekt, der gute Architekt, auch als Professor an einer Universität tätig. Ich sage nicht, daß das richtig oder falsch ist, nur, daß es bedeutet, daß eine Verbindung zum Ausbildungssystem besteht, und vielleicht gibt es in der Allgemeinheit ein zwischen einem und drei Prozent höheres kulturelles Bewußtsein für Architektur als Kunstform als hier in England; das kann in bezug auf die Einstellung der Öffentlichkeit zu neuen Ideen einen großen Unterschied machen.«

David Chipperfield (Mitte) bei einer Diskussion im Neuen Museum, Berlin.

David Chipperfield (centre) in discussion at the Neues Museum, Berlin.

»Ich glaube bei den Deutschen gibt es da eine Art romantischer Ader; sie mögen eine Idee und sie mögen die Vorstellung, daß man sich einer Sache verschrieben hat.« David Chipperfield

'There is a sort of romantic streak I think amongst the Germans in this way that they like an idea, and they like the idea that you are committed to something.' David Chipperfield

---

speak to in Berlin is interested in the new buildings. Berliners have nicknames for individual buildings and I read most of them as being friendly'. Michael Wilford: 'In Britain architecture only appears in the national popular press to be derided in some way because it's too expensive or because it's leaking or there is some kind of scandal. But in Germany it's there regularly, comprehensively written about in an intelligent way, and therefore understood and appreciated more by the general public'.

David Chipperfield: 'I think we are capable of producing very energetic, exciting and testing ideas. But we are not very good at putting them together with structure, and this is what I've enjoyed most about the people and organisations I have worked with in Germany who are interested in keeping these two things together'. Ian Ritchie: 'In the German-speaking world, the architect, the good architect, is also a professor at a university. I'm not saying that's right or wrong but that means there is a link to the education system and maybe there is between one and three per cent more cultural awareness of architecture as an art in the general populace than here, and that can make a vast difference in terms of the approach the public take towards new ideas'.

So does Britain export some of the world's most sought-after architects while not fully appreciating their talents at home? David Chipperfield: 'I've been asked to do one house in England. Germany has a more open attitude to the future, whereas I think in England there is an attitude that all the good things were in the past and we want to hang on to that. So when the Rolling Stones make an enormous amount of money the first thing they do is go out and buy an old house in Richmond. You know they are not going to commission a brand new house'.

So German clients seem to be more prepared to put their faith in modern architecture. Richard Rogers contrasts this to current architectural attitudes in Britain: 'We tend to say, yes, mistakes have been made, so let's retrench and go backwards rather than forwards, and that is a problem. The arguments we have continuously here are about style. The real question is not about style, it's about quality of life and how you achieve it'.

There is also the matter of the status of architecture and the architect. David Chipperfield: 'In Germany there is a demand that the architect performs. You are asked to be an architect. In Britain you have to smuggle it in through the back door. You are essentially seen as a professional consultant who will bring some design to the project. In Germany you are seen as a cultural captain, you are making these decisions and you can respond to that. There is a sort of romantic streak I think amongst the Germans in this way that they like an idea, and they like the idea that you are committed to something'. Richard Rogers also perceives a distinctive German attitude: 'In general, architecture in Germany is seen as of primary importance both to the quality of life aesthetically and the quality of life economically'.

But why should German clients hire British architects to such an extent? Michael Wilford: 'There is no doubt that German architectural graduates are very well trained. On the other hand, there is a certain inhibition in design terms. There is a great reluctance to relax, loosen up and let go. And that is where I think the British have scored. We are encouraged through the education system in this country to be more experimental, to be more bold, to take risks. And therefore, if clients want something different, want something to stand out, then they are happy to come to English architects to do that'. Nicholas Grimshaw: 'The kind of architecture we do in Britain is to a degree engineering-based and detail-based and that appeals to the people making good products in Germany'.

Given the huge success in Germany of foreign architects – not only the British – do German architects feel that too many of the plum jobs have gone to outsiders? Louisa Hutton spends most of her working time in Germany: 'It is a more democratic country than England, things are in general fairer and I think people are open to new ideas and new talent, so I don't think people really see it as a negative thing, even though they may feel a bit annoyed they haven't got the job themselves. But I think in general they are quite supportive and very outgoing'.

Meinhard von Gerkan, one of Germany's top architects, offers a different personal perspective: 'I suspect that Germany's great willingness to import foreign architects is due to a cultural and political inferiority complex. This may be a result of its history, or a subliminal compensation for the very pronounced German self-confidence in commercial affairs'. He also contrasts the marked success of British architects in Germany with the lack of German practices building in Britain: 'Seeing as all renowned British architects have not only had the occasional opportunity to build in Germany during the past decades but have been able to realise a considerable proportion of their creative work there, while in contrast not a single German architect has had the chance to leave even a splinter of his œuvre on British terrain, one asks oneself how such an aston-

Richard Rogers in seinem Londoner Büro.

Richard Rogers at his London practice.

Zaha Hadid hat zwei bemerkenswerte Projekte in Deutschland fertiggestellt.

Zaha Hadid has completed two remarkable projects in Germany.

»Die deutschen Bauherren können sich also die englischen Bauten in Deutschland als Verdienst anrechnen. Schließlich steht ihnen die Architektenschaft der ganzen Welt zur Auswahl.«
'So the German clients can take credit for the British buildings in Germany. After all, they have the world market to choose from.' Richard Rogers

Exportiert England also einige der weltweit gesuchtesten Architekten, ohne deren Talent zu Hause entsprechend zu würdigen? David Chipperfield: »In England wurde ich gebeten, ein einziges Haus zu bauen. In Deutschland steht man der Zukunft offener gegenüber, wohingegen ich glaube, daß in England eine Haltung herrscht, derzufolge alles Gute der Vergangenheit angehört, und das wollen wir erhalten. Wenn also die Rolling Stones eine Riesenmenge Geld verdienen, gehen sie als erstes hin und kaufen ein altes Haus in Richmond. Jeder weiß, daß sie kein nagelneues Haus in Auftrag geben werden.«

Es scheint also, als seien deutsche Bauherren eher bereit, der modernen Architektur Vertrauen zu schenken. Richard Rogers vergleicht dies mit den heute in England gängigen Einstellungen zu Architektur: »Wir neigen dazu zu sagen, ja, es wurden Fehler gemacht, laßt uns also kürzer treten und statt nach vorne lieber in die Vergangenheit sehen, und das ist ein Problem. Die Diskussionen, die hier stattfinden, drehen sich immer um Stil. Bei der wirklichen Frage geht es nicht um Stil, sondern um Lebensqualität und wie man sie erreicht.«

Dann gibt es da noch die Frage nach der Stellung der Architektur und des Architekten. David Chipperfield: »In Deutschland ist man daran interessiert, daß der Architekt eine Leistung erbringt. Es wird erwartet, daß man als Architekt in Erscheinung tritt. In England muß man das durch die Hintertür reinschmuggeln. Dort wird man im Grunde als fachkundiger Berater angesehen, der dem Projekt ein bißchen Design beifügt. In Deutschland gilt man als kulturelle Leitfigur, man trifft diese Entscheidungen und kann auf jenes reagieren. Ich glaube bei den Deutschen gibt es da eine Art romantische Ader; sie mögen eine Idee und sie mögen die Vorstellung, daß man sich einer Sache verschrieben hat.« Richard Rogers erkennt darüber hinaus eine typisch deutsche Einstellung: »Im allgemeinen hält man in Deutschland Architektur für außerordentlich wichtig, und zwar sowohl für die ästhetische wie für die ökonomische Lebensqualität.«

Weshalb aber vergeben so viele deutsche Bauherren Aufträge an britische Architekten? Michael Wilford: »Zweifellos sind die deutschen Absolventen eines Architekturstudiums sehr gut ausgebildet. Andererseits besteht in Fragen des Designs eine gewisse Hemmung. Es besteht wenig Neigung zu entspannen, sich zu lockern und den Dingen ihren Lauf zu lassen. Und ich glaube, in dem Punkt schneiden die Engländer besser ab. Wir werden von unserem Bildungssystem dazu angehalten, experimentierfreudiger und mutiger zu sein, Risiken einzugehen. Wenn Bauherren also etwas Besonderes wollen, etwas, das auffällt, dann wenden sie sich gerne an englische Architekten.« Nicholas Grimshaw: »Die Art von Architektur, die wir in England betreiben, basiert in gewissem Maß auf der Kenntnis von Technik und von Details, und das findet Anklang bei den Leuten, die in Deutschland Qualitätsprodukte herstellen.«

Sind angesichts des großen Erfolges auswärtiger – und nicht nur britischer – Architekten in Deutschland deutsche Architekten der Meinung, daß zu viele der hochdotierten Aufträge an Ausländer gegangen sind? Louisa Hutton verbringt einen Großteil ihres Arbeitslebens in Deutschland: »Es ist ein demokratischeres Land als England, es herrscht im allgemeinen eine größere Fairness, und ich glaube, die Leute stehen neuen Ideen und neuen Talenten offen gegenüber; ich denke also nicht, daß die Leute es als negativ empfinden, obwohl sie vielleicht ein bißchen ärgerlich sind, daß sie nicht selbst zum Zuge gekommen sind. Ich glaube aber, im allgemeinen sind sie sehr aufgeschlossen und recht bereit, einen zu unterstützen.«

Einer der führenden deutschen Architekten, Meinhard von Gerkan, führt eine andere persönliche Sichtweise ins Feld: »Ich vermute, daß Deutschland aus einem kulturpolitischen Minderwertigkeitskomplex heraus besonders offen ist, für den Import ausländischer Architekten. Dies mag eine Folge der Geschichte oder eine unterschwellige Kompensation zu dem sehr ausgeprägten deutschen Selbstbewußtsein in wirtschaftlicher Hinsicht sein.« Des weiteren stellt er dem offenkundigen Erfolg britischer Architekten in Deutschland den Mangel an Tätigkeit deutscher Architekturbüros in Großbritannien gegenüber: »Da alle namhaften zeitgenössischen britischen Architekten in den vergangenen Jahrzehnten in Deutschland nicht nur marginale Akzente hinterlassen haben, sondern einen wesentlichen Anteil ihres kreativen Schaffens verwirklichen konnten, im Gegensatz dazu aber nicht ein einziger deutscher Architekt auf britischem Terrain die Chance geboten bekam, einen Splitter seines Œuvres zu hinterlassen, fragt man sich, wie es zu einem solch erstaunlichen Ungleichgewicht kommen kann. Eine naheliegende Erklärung könnte in der fachlichen Überlegenheit der britischen Architektur gegenüber der deutschen Baukultur liegen. Bei aller nationalen Befangenheit, von der wir alle leider nie ganz frei sind, darf dies wohl bezweifelt werden, zumal die Erfolge deutscher Architekten bei internationalen Wettbewerben auch dagegen sprechen.«

In Wahrheit wird die hervorragende Qualität deutscher Architekten von keinem bezweifelt. Richard Rogers: »Ich würde deutsche Architekten in dieser ersten Liga gut ausgebildeter, einfallsreicher und sachkundiger Leute unter die allerbesten einreihen. Aber sie haben bisher noch nicht den Einfluß gewonnen, den man vielleicht hätte erwarten können. Wenn ich Deutscher wäre, würde ich vielleicht die Frage stellen, was ein paar Primadonnen nützen?« David Chipperfield hat eine

Louisa Hutton und Matthias Sauerbruch sind Partner in einem in London und Berlin ansässigen renommierten Architekturbüro.

Louisa Hutton and Matthias Sauerbruch, partners in a highly regarded architectural enterprise that spans London and Berlin.

Norman Foster mit David Nelson und Claude Engle mit dem Modell für den Plenarsaal und die Kuppel des Reichstages.

Norman Foster with David Nelson and Claude Engle at the mock-up for the Reichstag Plenary Chamber and Dome.

ishing imbalance could have come about. It would be simple to explain this as resulting from the superiority of British architecture over German building culture. Despite national bias, of which, sadly, none of us is entirely free, this may be doubted, for one thing because the successes of German architects in international competitions speak against it'.

In reality, no one doubts the outstanding quality of German architects. Richard Rogers: 'I would put German architects among the very best of that premier league of people who are highly trained, imaginative and professional. They are terrific people. But – and this could happen next year – they haven't as yet achieved the ascendancy one would have perhaps expected. I suppose if I were a German, I would argue, what good is a couple of prima donnas?' David Chipperfield has a similar viewpoint: 'How do you measure the health of an architectural culture? How do you take its temperature? We've got great stars, whereas I don't think Germany is as prolific in its stars, but I actually think the health of the basic architectural body is better because the system is more nurturing, it's more protective, it's less violently commercial. I think Germany is a better place to work at the moment. There is still the basis of a public structure for commissioning architecture'.

Even so, the fact remains of a large imbalance in the architectural trade between Britain and Germany. Meinhard von Gerkan views this as a case of Britain not yet giving German architects their proper due: 'Not even the European Union directives, which state that public building projects be opened to Europe-wide competition, have been able to alter the disinterested British attitude towards German architecture.' Richard Rogers puts things in a wider European context: 'Why don't we have more foreign architects? France, Germany and Spain are full of foreign architects. The EU regulations on architectural competitions for public buildings encourage anybody to compete if they want to'. Louisa Hutton, who has experience of both London and Berlin, sees other factors at work: 'Sauerbruch Hutton have done nearly forty competitions in the past ten years and we have won four, which is very lucky, but in England we haven't been given the opportunity to enter them, so I think there is too much of an old boy network and there is not enough recognition of latent talent'.

But ultimately it is British clients who decide which architects to commission; and if they have a preference for the homegrown article, then this does not mean that the British architectural profession is closed to foreign talent. Far from it, for there is in fact no shortage of architects from Germany working in Britain. The leading London practices employ a wealth of talented young Germans, many of whom eventually move on or return home having added a new dimension to their background and new clients to their portfolio. Indeed, the role of the client in the equation is crucial. For without a commission, no architect can perform his or her art in the only meaningful way, namely by building. Richard Rogers: 'England has the potential, but there is still a sort of lack of confidence and architects *per se* are only as good as the clients. So the German clients can take credit for the British buildings in Germany. After all, they have the world market to choose from'.

Nowhere was the global vision of a German client more evident than in the case of how the German government handled the rebuilding of the Reichstag. An international, invited competition was held to determine who would win the commission. This amounted to an architectural world championship. At first, Norman Foster suspected this might be merely for show: 'It would be a great exercise but probably a waste of time in one sense because how could a British architect win the competition for arguably the most important building in Germany and possibly in the evolution of Europe at that time?'[17]

Once Norman Foster realised he was in with a real chance, then he went for it in earnest and won convincingly. This example of a British architect rebuilding the new German parliament is often cited with a mixture of surprise and admiration. Naturally, the question has been put whether one can even imagine a German architect being awarded a commission to rebuild the Houses of Parliament at Westminster.

Richard Rogers: 'I was on the jury when Norman Foster won the Reichstag competition with the full backing of the parliamentarians and the architectural profession. It was very, very impressive. I think we could learn quite a lot. No one knew it was going to be a foreigner, let alone an Englishman. The fact that in the last group fifty per cent were foreign architects, that's pretty impressive'. Louisa Hutton was also impressed: 'I particularly like the German government effectively commissioning Foster. I think it is fantastic that their competition system is so open that an international architect wins a building that is obviously incredibly important'. David Chipperfield sees the Reichstag in a wider context: 'The reconstruction of Berlin is a politically sensitive thing and the participation of other cultures through their architects is seen to be an inevitable part of the story and a positive one. I think it is quite admirable that the Germans should somehow be attuned to that, be sensitive to that.'

Will Alsop, Leiter des erfolgreichen englisch-deutschen Architekturbüros Alsop & Störmer.

Will Alsop, Principal of the successful Anglo-German practice Alsop & Störmer.

ähnliche Meinung: »Wie beurteilt man den Gesundheitszustand einer Architekturkultur? Wie mißt man deren Temperatur? Wir haben große Stars, die meiner Meinung nach in Deutschland nicht so zahlreich sind, aber ich halte tatsächlich den Gesundheitszustand der architektonischen Basis für besser, weil das System pfleglicher ist, es ist schützender, weniger brutal kommerziell. Ich halte Deutschland augenblicklich für den besseren Arbeitsplatz. Es gibt da noch die Grundlage einer öffentlich geregelten Auftragsvergabe für Architektur.«

Trotz allem bleibt die Tatsache eines deutlichen Ungleichgewichts im architektonischen Austausch zwischen England und Deutschland bestehen. Nach Ansicht Meinhard von Gerkans läßt man deutschen Architekten in Großbritannien bisher keine Anerkennung widerfahren: »Selbst die Europanormen, die vorschreiben, daß öffentliche Bauvorhaben auch für Architekten europaweit auszuloben sind, haben die distanzierte Haltung gegenüber deutscher Architektur in Großbritannien nicht zu ändern vermocht.« Richard Rogers sieht die Angelegenheit in einem größeren europäischen Zusammenhang: »Warum gibt es in England nicht mehr Architekten aus dem Ausland? In Frankreich, Deutschland und Spanien gibt es überall ausländische Architekten. Die EU-Bestimmungen zu Architekturwettbewerben für öffentliche Gebäude ermutigen jeden Interessierten zur Teilnahme.« Die sowohl in London als auch in Berlin bewanderte Louisa Hutton erkennt andere bestimmende Momente: »Sauerbruch-Hutton haben sich im Laufe der letzten zehn Jahre an nahezu vierzig Wettbewerben beteiligt, von denen wir das Glück hatten, vier zu gewinnen. In England hat man uns nicht die Gelegenheit zur Teilnahme gegeben, ich glaube also, daß Beziehungen eine zu große Rolle spielen und daß verborgenes Talent nicht genügend anerkannt wird.«

Letzten Endes sind es jedoch die britischen Bauherren, die entscheiden, wen sie beauftragen, und wenn sie eine Vorliebe für heimische Kräfte hegen, bedeutet dies nicht, daß die britische Architektenschaft ein geschlossener, für Auswärtige nicht zugänglicher Zirkel ist. Ganz im Gegenteil, denn in England herrscht durchaus kein Mangel an dort tätigen, deutschen Architekten. Die führenden Londoner Büros beschäftigen eine Vielzahl begabter, junger Deutscher, von denen viele schließlich weiterziehen oder nach Hause zurückkehren, nachdem sie ihrem Werdegang eine neue Dimension und ihrer Projektmappe neue Auftraggeber hinzugefügt haben. Die Rolle des Auftraggebers ist bei dieser Gleichung tatsächlich von entscheidender Bedeutung. Ohne Auftrag kann nämlich kein Architekt seine bzw. ihre Kunst in der einzig sinnvollen Weise, nämlich durch Bauen, umsetzen. Richard Rogers: »England verfügt über das Potential, aber es besteht noch eine Art Mangel an Zutrauen, und Architekten sind per se nur so gut wie ihre Auftraggeber. Die deutschen Bauherren können sich also die englischen Bauten in Deutschland als Verdienst anrechnen. Schließlich steht ihnen die Architektenschaft der ganzen Welt zur Auswahl.«

Nirgendwo trat die globale Sichtweise eines deutschen Bauherrn deutlicher zutage als in der Art und Weise, wie die deutsche Regierung den Umbau des Reichstags handhabe. Um über die Vergabe des Auftrags zu entscheiden wurde ein internationaler, geschlossener Wettbewerb veranstaltet. Dies war gleichbedeutend mit einer Weltmeisterschaft der Architektur. Anfangs hegte Norman Foster den Verdacht, dies geschehe nur zur Schau: »Es wäre eine großartige Aufgabe, aber in mancher Hinsicht vermutlich reine Zeitverschwendung, denn wie könnte ein britischer Architekt den Wettbewerb gewinnen, bei dem es um das wohl wichtigste Bauwerk Deutschlands und das, aus damaliger Sicht, möglicherweise wichtigste Bauwerk für die Weiterentwicklung Europas ging?«[17]

Als Norman Foster jedoch erkannte, daß er tatsächlich gute Aussichten hatte, nahm er seine Beteiligung ernst und gewann schließlich. Dieses Beispiel eines britischen Architekten, der den Wiederaufbau des neuen deutschen Parlaments übernimmt, wird häufig mit einer Mischung aus Erstaunen und Bewunderung angeführt. Naturgemäß stellte sich die Frage, ob es überhaupt vorstellbar sei, daß ein deutscher Architekt den Auftrag zum Umbau der Houses of Parliament in Westminster erhielte.

Richard Rogers: »Ich saß in der Jury, als Norman Foster mit voller Unterstützung der Abgeordneten und der Architektenschaft den Reichstags-Wettbewerb gewann. Es war sehr, sehr beeindruckend. Ich denke, wir könnten einiges lernen. Keiner wußte, daß es ein Ausländer, geschweige denn ein Engländer sein würde. Die Tatsache, daß der letzten Gruppe fünfzig Prozent auswärtige Architekten angehörten, ist ziemlich eindrucksvoll.« Louisa Hutton zeigte sich ebenfalls beeindruckt: »Ich fand besonders gut, daß Foster tatsächlich von der deutschen Regierung beauftragt wurde. Es ist phantastisch, daß das deutsche Wettbewerbssystem so offen ist, daß ein internationaler Architekt den Auftrag für ein so offenbar unglaublich wichtiges Gebäude bekommt.« David Chipperfield sieht den Auftrag zum Umbau des Reichstags in größerem Zusammenhang: »Beim Wiederaufbau von Berlin geht es um eine politisch sensible Angelegenheit, und die Beteiligung anderer Kulturen durch deren Architekten wird als naturgemäß zugehöriger und positiver Teil der Sache verstanden. Ich halte es für durchaus bewundernswert, daß die Deutschen darauf irgendwie eingestellt und dafür empfänglich sind.«

Fosters Entwurfsphilosophie verkörpert im Hinblick auf das Reichstagsprojekt eine in Deutschland vorherrschende Stimmung, die die Vergangenheit akzeptiert und gleichzeitig mit Bestimmtheit hier den Beginn der Zukunft sieht.

Foster's design philosophy with regard to the Reichstag project reflects a prevailing mood in Germany that acknowledges the past, while saying quite firmly that the future begins here.

Die letzten Jahre des 20. und der Anfang des 21. Jahrhunderts werden im langen kulturellen Austausch zwischen England und Deutschland als eine bemerkenswert fruchtbare Zeit in die Geschichte eingehen, in der zahlreiche britische Architekten bei der baulichen Renaissance des wiedervereinigten Deutschland eine wesentliche Rolle spielten.

The end of the twentieth century and the start of the twenty-first will go down in the long cultural interaction between Britain and Germany as a remarkably fertile period, when so many British architects played a substantial part in the physical renaissance of a reunified Germany.

Nachdem die Architekturjury Fosters Entwurf als Gewinner des Reichstagswettbewerbs gekürt hatte, entdeckten die deutschen Parlamentarier in der Folge darin ein machtvolles Symbol ihrer ernsthaften Verpflichtung auf eine international und nicht national ausgerichtete Zukunft. Gibt es eine bessere Art, dies zu bekunden, als einem ausländischen Architekten den Umbau ihres Bundestages zu übertragen?

Abgesehen von Fragen der Nationalität, verkörpert Fosters Entwurfsphilosophie im Hinblick auf das Reichstagsprojekt eine in Deutschland vorherrschende Stimmung, die die Vergangenheit akzeptiert und gleichzeitig mit Bestimmtheit hier den Beginn der Zukunft sieht. Norman Foster: »Es heißt, die Geschichte der Vergangenheit zu respektieren und, wie in jeder anderen Epoche, einen klaren, achtbaren Bruch mit ihr zu vollziehen, für ein schärferes Bewußtsein der Vergangenheit und ein klareres Bewußtsein vom Einschnitt der Gegenwart.«[18]

Wie die folgenden Seiten zeigen, sollte Norman Fosters Arbeit am Reichstag keineswegs als glorreiche Einzeltat verstanden werden. Die letzten Jahre des 20. und der Anfang des 21. Jahrhunderts werden im langen kulturellen Austausch zwischen England und Deutschland als eine bemerkenswert fruchtbare Zeit in die Geschichte eingehen, in der zahlreiche britische Architekten bei der baulichen Renaissance des wiedervereinigten Deutschland eine wesentliche Rolle spielten. Außerdem sollte die Tatsache nicht übersehen werden, daß deutsche Architekten sowohl als Partner wie als Mitarbeiter zu den in diesem Band vorgestellten ›britischen‹ Gebäuden einen nicht zu unterschätzenden Beitrag geleistet haben.

Diese anglo-deutsche Erfolgsgeschichte muß allerdings auch im größeren Zusammenhang der sich deutlich globalisierenden, zeitgenössischen Architektur gesehen werden. Die Namen der Stars genießen quer über alle Kontinente dieser Erde hinweg Ruhm und Anerkennung. Sie sind die wahren Nachfolger der mittelalterlichen Baumeister, die ihrer erwählten Profession folgend, ständig geographische Grenzen und politische Schranken überschritten. Richard Rogers sieht in dieser internationalistischen Ausrichtung ein ermutigendes Zeichen für die Zukunft: »Wir sind in Europa. Wir stehen vor einem europäischen Schauplatz; und das Schöne an der Architektur ist, daß man keine Worte braucht. Die Bauten sprechen für sich.«

The architectural jury having selected Foster's scheme as the worthy winner of the Reichstag competition, German parliamentarians have subsequently discovered in this a powerful symbol of their whole-hearted commitment to an internationalist and not a nationalist future. For what better way could there be to demonstrate this than by inviting a foreign architect to rebuild their national parliament?

Questions of nationality aside, Foster's design philosophy with regard to the Reichstag project reflects a prevailing mood in Germany that acknowledges the past, while saying quite firmly that the future begins here. Norman Foster: 'It is to respect the history of the past and as in every other period of time to make a clear break from that in a good-mannered way so that the awareness of the past is sharper and the awareness of the intervention of the present is clearer'.[18]

As the following pages show, Norman Foster's work on the Reichstag should not be seen in splendid isolation. The end of the twentieth century and the start of the twenty-first will go down in the long cultural interaction between Britain and Germany as a remarkably fertile period, when so many British architects played a substantial part in the physical renaissance of a reunified Germany. Nor should one overlook the fact that German architects, both as partners and associates, have contributed massively to the 'British' buildings featured in this book.

But this remarkable Anglo-German success story must also be seen in the wider context of contemporary architecture, which is resoundingly global in scope. The star names enjoy fame and fortune across all the continents of the world. They are the true successors of the master masons of medieval Europe who constantly crossed geographical frontiers and political divisions in pursuit of their chosen profession. Richard Rogers sees in this internationalist dimension an encouraging sign for the future: 'We are in Europe now. We are looking at a European scene; and the beauty of architecture is that you don't need words. The buildings speak for themselves'.

ANMERKUNGEN
ENDNOTES

1. BBC, Omnibus, 7. Juni 1999.
2. Daniel Johnson, *The Daily Telegraph*, 29. Mai 1999.
3. Stefan Muthesius, *Das englische Vorbild*, München 1974, S. 43.
4. Anne D. Petersen, *Die Engländer in Hamburg 1814–1914: ein Beitrag zur hamburgischen Geschichte*, Hamburg 1993, S. 137.
5. David Bindman und Gottfried Riemann, *Karl Friedrich Schinkel – The English Journey*, New Haven und London, Yale University Press, 1993, S. 16 [dt. *Karl Friedrich Schinkel. Reise nach England, Schottland und Paris im Jahre 1826*, Berlin 1986.]
6. George Gilbert Scott sollte später etwas Ähnliches widerfahren, als er beim Bau des Außenministeriums in London auf Geheiß von Premierminister Lord Palmerston den von ihm bevorzugten gotischen Stil zugunsten einer italienisierenden Stilvariante aufgeben mußte.
7. Karl Friedrich Schinkel, *Erläuterungsbericht zu den Entwürfen*, 2. März 1824.
8. Es handelt sich um eine Replik des ›Turm der Winde‹.
9. Reinhard Wegner, *Karl Friedrich Schinkel: Lebenswerke – Die Reise nach Frankreich und England im Jahre 1826*, Berlin und München 1990, S. 114.
10. Muthesius' Titel lautete »Königlicher Regierungsbaumeister, zugeteilt der Kaiserlichen Botschaft«.
11. Jacob Falke, »Das englische Haus« in: *Zur Kultur und Kunst*, Wien 1878 und Robert Dohme, *Das englische Haus, eine kultur-und baugeschichtliche Studie*, Braunschweig 1888.
12. Kay Mann, *London: The German Connection*, o.O., 1993, S. 86.
13. Wie Anm. 12.
14. Kristiana Hartmann, *Deutsche Gartenstadtbewegung*, München 1976.
15. Eine Ausnahme stellt das 1924 von Peter Behrens errichtete Landhaus New Ways in Northampton dar.
16. Tim Benton, »The Myth of Function«, in: Paul Greenhalgh (Hg.), *Modernism in Design*, London 1990, S. 51.
17. BBC, Omnibus, 7. Juni 1999.
18. Wie Anm. 17.

1. BBC, Omnibus, 7 June 1999.
2. Daniel Johnson, *The Daily Telegraph*, 29 May 1999.
3. Stefan Muthesius, *Das englische Vorbild*, (Prestel, Munich, 1974), p. 43.
4. Anne D. Petersen, *Die Engländer in Hamburg 1814–1914: ein Beitrag zur hamburgischen Geschichte*, (Bockel Verlag, 1993), p. 137.
5. David Bindman and Gottfried Riemann, *Karl Friedrich Schinkel – The English Journey*, (New Haven and London, Yale University Press, 1993), p. 16.
6. Something similar later befell George Gilbert Scott who was obliged to drop his preferred Gothic style for the Foreign Office in London in favour of something in the Italianate manner as ordained by the Prime Minister, Lord Palmerston.
7. Karl Friedrich Schinkel, *Notes on Sketches for the Friedrichswerdersche Kirche*, 2 March 1824.
8. A replica of the Tower of the Winds.
9. R. Wegner, *Karl Friedrich Schinkel: Lebenswerke – Die Reise nach Frankreich und England im Jahre 1826*, (Berlin & Munich, 1990), p. 114.
10. Muthesius was known as the 'architect to the Kaiser, seconded to the imperial embassy'.
11. Jacob Falke, 'Das englische Haus' in *Zur Kultur und Kunst*, (Vienna, 1878); and Robert Dohme, *Das englische Haus, eine kultur- und baugeschichtliche Studie*, (Brunswick, 1888).
12. Kay Mann, *London: The German Connection*, (KT Publishing, 1993), p. 86.
13. Ibid.
14. Kristiana Hartmann, *Deutsche Gartenstadtbewegung*, (Munich, 1977) refers to Howard as 'einen trockenen Pragmatiker'.
15. An exception is New Ways, Northampton by Peter Behrens in 1924.
16. Tim Benton, 'The Myth of Function', in Paul Greenhalgh (ed.), *Modernism in Design*, (London, Reaktion Books, 1990), p. 51.
17. BBC, Omnibus, 7 June 1999.
18. Ibid.

DIE BAUTEN
THE BUILDINGS

DER REICHSTAG – NEUER DEUTSCHER BUNDESTAG, BERLIN
THE REICHSTAG – NEW GERMAN PARLIAMENT, BERLIN

Foster and Partners, 1995–1999

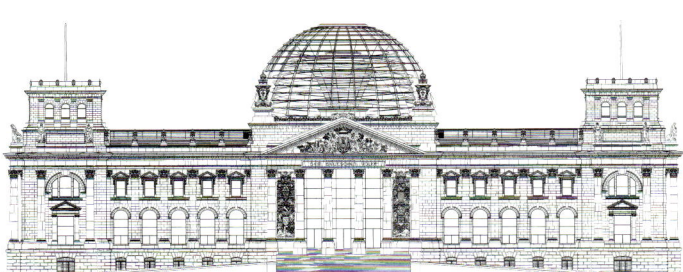

Westfassade. West elevation.

Ansichten des Entwurfsmodells.
Model views of competition scheme.

Als die Entscheidung gefallen war, das deutsche Parlament von Bonn nach Berlin zu verlegen und es im historischen Reichstag unterzubringen, sah der ursprüngliche Bauauftrag 34 000 m² umbauten Raum vor, von dem – so der erste Entwurf Fosters – ein Gutteil in einem neuen Podiumssockel untergebracht war, der das bestehende Bauwerk umgeben und von einem großen Dach überfangen werden sollte (vgl. Abb. links unten). Im zweiten Stadium des Wettbewerbs ging es um bedeutend weniger Raum, so daß ein völlig neuer Entwurf notwendig wurde. Dabei gelang es, sämtliche Räumlichkeiten innerhalb des alten Reichstagsgebäudes unterzubringen. Der endgültige Entwurf sah eine Glaskuppel vor, die dosiertes Tageslicht in den darunterliegenden Plenarsaal reflektiert und darüber hinaus als natürliches Belüftungssystem verbrauchte Luft abzieht. Im Scheitel der Kuppel befindet sich zudem eine über spiralförmige Rampen erreichbare erhöhte Aussichtsplattform. Von hier aus bieten sich nicht nur wunderbare Panoramablicke über Berlin, sondern die Besucher stehen buchstäblich über den ihnen verantwortlichen Politikern. Der Reichstag birgt darüber hinaus eine Fülle Symbolik anderer Art in einem einzigartigen architektonischen Zusammenspiel, bei dem sich Vergangenheit, Gegenwart und Zukunft begegnen und vermischen.

When the decision was made to move the German Parliament from Bonn to Berlin and to relocate it in the historic Reichstag, the initial brief was for 34,000m² of space, most of which was housed according to the first Foster scheme in a new podium that wrapped around the existing building and sheltered under a large roof (see images left). The second stage competition asked for significantly less space so that it was necessary to start the design all over again. In this, the entire accommodation could be fitted within the walls of the old Reichstag. The final design incorporates a glass dome, which deflects controlled daylight into the Plenary Chamber below and also serves to draw out air as a natural ventilation system. The dome also contains an elevated viewing deck at the apex with access by helical ramps. Apart from having the best panoramic views over Berlin, the people are raised above the politicians who are answerable to them. The Reichstag is full of other symbolism too in a unique architectural cohabitation where past, present and future meet and mingle.

»In der ersten Phase war es fast so, als hätte jemand gesagt: ›Entwirf uns einen sehr großen Bus.‹ – Dann, in der zweiten Phase, hieß es: ›Ändere es ab. Wir wollen stattdessen ein Auto. Ein sehr wichtiges Auto, aber wir wollen nur ein Auto.‹ – Wir konnten es nicht abändern. Wir fingen stattdessen ganz von vorne an.« Norman Foster

'At the first stage it was almost as if someone had said: "Design us a very large bus." Then, at the second stage, they were saying: "Modify it. We want a car instead. A very important car, but we only want a car." We couldn't modify it. We started again, completely from scratch.' Norman Foster

Ererbtes trifft auf High-tech. Das großartige Portal des Reichstags wurde erhalten; sowohl gewählte Politiker als auch die Allgemeinheit gelangen so in das moderne Herz des Gebäudes. Unter der technischen Raffinesse der Glaskuppel erscheint die vertraute, neoklassizistische Fassade als beruhigend traditionelles Element.

Heritage meets high-tech. The grand ceremonial entrance of the Reichstag has been retained to welcome both elected politicians and the general public into the modern heart of the building. The familiar neo-classical façade strikes a reassuringly traditional note beneath the technological sophistication of the glass dome.

»Ich wollte unter gar keinen Umständen an der Nachbildung der historischen Kuppel beteiligt sein. Es kam überhaupt nicht in Frage: nichtssagend, anachronistisch, völlig bedeutungslos für das, was wir taten und für die Rolle Deutschlands und seinen symbolischen Stellenwert zu dieser Zeit.« Norman Foster

'I felt absolutely passionately that I could not be party to the recreation of the historic dome. It would be totally out of the question: vacuous, anachronistic, no relevance to what we were doing and the role of Germany, its symbolism at this time.' Norman Foster

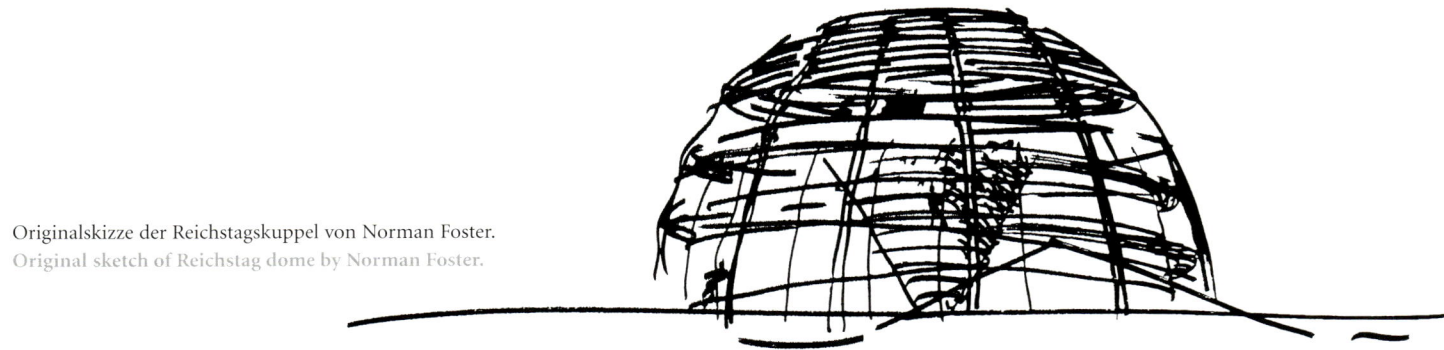

Originalskizze der Reichstagskuppel von Norman Foster.
Original sketch of Reichstag dome by Norman Foster.

Ingenieurkunst. Eine täuschend simple Skizze ergab ein höchst raffiniertes Werk der Technik. Für die Kuppel des Reichstages experimentierte Foster mit verschiedenen Spielarten von Formen und Strukturen, ehe er sich für den endgültigen Entwurf entschied.

Art into engineering. A deceptively simple sketch gave birth to a highly sophisticated work of technology. Foster experimented with a variety of shapes and structures for the dome of the Reichstag before deciding on the definitive design.

Regierung und Kultur Government and Culture

Ökologie und Innovation gehen Hand in Hand. Das innere Geheimnis von Fosters Kuppel liegt in einem konischen Gebilde (oben). Es erfüllt eine Reihe von Funktionen: Es soll verbrauchte Luft aus dem untenliegenden Plenarsaal abziehen und mittels gebogener Spiegel Tageslicht nach unten auf die Parlamentarier reflektieren. Außerdem bezieht es mit Hilfe von Photovoltaikzellen Energie aus dem Tageslicht und speichert sie für den späteren Gebrauch im Heizungssystem. Der Ausstoß von Treibhausgas läßt sich so um vierundneunzig Prozent reduzieren.

Ecology joins forces with innovation. The inside secret of Foster's dome resides in the carrot-shaped structure (above). This has a number of functions: to extract stale air from the Plenary Chamber below as well as to deflect natural light via curved mirrors down onto the Members of Parliament. The structure also draws energy from daylight through photovoltaic cells and stores it for later use in the heating system. A ninety-four per cent reduction in greenhouse gas emissions has been achieved.

Innenansicht der Reichstagskuppel von der Besuchergalerie (links) und Außenansicht von der Dachterrasse (rechts).

Internal view of the Reichstag dome from the visitors' gallery (left) and external view from the roof terrace (right).

Regierung und Kultur Government and Culture

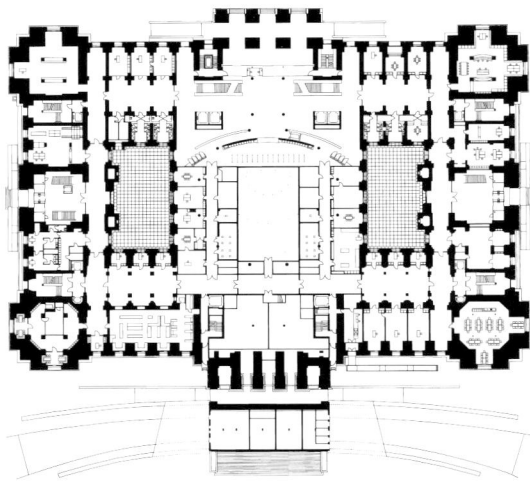

Grundriß Erdgeschoß. Ground-floor plan.

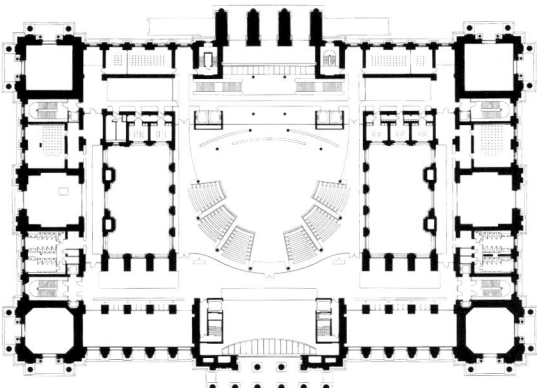

Grundriß Mezzaningeschoß. Mezzanine-floor plan.

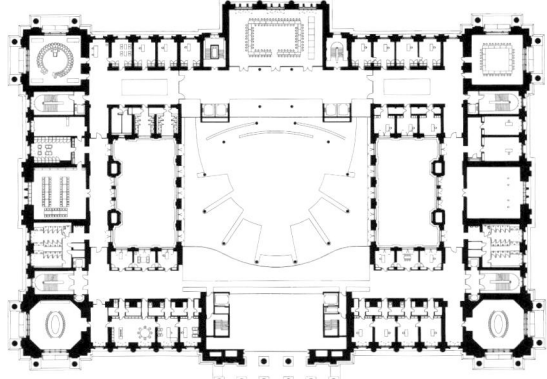

Grundriß zweites Obergeschoß. Second-floor plan.

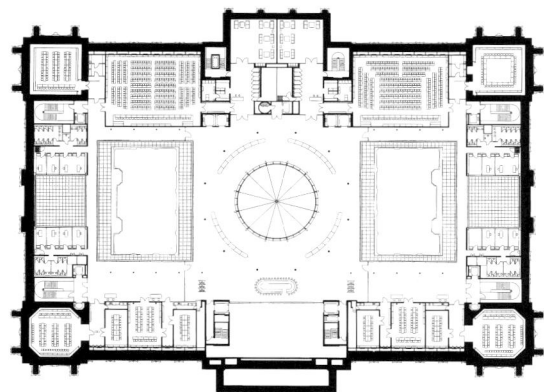

Grundriß drittes Obergeschoß. Third-floor plan.

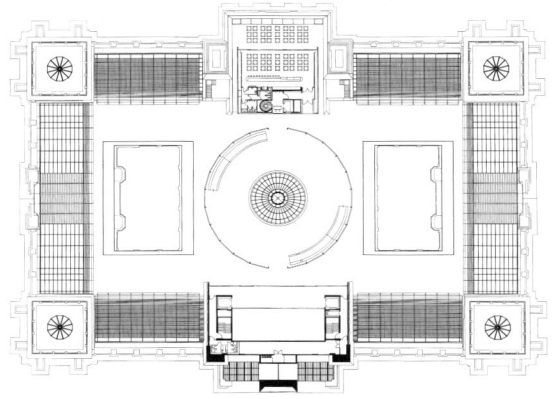

Grundriß viertes Obergeschoß. Fourth-floor plan.

Die Grundrisse lassen erkennen, wie sich ein völlig neues Gebäude paßgenau in die Hülle des alten einfügt. Die Klarheit der Anlage des ursprünglichen Reichstagsbaues lieferte einen soliden, aus dem neunzehnten Jahrhundert stammenden Rahmen für den kühnen Entwurf des zwanzigsten Jahrhunderts. Es bieten sich großartige Ausblicke hinunter in den Plenarsaal, der das Zentrum des Gebäudes einnimmt.

A series of plans reveal how an entirely new building has dropped neatly into the shell of the old. The clarity of the original Reichstag layout provided a rational nineteenth century framework for a daring twentieth-century design. There are sensational views (right) down into the Plenary Chamber, which occupies the inner core of the structure.

Regierung und Kultur Government and Culture

Auch der von Tageslicht erhellte Plenarsaal verweist symbolisch auf die politische Transparenz des neuen Reichstages. Die von Foster vorgeschlagene Ausstattung wurde in zwei wichtigen Punkten geändert. Die grauen Sitzbezüge mußten blauen Polstern weichen, und der alte Adler wurde zu Lasten von Fosters verschlankter Fassung beibehalten.

The natural light enjoyed by the Plenary Chamber is also symbolic of the political transparency of the new Reichstag. The décor proposed by Foster underwent two major changes. The grey colour for the seating was dropped in favour of blue, and the old design of the eagle was retained at the expense of Foster's slimmed-down version.

Regierung und Kultur Government and Culture

Der Beschluß der Parlamentarier, den Reichstag zu einem lebenden Museum deutscher Geschichte zu machen, indem man die Verkleidung entfernte, um Geschoßspuren, verkohltes Holz und die Graffiti der russischen Besatzer freizulegen, erwies sich als umstritten. Nicht jeder hält dies für eine angemessene Art, sich der Vergangenheit zu erinnern.

The decision of the Parliamentarians to make the Reichstag a living museum of German history by peeling away the fabric to reveal shell marks, charred timber and the graffiti of the Russian occupation has proved controversial. Not everyone agrees that this is an appropriate way to remember the past.

»Es erscheint immer noch unglaublich, daß das deutsche Parlament einen Wettbewerb durch das Sperrfeuer der Mediendiskussion steuern und schließlich britische Architekten mit einem Projekt betrauen konnte, das dem Herzen der Nation so nahe steht. Es sagt viel aus über die Aufgeschlossenheit der deutschen Demokratie, und dieser Vertrauensbeweis inspiriert uns als Architekten auch weiterhin.« Norman Foster

'It still seems incredible that the German Parliament could run a competition through the gauntlet of media debate and finally appoint British architects for a project which is so close to the heart of the nation. It tells much about the open-minded strength of German democracy, and this act of faith continues to be an inspiration for us as architects.' Norman Foster

STAATSGALERIE STUTTGART, STUTTGART
STAATSGALERIE STUTTGART, STUTTGART

James Stirling, Michael Wilford and Associates, 1977–1984

Dieser Bau lenkte die Aufmerksamkeit einer breiteren Öffentlichkeit auf die reizvollen Möglichkeiten postmoderner Architektur. James Stirling lehnte gleichwohl das Etikett ›postmodern‹ stets ab und nahm für sich in Anspruch, einfach ein Vertreter ›moderner‹ Architektur zu sein. Etwas Vergleichbares hätte schon einige Jahre früher entstehen können, aber Stirlings Entwurf aus dem Jahre 1975 für ein Museum in Düsseldorf wurde abgelehnt. Auf jeden Fall brachte Stuttgart den für die Realisierung eines solch wegweisenden Projekts nötigen Vertrauensvorschuss auf. Das zwar zur Zeit seiner Erbauung keineswegs unumstrittene Gebäude half mit, die Position Stuttgarts als eines der kulturell führenden Zentren Deutschlands zu stärken. Im größeren europäischen Zusammenhang gesehen, spielte die Staatsgalerie darüber hinaus eine entscheidende Rolle, als es darum ging, über die traditionelle Vorstellung vom Museum als Ort der Aufbewahrung von Kunstwerken hinauszugehen und das Museum als eigenständiges Kunstwerk zu betrachten.

This building brought the attention of a wider public to the exciting possibilities of post-modern architecture. James Stirling, however, always rejected the 'post-modern' label, claiming that he was simply an exponent of 'modern' architecture. Something in the same genre might have been built a couple of years earlier, but Stirling's scheme of 1975 for a museum in Düsseldorf was turned down. At any rate, Stuttgart took the enormous leap of faith necessary to realise such an epoch-making project. The building, although not without its critics at the time, helped to boost the standing of Stuttgart as one of the leading cultural cities in Germany. Seen in the wider context of Europe, the Staatsgalerie also played a crucial role in going beyond the traditional idea of the museum simply as a receptacle for housing works of art and made the museum a work of art in its own right.

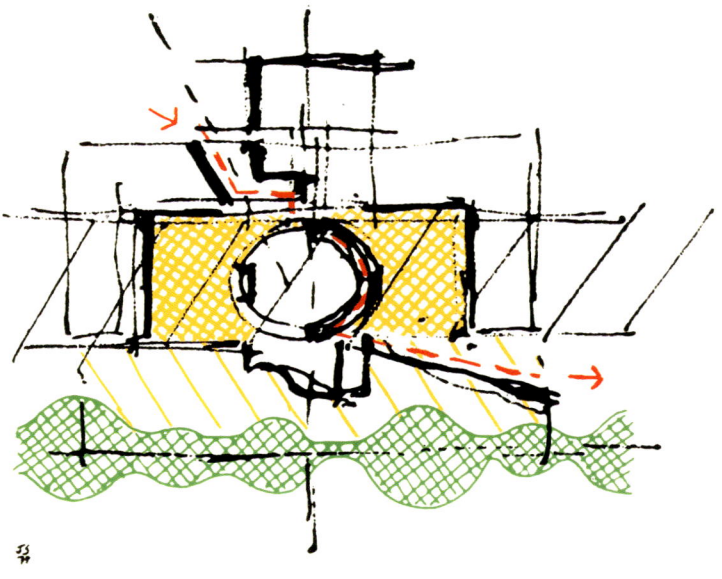

Originale Entwurfsskizze von James Stirling.
Original concept sketch by James Stirling.

Regierung und Kultur Government and Culture

Im Inneren der Staatsgalerie gestaltet sich das Zusammenspiel der architektonischen Komponenten sehr viel zurückhaltender. Der Besucher trifft auf viele vertraute Ansichten, die Architektur läßt den ausgestellten Kunstwerken Raum und übertönt sie nicht.

The architectural games are more subdued inside the Staatsgalerie. Visitors encounter much that is familiar and the building does not seek to upstage the works of art on display.

Regierung und Kultur Government and Culture

»Es ist etwas Ungewöhnliches gewesen, und die Stuttgarter waren sehr schnell davon überzeugt, nachdem sie sahen, wieviel junges Publikum hier den Zugang zur Kunst gefunden hat.« Roswitha Wenzl, Stuttgart Marketing

'It was something out of the ordinary, and the people of Stuttgart were quickly won over when they saw how many young people found through this building a way into art.' Roswitha Wenzl, Stuttgart Marketing

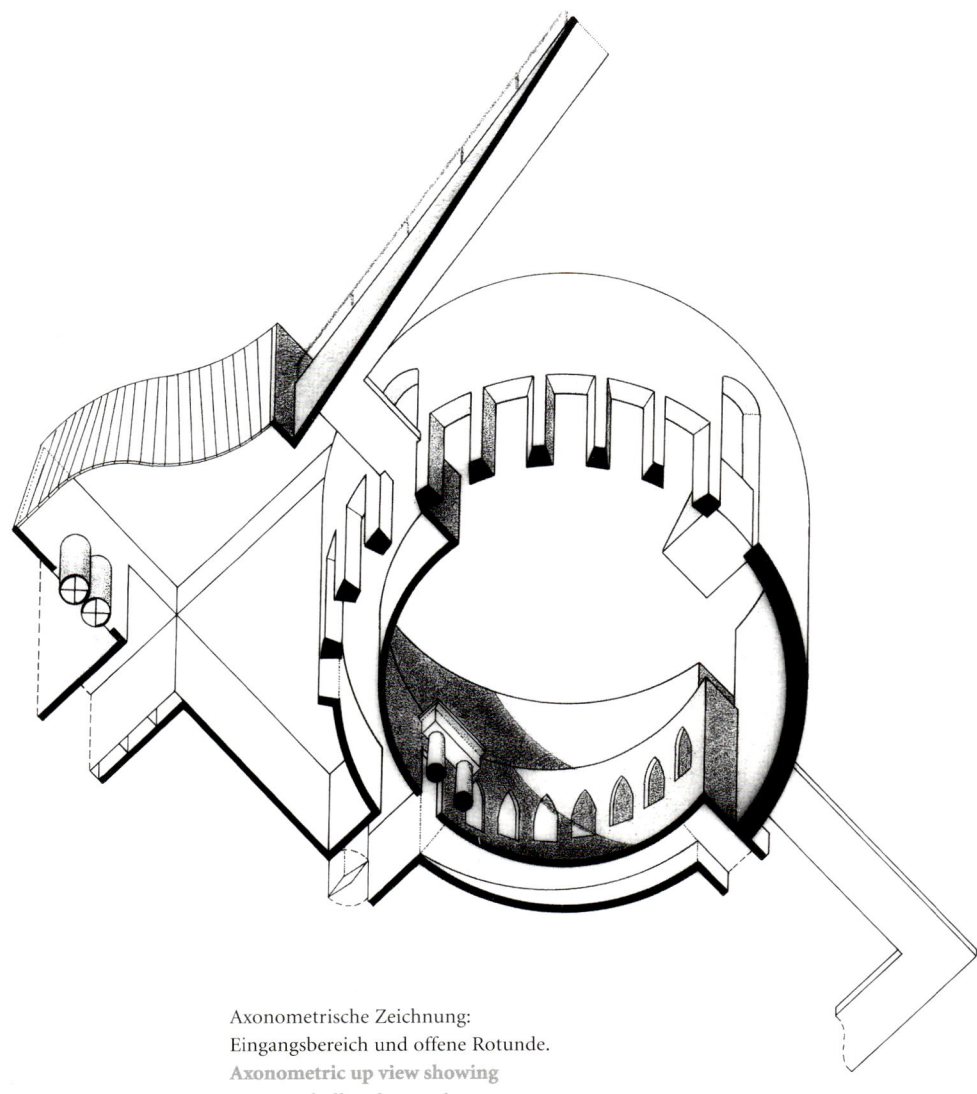

Axonometrische Zeichnung: Eingangsbereich und offene Rotunde.
Axonometric up view showing entrance hall and rotunda.

»Ich bin mit meinem dreijährigen Neffen, der nicht viel von Kunst versteht, kürzlich mal reingegangen, und ich habe bemerkt, daß er richtig Spaß hat. Und wenn wir später daran vorbeigefahren sind, hat er es immer wieder erkannt.« Karin Storz, Stuttgart Marketing

'Recently I went in with my three-year-old nephew who doesn't understand too much about art and I noticed that he really had fun. Afterwards, whenever we drove past he always recognised it.' Karin Storz, Stuttgart Marketing

»Die Diskussion um die Neue Staatsgalerie setzte modelhaft einen Streit zwischen zwei scheinbar unüberwindbaren Bau-Ideologien in Gang: zwischen einer dem Funktionalismus verpflichteten Architekturtradition, die sich in Stuttgart vor allem mit der Errichtung der Weißenhofsiedlung (1927) etabliert hatte, und einer aus Großbritannien importierten ›Postmoderne‹ mit ihrer Vorliebe für Stil-Collagen. Erst die internationalen Pressestimmen zur Eröffnung am 9. März 1984 zollten dem Stirling-Bau weltweit Beachtung. Das internationale Ansehen der Staatsgalerie bestätigt, daß der in den siebziger Jahren zu Zeiten allgemeiner wirtschaftlicher Rezession beschlossene Neubau eine lohnende Investition in die Zukunft war.« Pressemitteilung, Staatsgalerie Stuttgart, 1994

'The discussion surrounding the new Staatsgalerie sparked off a battle between two seemingly irreconcilable building ideologies: on the one hand the Functionalist tradition of architecture that had established itself in Stuttgart with the Weißenhofsiedlung (1927), and on the other hand a post-modernism imported from Great Britain with its preference for stylistic collages. Only when the international press aired its views after the opening on 9 March 1994 did Stirling's building gain world-wide regard. The international reputation of the Staatsgalerie confirms that the decision to construct a new building in the 1970s at a time of general economic recession was a worthwhile investment.' Press release, Staatsgalerie Stuttgart, 1994.

Die S-förmige Fassade setzt sich auch im Inneren der Staatsgalerie fort.

The S-shaped façade also makes its presence felt inside the Staatsgalerie.

Regierung und Kultur Government and Culture

MUSIKHOCHSCHULE, STUTTGART
MUSIC SCHOOL, STUTTGART

James Stirling, Michael Wilford and Associates, 1987–1996

Dieses Gebäude ergänzt Stuttgarts ›Kulturmeile‹ in eindrucksvoller Weise. Die Musikhochschule umfaßt in einem linearen Trakt entlang der Urbanstraße neun Geschosse mit Unterrichts- und Übungsräumen. Das Zentrum des Gebäudes markiert ein runder Turm, der stark an den Schornstein eines Dampfers erinnert. In dem Turm sind eine Konzerthalle und die Bibliothek untergebracht. Von der bekrönenden Dachterrasse mit Garten bieten sich herrliche Ausblicke über die Stadt. Dieser Bauteil fungiert darüber hinaus als Lichtschacht, der Tageslicht in die darunterliegende Bibliothek leitet. Als Pendant zur Staatsgalerie setzt die Musikhochschule deren Wandverkleidungen mit Sandstein, Travertin und Putz sowie die Abfolge halb umschlossener Außenräume fort, die sich vor dem Abhang zur Stadt hin öffnen. Die ganze architektonische Anlage wird mit dem in der Form eines Konzertflügels geplanten Historischen Museum vervollständigt, das auf dem verbleibenden Teil des Geländes entstehen soll.

This building represents a striking addition to Stuttgart's 'Cultural Mile'. The Music School comprises nine floors of teaching and practice rooms accommodated in a linear building fronting Urbanstrasse. The focus of the building is a cylindrical tower strongly suggestive of the funnel of a steamship, which contains the concert hall and library and is topped by a roof terrace and garden enjoying magnificent views over the city. The structure also provides a well of natural light that penetrates down to the library below. The Music School mirrors the Staatsgalerie by continuing the sandstone, travertine and stucco wall finishes and continuing the series of external semi-enclosed spaces that open out from the hillside towards the city. The whole architectural composition will be complete when the History Museum, in the shape of a grand piano, is built on the remaining portion of the site.

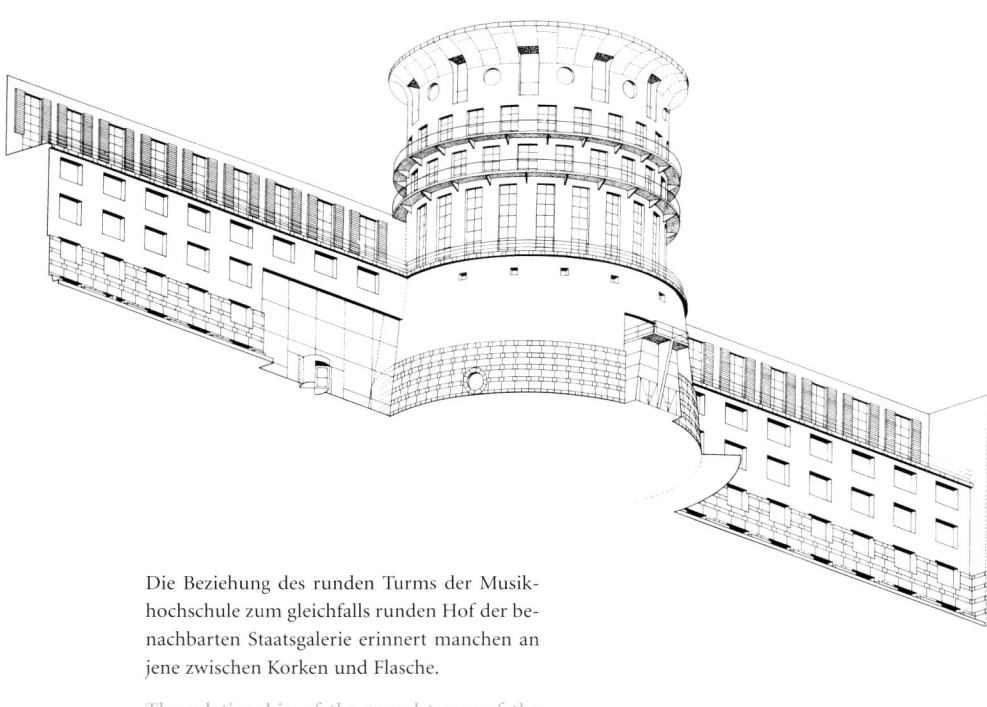

Die Beziehung des runden Turms der Musikhochschule zum gleichfalls runden Hof der benachbarten Staatsgalerie erinnert manchen an jene zwischen Korken und Flasche.

The relationship of the round tower of the Music School to the circular courtyard of the Staatsgalerie next door has been likened to pulling a cork out of a bottle.

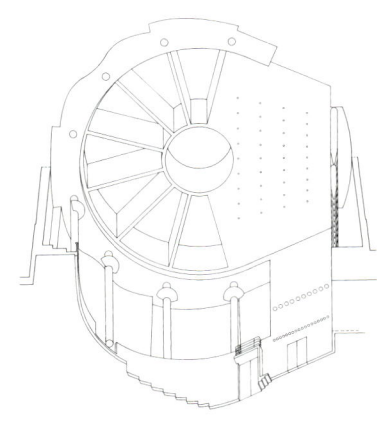

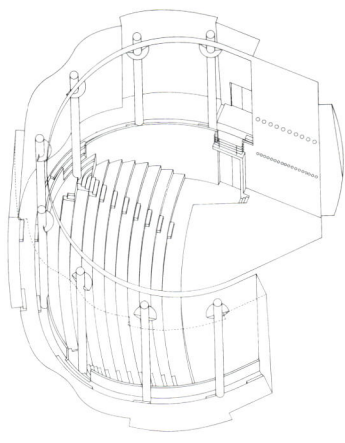

Vier Axonometrien der hochschuleigenen Konzerthalle.
Four axonometrics of the Music School concert hall.

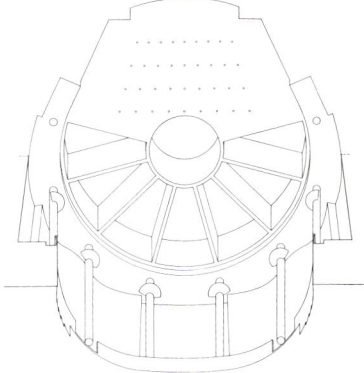

In der Ausstellungsgalerie der Musikhochschule ergeben sich schöne Licht- und Schatteneffekte.

The exhibition galleria of the Music School makes an interesting play of light and shade.

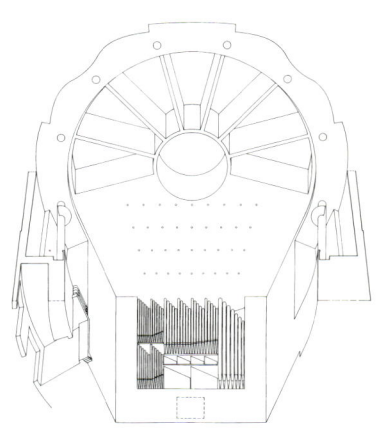

Regierung und Kultur Government and Culture

Die Aufführungsbedingungen der Musikhochschule entsprechen modernsten technischen Maßstäben. Stuttgart erhielt so einen Konzertsaal von internationaler Bedeutung. Neben dem Hauptsaal (unten) gibt es noch eine Reihe weiterer kleiner Übungsräume, die die Einrichtung vervollständigen.

The performance conditions enjoyed by the students of the Music School are of the highest contemporary technical standards. Stuttgart has acquired thereby a venue of international significance. In addition to the main concert hall (above) there are also a number of smaller practice rooms which complete the musical facilities.

LANDESGARTENSCHAU, WEIL AM RHEIN
REGIONAL GARDEN SHOW, WEIL AM RHEIN

Zaha M. Hadid with Schumacher, Mayer, Bährle, 1997–1999

The state of Baden-Württemberg maintained its reputation for being at the cutting edge of architectural innovation when it selected Zaha Hadid to build a pavilion as an event and exhibition space for its regional garden show in Weil am Rhein, which occupies a new park on the site of a disused gravel quarry to the south of the town. The project was conceived as a landscape counterpoint to the renowned architectural complex created by Vitra to the north; and it was Zaha Hadid's acclaimed Fire Station for Vitra that influenced the choice of those responsible for the Landesgartenschau. Her new creation, known as Landscape Formation One, fulfils the promise of its name by emerging as an almost natural form from the ground on which it stands. The architect refers to the building not in conventional terms as a structure but as a 'space-bundle' not to be seen in isolation but 'as part of a sequence of projects that try to elicit new fluid spatialities from the study of natural landscape formations such as river deltas, mountain ranges, forests, deserts, canyons, ice floes, oceans and so on'. The opening of this building was greeted as a maturing of the Zaha Hadid style with its emphasis on confident understatement rather than exuberant fireworks.

Das Bundesland Baden-Württemberg wurde seinem Ruf als Vorreiter in Sachen innovative Architektur gerecht, als es Zaha Hadid damit beauftragte, für die Landesgartenschau in Weil am Rhein einen Pavillon zu entwerfen, der als Raum für Aktionen und Ausstellungen dienen sollte. Für die Gartenschau wurde auf dem Gelände einer ehemaligen Kiesgrube am Südrand der Stadt ein neuer Park angelegt. Das Projekt wurde als landschaftliches Gegenstück zu dem berühmten, im Norden der Stadt gelegenen Architekturensemble von Vitra konzipiert, dessen vielgerühmte, von Zaha Hadid entworfene Feuerwache die Verantwortlichen der Gartenschau beeinflußte. Ihr neues, als ›Landscape Formation One‹ bekanntes Werk wird seinem Namen gerecht, indem es aus dem Boden, auf dem es steht, gleichsam wie eine natürliche Form aufsteigt. Die Architektin spricht von dem Bau nicht in herkömmlichen Begriffen als einer Konstruktion, sondern als einem »Raum-Bündel«, das nicht isoliert, sondern als »Teil einer Folge von Projekten« gesehen werden soll, »die neue fließende Räumlichkeiten aus dem Studium natürlicher Landschaftsformen wie Flußdeltas, Gebirgszüge, Wälder, Wüsten, Canyons, Eisschollen, Meere und so weiter entwickeln wollen.« Bei seiner Eröffnung wurde dieser Bau als Beispiel des gereiften Stils von Zaha Hadid gefeiert, dessen Schwergewicht nicht auf überschwenglichen Effekten, sondern auf bewußtem Understatement liegt.

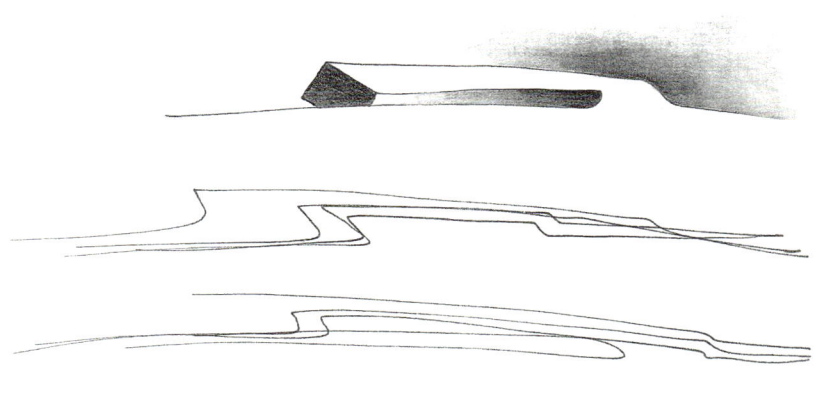

Wie der Name andeutet, geht es bei ›Landscape Formation One‹ weniger um einen Fremdkörper in der Landschaft als um eine Erweiterung der Landschaft selbst. Das Gebäude behauptet seine eigene architektonische Identität und erweckt gleichzeitig den Eindruck, es handele sich um eine mit ihrer Umgebung verbundene, natürliche Formation.

As the name suggests, Landscape Formation One sets out to be not so much an alien object in the landscape as an extension of the landscape itself. The building asserts its own architectural identity while creating the impression of being a natural feature linked to its surroundings.

Diese Studie läßt die Nähe des endgültigen Bauwerks zum vorbereitenden Konzept erkennen. Das fertige Gebäude zeichnet sich durch die gleiche enge Linienführung und den gleichen Ortssinn aus wie die frühen Skizzen.

This painting shows the closeness of the final product to the preliminary concept. The finished building has all the tightness of line and sense of direction so readily apparent in the initial sketches.

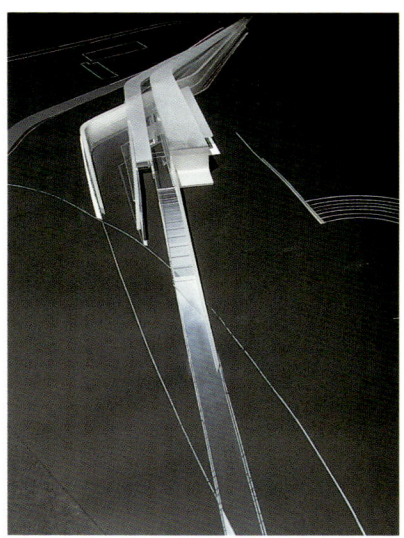

Aufsichten zeigen die geschmeidigen Umrisse des sanft aus dem Boden aufsteigenden, flachen Gebäudes. Der geschwungene Fußweg, der genau über das Dach führt, verstärkt die scheinbar natürliche Wirkung des Baukörpers, der sich geschickt gleichermaßen als Ziel wie auch als Weg präsentiert. Modelle (links) geben dem gleichen Gedanken Ausdruck.

Elevated views show the smooth contours of the low-lying building emerging gently from the ground. The sinuous walkway that runs right across its roof enhances the quasi-natural effect of the structure that cleverly presents itself both as a destination and as a route. Models (left) express the same idea.

Regierung und Kultur Government and Culture

»Das Raum-Bündel verwirklicht einige der Aspekte von Landschaft, die wir als die befreiendsten erkannt haben: Die Gestalt unseres Gebäudes ist nicht begrenzt. Es blutet buchstäblich aus und löst sich in der umgebenden Landschaft auf. Es erhebt sich allmählich aus dem Wegegewirr und überläßt es dem Besucher, anhand seiner oder ihrer eigenen Perspektive, Anfang und Ende zu erkennen und zu bestimmen.« Zaha Hadid

'The space-bundle realises some of the aspects of landscape that we have identified as most liberating: the figure of our building is not contained. It literally bleeds out and dissolves into the surrounding landscape. It emerges gradually from the tangle of paths, leaving it to the visitor to define and realise its beginning and end, according to his or her own perspective.' Zaha Hadid

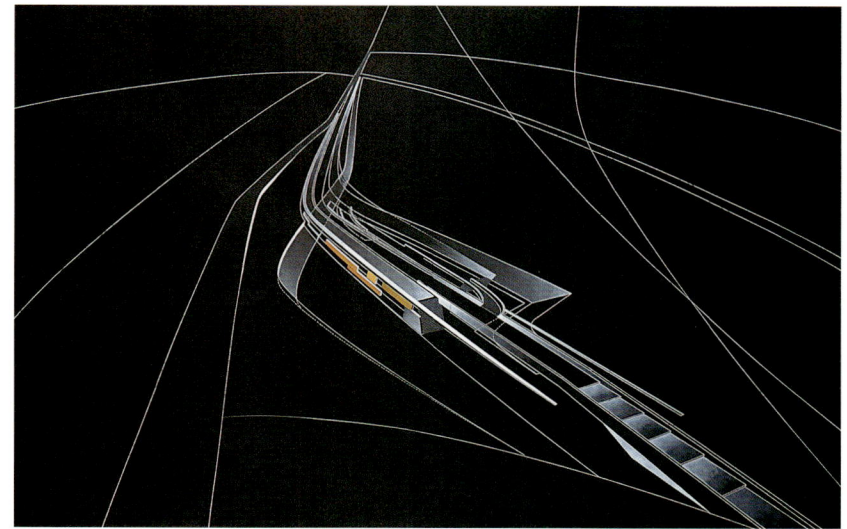

Dynamische Studie. Dynamic painting.

Der zweckmäßige Charakter der Betonelemente des Baus schafft eine charakteristische, kraftvolle Geometrie. Die innere Anordnung scheint ein Eigenleben anzunehmen, das etwas mit der primitiven Struktur einer megalithischen Kammer aus prähistorischer Zeit gemein hat. Das Spiel von Licht und Schatten gestaltet sich höchst dramatisch.

The purposeful character of the concrete building elements creates a distinctive muscular geometry. The internal arrangement appears to acquire a life of its own that has something in common with the primitive structure of a megalithic chamber in prehistoric times. The interplay of light and shade is highly dramatic.

Beton wird auf verschiedene Weise geformt, um Bauteile von großer Prägnanz zu erzeugen.

Concrete is shaped in various ways that create building elements with powerful impact.

WISSENSCHAFTSZENTRUM FÜR SOZIALFORSCHUNG, BERLIN
SOCIAL SCIENCE RESEARCH CENTRE, BERLIN

James Stirling, Michael Wilford and Associates, 1984–1988

Der von den Berlinern mit dem Spitznamen ›Hochzeitstorte‹ belegte Anbau des Wissenschaftszentrums für Sozialforschung weist die bekannten Merkmale von James Stirlings lebhafter architektonischer Phantasie auf. Die postmoderne Verspieltheit dieses bemerkenswerten Gebäudes steht in denkbar scharfem Kontrast zur würdigen Fassade des Altbaus, einem Produkt des preußischen 19. Jahrhunderts. Der Schlüssel zum Verständnis des Wissenschaftszentrums ist nicht ganz leicht zu finden. Die nach Art eines Campus um ihre jeweiligen Innenhöfe gruppierten Bauten weisen zahlreiche, nur mit Zeitaufwand zu enträtselnde, ironische Bezüge auf, angefangen bei gotischen Bögen bis hin zu griechischen Kapitellen. Wie bei allem, was von konventionellen Normen abweicht, stößt auch Stirlings Werk sowohl auf wütende Reaktionen wie auf Begeisterung. Als der Architekt sah, was überall in Berlin gebaut wurde, bezeichnete er sich selbst als stolz, Teil dieses faszinierenden Architekturzoos zu sein.

Nicknamed 'the wedding cake' by Berliners, the extension to the Social Science Research Centre bears the familiar signs of James Stirling's vivid architectural imagination. The post-modern playfulness of this remarkable building forms a complete contrast to the worthy nineteenth-century Prussian façade of the parent structure. Finding a key to understanding the Social Science Research Centre is no straightforward matter. The buildings grouped in campus style around their courtyards are full of ironic references from Gothic arches to Greek capitals that take time to decipher. As with all departures from conventional norms, Stirling's work has the capacity to exasperate as well as to delight. When the architect saw what was being built all around in Berlin, he declared himself proud to be part of the most fascinating architectural zoo.

»Schiebt uns hier ein genialer Requisiteur auf einem der Schauplätze des großen ›Kulturforums‹ die Kulissen einer Bühne zurecht, auf der neue, zeitgemäße Stücke fröhlicher Wissenschaft aufgeführt werden?« Dr. Georg Thurn, Forschungsplanung und Forschungskoordination, Wissenschaftszentrum

'Do we have here a master of props arranging the scenery on one of the stages of the great "Culture Forum" on which new and contemporary works of joyful science will be performed?' Dr G. Thurn, Research Policy and Coordination, Social Science Research Centre

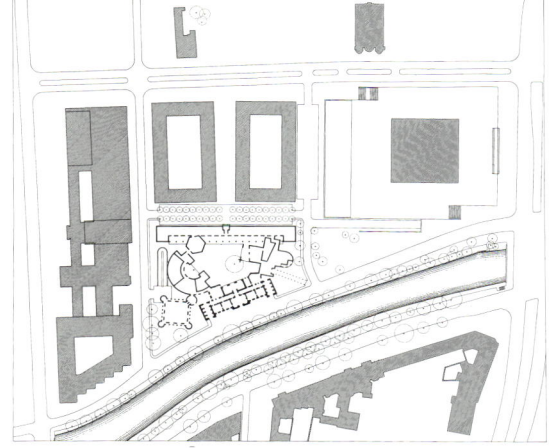

Lageplan. Site context plan.

Als man ihn mit den angeblich unseligen historischen Assoziationen der Fenster konfrontierte, machte James Stirling völlig lautere Absichten geltend. Die unverhältnismäßig schweren Fensterumrahmungen sollten im größeren Zusammenhang der beständigen Vorliebe des Architekten für das Unerwartete gesehen werden; hier unternahm er mit Hilfe von Masse und Volumen den Versuch, den Betrachter in einem Zustand gespannter Ungewißheit zu halten.

When confronted with the supposedly unfortunate historic associations of the windows, James Stirling claimed to be completely innocent in his intentions. The disproportionately heavy lintels should be seen in the wider context of the architect's constant predilection for doing the unexpected with mass and volume in a calculated attempt to keep the viewer in a state of uncertainty and suspense.

Grundriß drittes Obergeschoß. Third-floor plan.

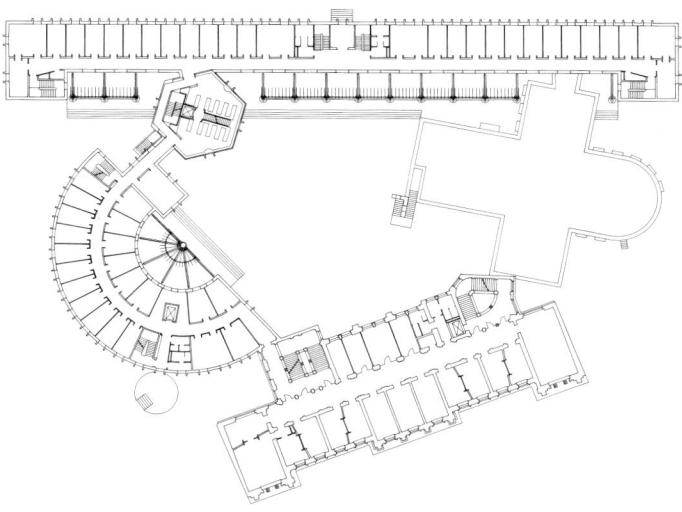

»Zu Anfang waren die Ansichten sehr geteilt. Es gab Kritiker und Skeptiker, die sagten, wir wollen in keinem dysfunktionalen, postmodern-manieristischen Gebäude arbeiten. Wir wollen die klare, bodenständige, progressive Tradition einer aufgeklärten Moderne und können das nicht akzeptieren. Dann gab es die anderen, die von Anfang an dachten: ›Also, das hier ist etwas anderes, es stimmt optimistisch, ist etwas besonderes, und wir fühlten uns sofort wohl.‹ Viele der anfangs Skeptischen wurden bekehrt und teilen jetzt dieses Gefühl, daß hier etwas Besonderes, etwas Anregendes passiert. Inzwischen hat es sich sehr bewährt.« Dr. Georg Thurn, Forschungsplanung und Forschungskoordination, Wissenschaftszentrum

'At the beginning people were very much divided. There were critics and sceptics who said we do not wish to work in a dysfunctional, post-modern building of the Mannerist type. We want the clear, down-to-earth, progressive Enlightenment/Modernist tradition and we cannot accept this. Then there were the others who from the beginning thought: "Well, this is different it's elating, it's special, and we are happy right away." Many of the others have become converted and now share this feeling of something special and stimulating happening here. It has more than stood the test of time.' Dr G. Thurn, Research Policy and Coordination, Social Science Research Centre

Grundriß erstes Obergeschoß. First-floor plan.

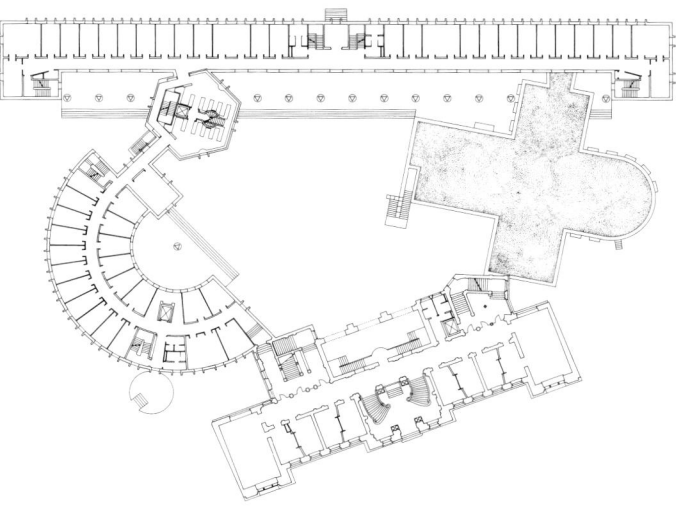

Grundriß Obergeschoß. Upper-level plan.

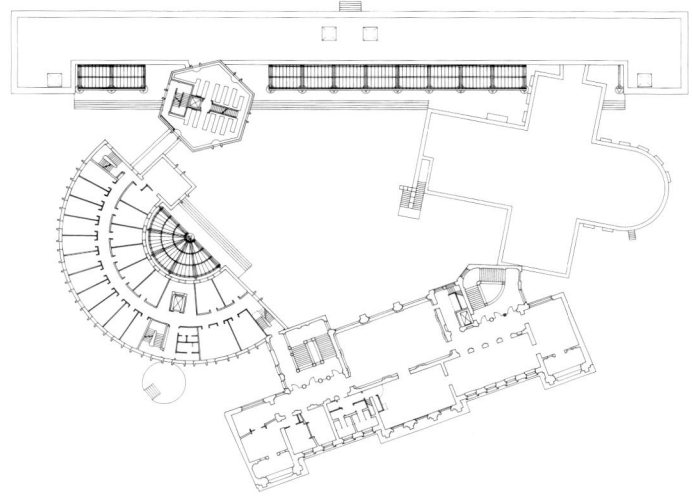

Die Bibliothek des Wissenschaftszentrums ist auf mehreren Ebenen in einem runden Bücherturm untergebracht, der von ferne an einen Elfenbeinturm erinnert, in dem Forscher, abgeschirmt von Lärm und Trubel des Alltags, über die Zukunft nachdenken können.

The library of the Social Science Research Centre is housed on several layers in a round book tower that is vaguely suggestive of an ivory tower in which academic researchers might meditate on the future, well shielded from the noise and clamour of today's world.

Das Wissenschaftszentrum ist voller unerwarteter Details und stilistischer Überraschungen. In scharfem Gegensatz zur Außenfassade mit ihren schweren Fensterstürzen und -laibungen sind die hofseitigen Fensterumrahmungen in geradezu minimalistischer Weise reduziert. Auf dem transparenten Vordach sammelt sich das Regenwasser wie in einer geöffneten Blüte. Der mächtige Stützpfeiler verjüngt sich unmittelbar vor dem Zusammentreffen mit dem Dach zu einem schlanken Halm. Bedingt durch seine gebogene Form wirft der Baukörper einen Schatten auf sich selbst und erinnert so an eine Sonnenuhr.

The Social Science Research Centre is full of unexpected features and stylistic surprises. In stark contrast to the external façade with heavy lintels, the window surrounds on the courtyard side are pared down in almost Minimalist fashion. The transparent canopy collects rainwater like an open flower. The thick supporting column suddenly tails off into a slender stem just before the point of contact. The curved building casts a shadow across itself in a manner reminiscent of a sundial.

STAATSARCHIV, HAMBURG
STATE ARCHIVES, HAMBURG

Alsop & Störmer, 1994–1997

Der Lesesaal des Staatsarchivs bietet etwa 50 Plätze, an denen Besucher die historischen Dokumente der Sammlung studieren können. Im Gegensatz zum kühlen Erscheinungsbild des Depots, entstand hier ein lebendiger Treffpunkt mit der Geschichte mit einer in einem warmen Orangeton gehaltenen Innenausstattung. Nur die Servicetheke hebt sich durch ihre weiße Farbe ab.

The reading room of the State Archives offers about 50 seats where visitors are able to study the historic documents of the collection. In contrast to the cool aspect of the storage building, this space represents a livelier meeting point with history. This is the reason for the overall treatment of the décor in a warm orange colour. Only the serving counter has been prominently picked out in white.

Das neue Staatsarchiv in Hamburg besteht aus zwei Hauptgebäuden: dem Bau, in dem Depot und Konservierungsstelle untergebracht sind sowie dem Verwaltungsbau, in dem sich Forschungseinrichtungen, Lesesaal und die Cafeteria befinden. Das Archivgebäude im Zentrum des Geländes enthält annähernd 30 km Akten, die in einem freistehenden, kastenförmigen Bau ohne jegliche Öffnungen untergebracht sind, um ein gleichbleibendes Klima im Inneren zu gewährleisten. Er ist mit durchscheinendem, vielfältig strukturiertem Glas verkleidet, wodurch der Eindruck eines Eiswürfels entsteht. Mit diesem Bild soll die elementare Funktion des Staatsarchivs als Ort der dauerhaften Bewahrung von Geschichte symbolisiert werden. Die blau abgesetzten Schächte, die der vertikalen Erschließung dienen, fügen dem allgemeinen Eindruck eine Farbkomponente hinzu.

The new development for the State Archives in Hamburg consists of two main buildings: the archive for storage and preservation and the administration building which accommodates research, reading and catering facilities. The archive building in the centre of the site contains approximately 30km of files in a solitary box-like structure without any openings, in order to maintain a constant climate inside. It is clad in translucent glass in a variety of textures to create the appearance of an ice cube. This image was intended to symbolise the basic function of the State Archives as a place for the permanent conservation of history. The blue rendered cores providing vertical circulation add a dash of colour to the overall impact.

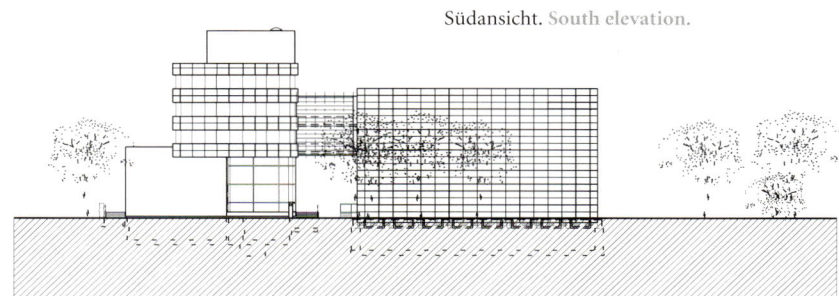

Südansicht. South elevation.

Obgleich sich die beiden benachbarten Gebäude des Staatsarchivs durch die jeweils verwendeten Materialien unterscheiden, ergibt sich im Hinblick auf Maßstab und harmonisches Nebeneinander ein geschlossener Eindruck. Die unterschiedliche Strukturierung der durchscheinenden Glaspaneele läßt eine Fassade entstehen, die dem Auge im Rahmen des insgesamt einheitlich wirkenden Entwurfs eine interessante Vielfalt bietet.

The two adjacent buildings that make up the State Archives, although contrasting in their materials, present a homogeneous picture in terms of scale and harmonious juxtaposition. The different textures of the translucent glass panels contribute to a façade that offers the eye a diversity of interest within the overall unity of design.

Brücken aus Stahl und Glas (rechts) verbinden den Verwaltungsbau mit dem Archivblock, der einige, für die Geschichte der Stadt Hamburg bedeutende Texte zur Schau stellt, die durch die Glasfassade hindurch deutlich zu sehen sind. Auf diesem Foto (unten links) ist ein Auszug aus der im zwölften Jahrhundert verfaßten ›Burspraake‹ zu sehen, die der ansässigen Bauernschaft zum ersten Mal Rechte einräumte.

Bridges of steel and glass (above right) connect the administration building to the archive block which displays some important texts of Hamburg city history that are clearly visible through the glass façade. This photo (above left) shows an extract from the twelfth century 'Burspraake' in which rights were first granted to the local peasantry.

Regierung und Kultur Government and Culture

BRITISCHE BOTSCHAFT, BERLIN
BRITISH EMBASSY, BERLIN

Michael Wilford and Partners, 1995–2000

Aufriß Wilhelmstraße mit Britischer Botschaft und Brandenburger Tor. Elevation to Wilhelmstrasse showing British Embassy and Brandenburg Gate.

Mit der Wiedervereinigung Deutschlands und dem Umzug der Bundesregierung von Bonn nach Berlin, ergab sich für die Britische Botschaft die einzigartige Chance, sich den Herausforderungen der Zeit zu stellen. Das frühere Gebäude war zerstört, das Grundstück jedoch noch vorhanden, da es, bedingt durch seine Lage an der Berliner Mauer, nicht bebaut werden konnte. Also war der Weg frei für die britische Diplomatie, an genau dem gleichen Ort in der Wilhelmstraße, an dem sie bis zum Ausbruch des Zweiten Weltkrieges residiert hatte, einen neuen Anfang zu machen. Im Gegensatz zum stilistischen Freistil, der die Wiedergeburt des Potsdamer Platzes charakterisiert, unterlag das Gebiet um Pariser Platz und Brandenburger Tor strengen Planungsrichtlinien. Hier sollten traditionelle urbane Werte von größter Bedeutung sein. Gleichwohl wollte die Britische Botschaft ihre Zugehörigkeit zum neuen Berlin klar zum Ausdruck bringen. Die Berücksichtigung dieser Kriterien bieten den Schlüssel für Michael Wilfords Vorgehen bei seinem erfolgreichen Entwurf für ein Gebäude, das Berlins Geschichte respektiert und zugleich einen kühnen Sprung in die Zukunft wagt.

With the reunification of Germany and the transfer of the Federal Government from Bonn to Berlin a unique opportunity was offered to the British Embassy to meet the challenge of the age. The former building had been destroyed but the site was still available, having been saved from development by the Berlin Wall. So the way was open for British diplomacy to make a fresh start on the exact location on the Wilhelmstrasse it had occupied until the outbreak of war in 1939. In contrast to the stylistic free-for-all that characterised the rebirth of Potsdamer Platz, this area around Pariser Platz and the Brandenburg Gate was subject to stricter planning guidelines. Here, traditional urban values were to be of the utmost importance. Yet the British Embassy wanted to make a clear statement that it belonged very much to the new Berlin. Resolving these criteria provides the key to the approach of Michael Wilford in his successful design for a building that respects Berlin's past while taking a bold leap into the future.

»Eine Botschaft dient einer höchst öffentlichen Funktion, sie soll die Bürger Deutschlands willkommen heißen und Großbritannien ihnen gegenüber vertreten. Also haben wir eine ziemlich große Öffnung in die Steinfassade geschnitten, so daß die öffentlichen Bereiche, fast wie Zähne in einem offenen Mund, auch draußen sichtbar sind. Die Fassade liefert so buchstäblich eine Darstellung des Geschehens im Gebäudeinneren.« Michael Wilford

'An Embassy has a very public function, to welcome the citizens of Germany and to represent Britain to them. So we have cut a rather large opening through the stone façade allowing the public spaces to grin through almost like teeth in an open mouth. So the façade is a very literal representation of what is happening inside the building.' Michael Wilford

Die Innengestaltung des Gebäudes tritt in Gestalt reizvoller, farbiger Formen hervor, die die im Inneren herrschende Moderne ahnen lassen. Das hellblaue, dreieckige Cockpit dient als Informationszentrum, wohingegen in dem daneben liegenden, purpurfarbenen Rund Konferenzeinrichtungen untergebracht sind. Die Tatsache, daß die Britische Botschaft und das Brandenburger Tor mit dem gleichen Stein verkleidet sind, verdeutlicht den einfühlsamen Umgang mit dem städtischen Umfeld.

The internal style of the British Embassy protrudes in the form of intriguing, colourful shapes that hint at the modern vision lying within. The triangular cockpit in light blue above the main entrance serves as an Information Centre, while the purple drum beyond accommodates conference facilities. Acutely sensitive to the urban fabric of the surrounding area, the British Embassy is clad in the same stone as that used for the Brandenburg Gate.

Modellphoto mit Eingangshof und Wintergarten.
Modelshot showing Entrance Court and Wintergarden.

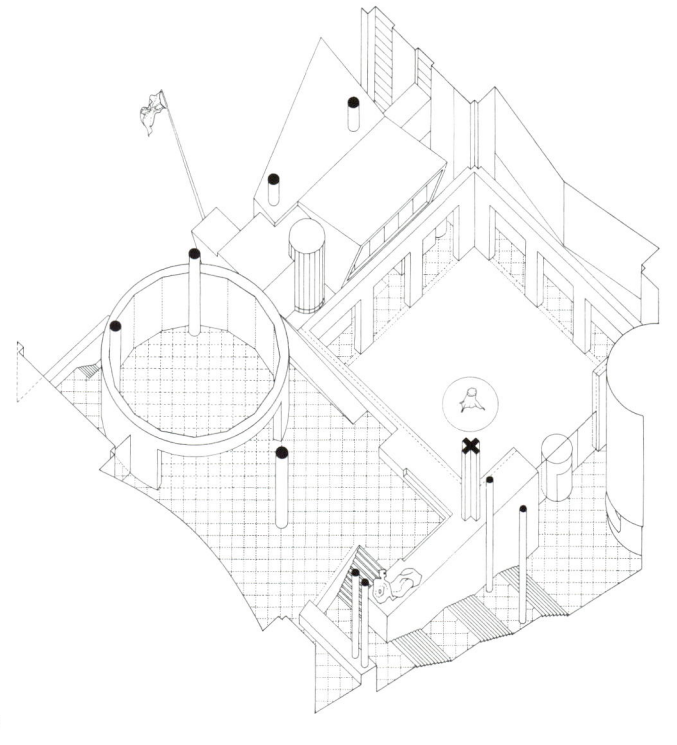

»Das Gebäude ist für jeden sofort verständlich, der es von der Straße her betritt, wo die vorspringenden Formen andeuten, daß im Inneren etwas ganz Besonderes, vielleicht sogar Spannendes zu erwarten ist. Unsere Analyse der Geschichte Berlins ergab, daß dieser Gebäudetyp mit einem zentralen Innenhof typisch für die Stadt ist.« Michael Wilford

'Everybody understands the building once they have entered from the street where the projecting forms give a clue of something really special and perhaps exciting happening inside. Our study of the history of Berlin revealed that this building type with the courtyard in the centre is characteristic of the city.' Michael Wilford

Axonometrie von Wintergarten und Eingangshof (oben). Blick über den Eingangshof zum Wintergarten (unten).
Down axonometric of Wintergarden and Entrance Court (top). View across Entrance Court to Wintergarden (bottom).

Regierung und Kultur Government and Culture

Sobald der Besucher das Gebäude betritt, erblickt er eine imposante Freitreppe zum Piano Nobile, wo sich die hauptsächlichen öffentlichen Bereiche wie Wintergarten und Informationszentrum befinden. Diese fulminante Wegführung läßt ein Gefühl der Erwartung aufkommen, und die einladende Geste unterstreicht den offenen, transparenten Charakter der neuen Britischen Botschaft, der in deutlichem Gegensatz zu überkommenen Vorstellungen von diplomatischer Geheimhaltung und Absonderung steht.

Once inside the building, the visitor catches an enticing glimpse of a Grand Staircase leading up to the piano nobile where the main public areas such as the Wintergarden and the Information Centre are located. This dramatic processional route creates a keen sense of anticipation, and this invitation to explore reinforces the open, transparent character of the new British Embassy that stands in marked contrast to traditional notions of diplomatic privacy and seclusion.

»Dieser Raum war nicht Bestandteil der ursprünglichen Ausschreibung, aber nach der Analyse von Botschaftsgebäuden und nachdem wir verstanden hatten, wie dieses hier genutzt werden sollte, waren wir der Meinung, ein gemeinschaftlicher Innenraum für Bankette oder Tagungen wäre wichtig. Die in der Ausschreibung vorgesehenen Bereiche für Konferenzräume, Bücherei, Speisezimmer und Bar sind dann auch um diesen Wintergarten herum angeordnet, der sehr hell und bei jedem Wetter zu nutzen sein wird.« Michael Wilford

'The Wintergarden wasn't in the original brief, but we felt after studying embassies and understanding how this one was intended to be used that it was important to have an indoor communal space that could be used for banquets or conventions. The spaces that were in the brief for a conference room, a commercial library, a dining room and a bar are actually distributed around this Wintergarden which will be very light and can operate in all weathers.' Michael Wilford

Regierung und Kultur Government and Culture

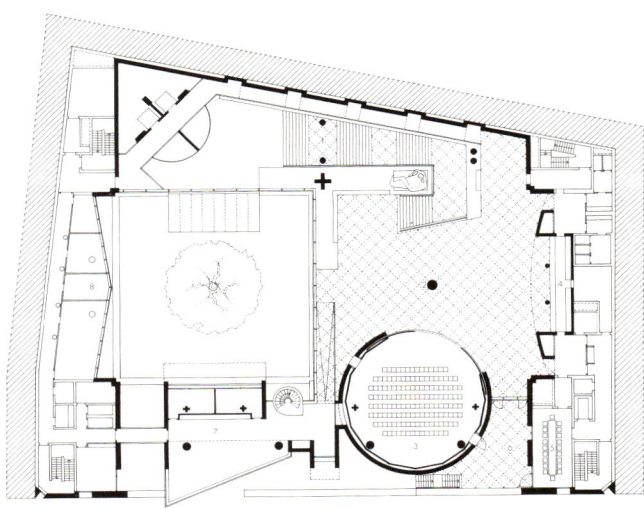

Grundriß des zweiten Obergeschosses.
Second-floor plan.

Zentraler Bereich der Botschaft ist der von Tageslicht erfüllte Wintergarten, durch dessen großflächige Fenster man den Eingangshof überschaut. Einer Piazza im Gebäudeinneren gleich fungiert er als zentraler Treffpunkt. Darüber hinaus wurde der überdachte Raum im Hinblick auf Flexibilität und Multifunktionalität konzipiert und eignet sich gleichermaßen für Empfänge, wie für Präsentationen und Ausstellungen. Von der ersten Büroetage überblickt man den Wintergarten, so daß sich hier Beschäftigte wie Besucher der Anwesenheit der jeweils anderen Gruppe bewußt sind.

The Wintergarden, bathed in natural light from above and overlooking the Entrance Court through generous windows, forms the focus of the Embassy. Like an internal piazza it provides a place for everyone within the building to meet and mingle. This covered space was also designed to be highly flexible and multi-functional, equally suitable for hosting receptions, presentations or exhibitions. The first floor of offices enjoy fine views directly into the Wintergarden, thus giving both staff and visitors a sense of one another's presence.

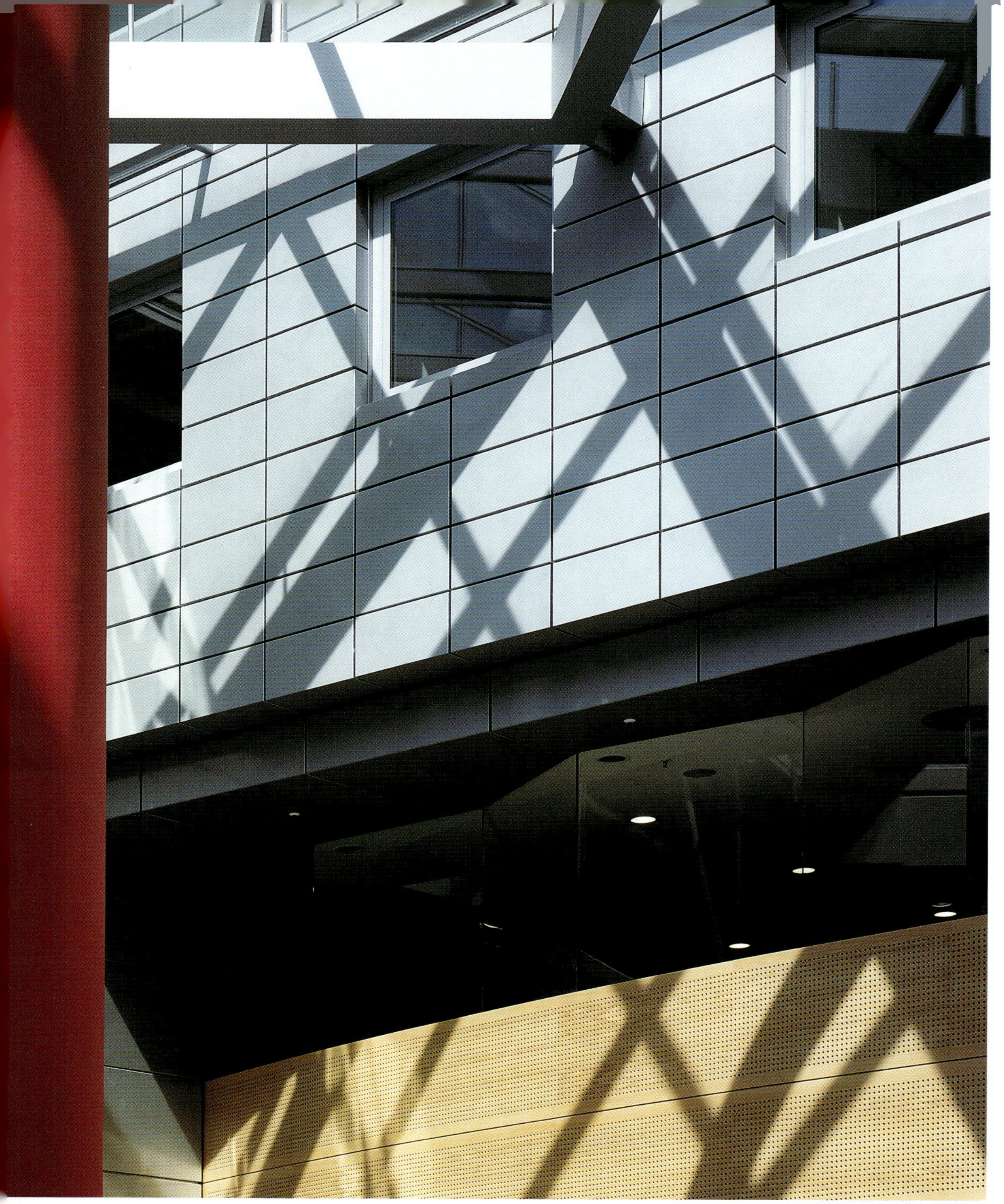

Die verschiedenen Bereiche der Botschaft sind stark aufeinander bezogen. Von bestimmten Standpunkten aus lassen sich Wintergarten, Eingangshof und Freitreppe mit einem Blick erfassen. Vom Eingang auf Straßenniveau bis hinauf zum Piano Nobile eröffnet sich mit jedem Schritt eine verwirrende Vielfalt von Ansichten. Dieser Eindruck eines sich entfaltenden architektonischen Schauspiels macht den eigentlichen Geist des Gebäudes aus.

The different parts of the Embassy interrelate to a high degree. From certain vantage points one can encompass Wintergarden, Entrance Court and Grand Staircase in a single glance. A dazzling variety of perspectives open up at every turn all the way from the entrance at street level right up to the piano nobile. This sense of an architectural drama unfolding defines the essential spirit of the building.

Blick auf Bürofenster vom Wintergarten aus. Office windows seen from the Wintergarden.

Die im ganzen Bau zu findende Vielzahl überraschender Details lassen den Besuch in der Britischen Botschaft zu einem reizvollen visuellen Erlebnis werden. Schon im Außenbau ist die kühne Verwendung von Farbe sichtbar, die sich im Inneren fortsetzt. Bestimmten Elementen zugeordnete, unterschiedliche Farbtöne erleichtern es, die Funktionalität des Gebäudes zu verstehen.

A wealth of eye-catching details throughout the structure make the British Embassy an exciting visual experience. The dashing use of colour apparent from the entrance gate outside (right) finds a continuation inside. The various shades defining certain elements make it easier to read and understand the functionality of the building.

Regierung und Kultur Government and Culture

WOHNUNGEN DAIMLER CHRYSLER, POTSDAMER PLATZ, BERLIN
DAIMLER CHRYSLER APARTMENTS, POTSDAMER PLATZ, BERLIN

Richard Rogers Partnership, 1993–1999

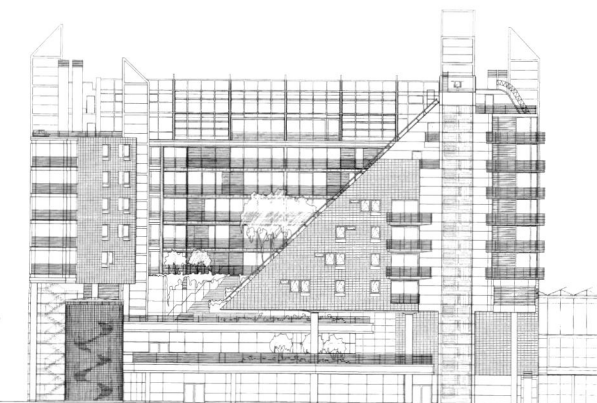

Erste Entwurfsskizze von Laurie Abbott.
Zeichnung (unten): Fassade an der Linkstraße.
First concept sketch (above) by Laurie Abbott.
Drawing (below): the Linkstrasse elevation.

Dieses, als B8 bekannte, markante Wohnhochhaus ist von entscheidender Bedeutung für das Mischnutzungskonzept im Daimler-Chrysler-Sektor des Potsdamer Platzes; ebenso wie die benachbarten Bürobauten B4 und B6 entstand es nach einem Entwurf der Richard Rogers Partnership. Obgleich sich auch dieser Bau an die allgemeinen Abmessungen des Kontexts hält, ist die Wohnfunktion durch die ins Auge fallende Verwendung von im Wohnhausbau gebräuchlichen Terrakottafliesen und anhand der Balkone sofort erkennbar. Der Baukörper ist geschickt plaziert, um einen optimalen Sonneneinfall und Panoramablicke auf den benachbarten Park zu gewährleisten. Die verglasten Bereiche der nach Nordosten und Nordwesten gelegenen Gebäudeseiten sind vergleichsweise klein bemessen, was den Wärmeverlust in den Wintermonaten verringert. Wintergärten an den beiden nach Süden gerichteten Seiten sorgen für größtmögliche Nutzung passiver Sonnenenergie. Auf Schienen gleitende Aluminiumjalousien verhindern in den Sommermonaten zu starken Sonneneinfall und daraus folgende Überhitzung. B8 konnte sich bereits als prestigeträchtige Adresse an Berlins neuer Linkstraße etablieren.

Essential to the mixed-use concept of the Daimler Chrysler sector of the Potsdamer Platz is this striking apartment block known as B8, located directly alongside the office buildings B4 and B6, which were also designed by the Richard Rogers Partnership. Although respecting similar overall dimensions to its neighbours the residential function of B8 is readily apparent from the prominent use of domestic style terracotta tiles and balconies. The building mass has been cleverly situated in order to benefit from solar orientation and to optimise panoramic views onto the adjacent park. The glazing areas to the north-east and north-west façades are comparatively small, which reduces heat loss during the winter months. Winter gardens on the two southerly elevations maximise the passive use of solar energy. Sun shading provided by aluminium louvres on sliding tracks prevents overheating in summer. B8 is already established as a prestigious address on Berlin's new Linkstrasse.

Die klare, dynamische Linienführung paßt zum modernen Urbanismus des Potsdamer Platzes. Eckige und runde Formen vereinen sich zu dramatischer Wirkung. Das von Läden und Geschäften belegte Erdgeschoß macht die Linkstraße zu einer lebendigen, urbanen Straße.

The crisp, dynamic lines are in tune with the modern urbanism of the Potsdamer Platz. Angular and rounded forms combine with dramatic effect. The ground floor occupied by shops and businesses gives Linkstrasse the quality of a living street.

In einer Reihe verschiedenartiger Wohnungen stehen insgesamt 16 300 m² Wohnfläche zur Verfügung. Die Grundrisse wurden flexibel gestaltet, so daß die Bewohner den Innenraum ihren persönlichen Bedürfnissen anpassen können.

16,300m² of living accommodation have been provided in a varied series of apartments. The layouts are kept as flexible as possible so that users can adapt the interior according to their individual requirements.

In allen Wohnungen sind Wohn- und Eßraum unmittelbar auf die Küche als den zentralen Raum bezogen. Die großzügig verglasten Fronten nutzen das Tageslicht optimal aus.

In all cases the living and dining areas relate directly to the kitchen as a central focal point. The use of floor-to-ceiling glazing optimises the benefits of natural light.

Von dem erhöhten Fußweg auf der Mezzaninebene aus gesehen erscheint das vorkragende Profil des pyramidenförmigen Teils von B8 besonders eindrucksvoll.

The exciting profile of the pyramid-shaped section of the B8 building is particularly dramatic when viewed from the elevated walkway at mezzanine level.

Der hohe Anteil von Glas an den nach Südwesten und Südosten gelegenen Fassaden führt zu einer Hierarchie der Räume, derzufolge sich die Wohnräume zum Innenhof hin, die Mehrzahl der Schlafräume zum Nordosten und Nordwesten hin öffnen.

The high proportion of glazing to the southwest and south-east elevations results in a hierarchy of spaces with the living areas opening onto the courtyard and the majority of bedrooms situated on the north-east and north-west sides.

Die insgesamt südöstliche Ausrichtung des Gebäudes gestattet maximale Sonneneinstrahlung in den Innenhof. Er bietet den Bewohnern mitten im Herzen von Berlin eine willkommene grüne Oase.

The general south-easterly orientation of the building allows optimum sunlight to penetrate the courtyard. This provides a welcome green oasis for the residents right in the heart of Berlin.

Die Skizze verdeutlicht die für größtmöglichen Lichteinfall abgetreppte Form des Gebäudes.

This sketch illustrates the stepping down of the building in order to admit light.

WOHNHAUS
PRIVATE HOUSE

Foster and Partners, 1992–1994

Das Wohnhaus für eine junge deutsche Familie entstand auf einem nach Süden ausgerichteten Grundstück, das unbehinderte Ausblicke ins Tal bietet. Das Gelände fällt 18 Meter unter das Straßenniveau ab, so daß die Dachterrasse mit Parkplatz für vier Fahrzeuge auf der Straßenseite zur Eingangsebene wird. Eine teilverglaste Stahlkonstruktion über der Terrasse bietet geschützten Zugang zum Haupteingang und den beiden östlich und westlich davon gelegenen Seiteneingängen. Von dieser Ebene führt eine Rampe durch die Ebenen des Hauses hinunter zur Gartenterrasse. Auf der unteren Gartenebene öffnet sich das Haus nach Süden mit Wohnbereichen, Schlafzimmern und Eßbereichen, die den Garten überblicken. Auf der oberen Ebene befinden sich eine Wohnung für eine Haushälterin, vier Kinderschlafzimmer sowie eine kleine Bibliothek. Die vollständig mit abwechselnd transparenten und lichtdurchlässigen Scheiben verglaste Südfassade sorgt für differenzierten Lichteinfall. Die ungewöhnliche Kombination von innerer und äußerer Wegeführung ermöglicht der Familie und ihren Freunden ein außergewöhnliches Maß an Gemeinsamkeit und respektiert gleichzeitig die Privatsphäre des Einzelnen.

A private house for a young German family has been built on a south-facing site with uninterrupted valley views. The site falls 18 metres below street level, so the roof terrace, with space for four parked cars, becomes the arrival level from the street. Above the terrace, a partially glazed steel structure provides covered access to the main entrance and the two side entrances to east and west. From this level a ramp leads down through the levels of the house to the lower garden terrace. At lower garden level, the house opens out towards the south with living areas, bedrooms and dining areas overlooking the garden. The upper level includes a housekeeper's flat, four children's bedrooms and a small library. The southern façade is completely glazed with alternating transparent and translucent panels to vary the quality of light and transparency. The unusual combination of inside and outside circulation enables the house to offer the family and its friends an exceptional degree of community, as well as respecting the privacy of the individuals.

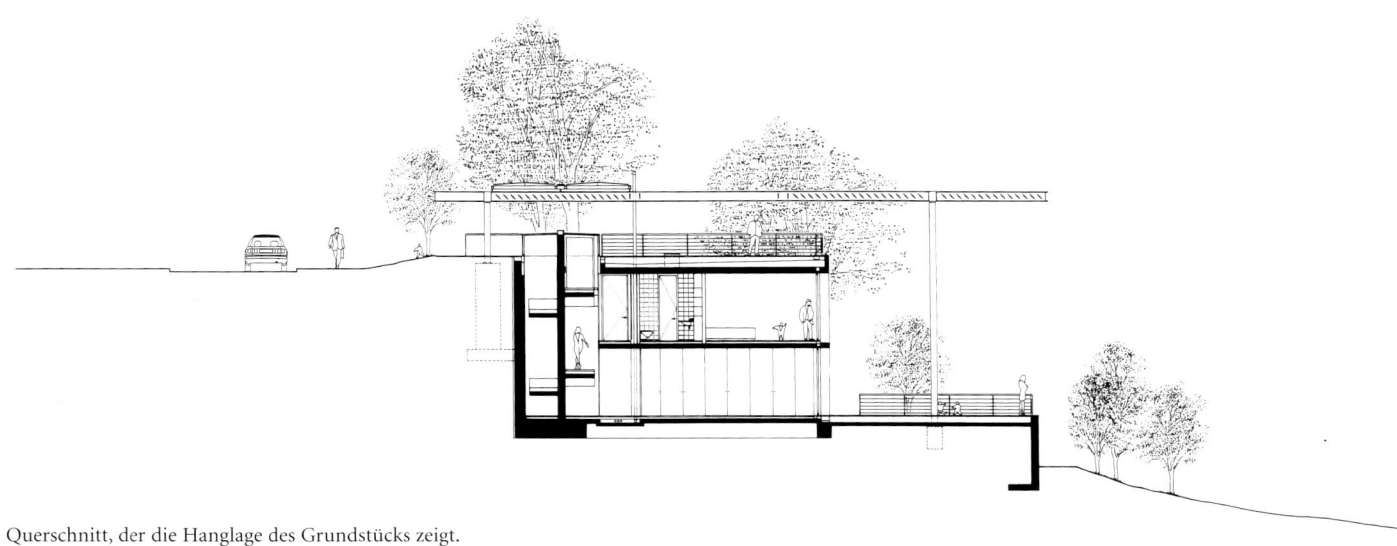

Querschnitt, der die Hanglage des Grundstücks zeigt.
Cross-section shows the hillside nature of the site.

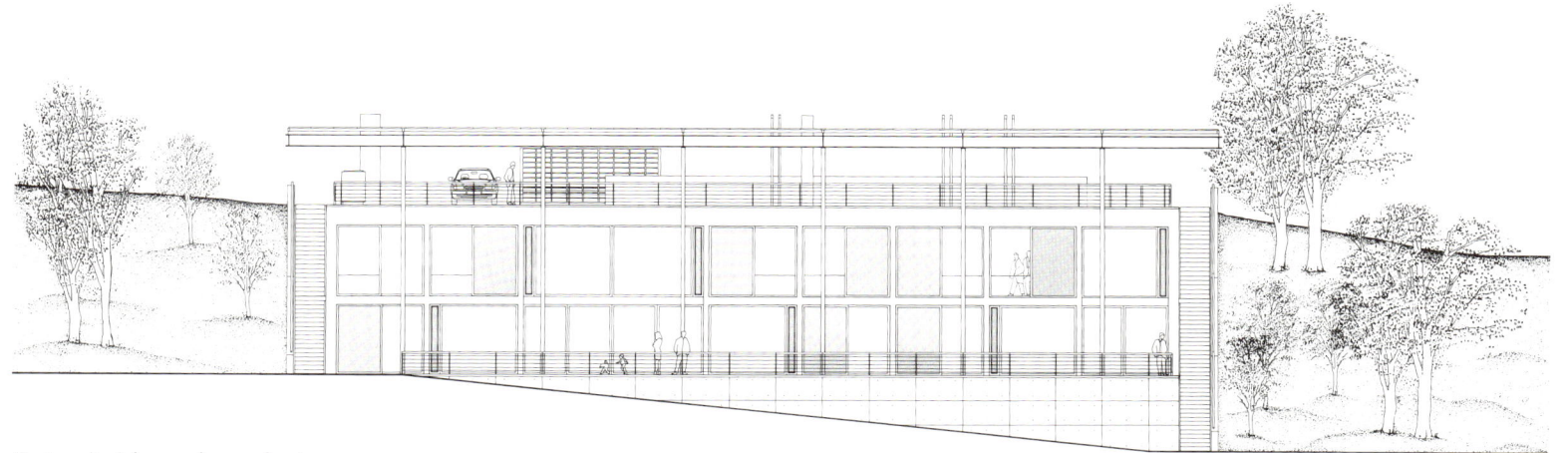

Gartenseite (oben und ganz oben).
The garden elevation (top and above).

Der Hauptwohnbereich mit dem von Büchern gerahmten Kamin und der offenen Küche zu Seiten des doppelgeschossigen Wohnraums ist der Familie zugedacht. Der Besitzer hat ein persönliches Interesse am Kochen, das sich in einer professionell ausgestatteten Küche mit einem leistungsstarken Abluftsystem niederschlägt.

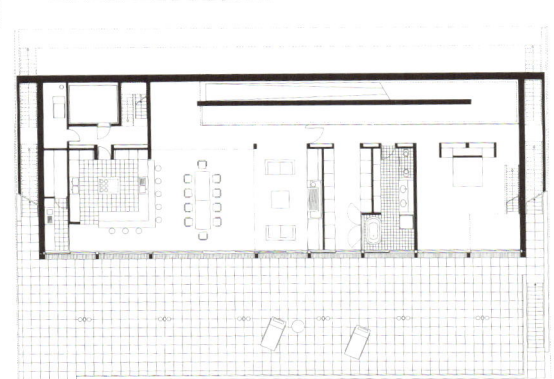

Untere Ebene. Lower-level plan.

The main living area is the family domain containing the book-lined hearth and the open kitchen either side of a double-height living space. The owner has a personal interest in cooking that is reflected in a professionally equipped kitchen with a very efficient extraction system.

WOHNHAUS
PRIVATE HOUSE

David Chipperfield Architects, 1994–1996

Der Backsteinbau ist um einen nach Süden gelegenen Hof angeordnet. Für den Bau, mit dem der Architekt sein Anliegen verfolgt, Raum zu schaffen sowie Innen- und Außenbereiche zu differenzieren, ist das Material von entscheidender Bedeutung. Die Vorstellung einer Backsteinvilla wird zur *idée fixe*, in der sich materielle Festigkeit, die vage Erinnerung an Häuser der frühen Moderne von Mies van der Rohe und Mendelsohn sowie eine mit dem Umfeld der begrünten Vorstadt kompatible Stofflichkeit vereinen. Ein anderes, hier wie in anderen neuen Werken Chipperfields erkennbares Anliegen betrifft die Beschaffenheit des Materials: den bewußten Zusammenprall ungewöhnlicher Materialien mit glatten, mechanischen Oberflächen. Bei diesem Projekt deutet der Kontrast zwischen den großen, stahlgerahmten Glasflächen und den stark strukturierten, handgearbeiteten Backsteinen auf eine Kritik an der Tendenz zu immer perfekteren Oberflächen und zur Neutralisierung der Baumaterialien hin.

The building is in brick and organised around a south-facing courtyard. While pursuing the architect's defined concerns of room-making and inside/outside space, the material is a determining element. The idea of a brick villa becomes an *idée fixe*, combining physical solidity, a vague memory of early Modernist houses by Mies van der Rohe and Mendelsohn, and a materiality consistent with the leafy suburban surroundings. Another concern apparent here as in other recent work by Chipperfield is that of texture: the conscious collision of erratic materials with smooth mechanical surfaces. In this project the contrast between the large expanses of steel-framed glazing and the highly textured handmade brickwork offers a criticism of the developing tendency towards the perfection of finishes and the neutralisation of building materials.

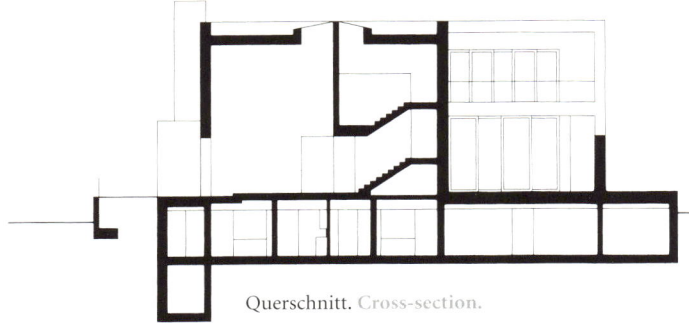

Querschnitt. Cross-section.

Die Backsteinfassade findet ihre Entsprechung in der Treppe, die in einer wahren Backsteinkaskade von der Straße zum Garten führt.

The brick façades find an echo in the staircase which flows in a cascade of brickwork from street level down to the garden.

»Den Leuten, die unsere Arbeit mögen, gefällt die Vorstellung einer einfachen modernen Architektur, bei der die Räume gut konzipiert und angeordnet sind und bei der Tageslicht und das Material eine wichtige Rolle spielen.« David Chipperfield

'The people who are attracted to our work like the idea of simple modern architecture where the spaces are well ordered and conceived and there is a large use of natural light and a strong material idea.' David Chipperfield

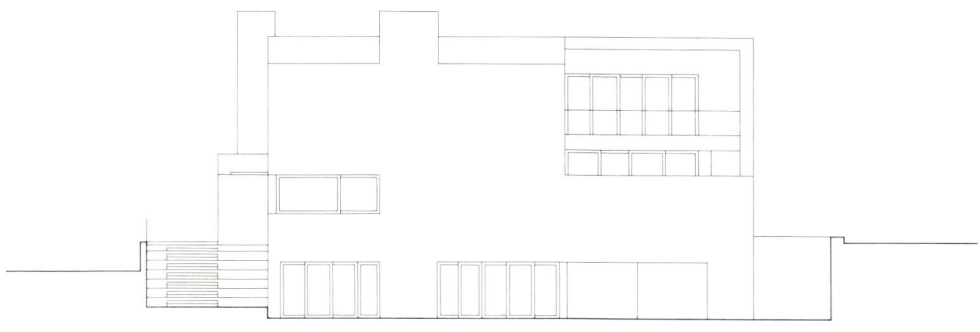

Seitenansicht. Front elevation.

Haus und Wohnen Housing

»Jedesmal wenn eine Wahl zu treffen war, setzten sich die Auftraggeber ernsthaft damit auseinander und wählten häufig die teurere, qualitätvollere Variante. Da ging es nicht um Effekthascherei. So war beispielsweise der Backstein aus dem wir das Haus bauten, enorm teuer, und sie hätten einen viel billigeren wählen können, weil der Unterschied nicht sofort ins Auge fällt. Ich glaube, es ist eine Sache, sein Haus mit Travertin verkleiden zu lassen, aber sehr guten Backstein zu verwenden, ist etwa so, als wenn man sehr teure Unterwäsche trägt. Versteht das irgend jemand wirklich? Irgendwie habe ich dieses Qualitätsbewußtsein bewundert.« David Chipperfield

'Every time there was a choice to be made the clients seriously considered things and quite often they would take the more expensive option that had more quality. These weren't showy decisions. For instance, the brick that we built the house out of was phenomenally expensive and they could have chosen a much cheaper one because it's not very showy. I mean, it's one thing to cover your house in travertine, but just to use a very good brick is sort of like having very expensive underwear I guess. Is anyone going to really understand it? I rather admired that commitment to quality.' David Chipperfield

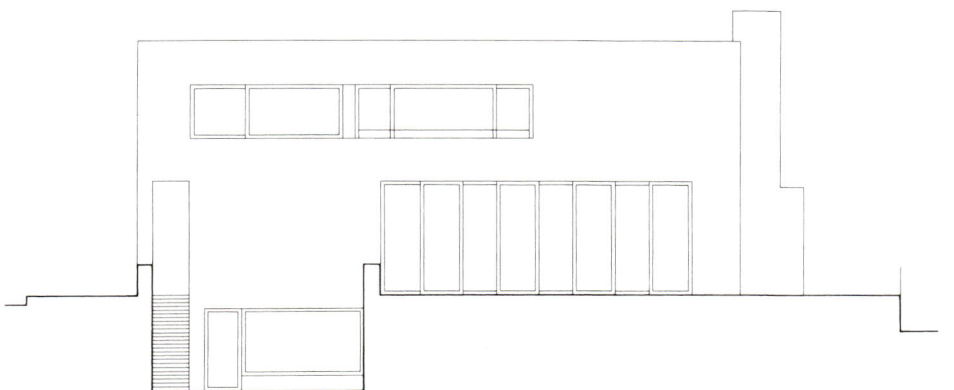

Gartenquerschnitt. Garden elevation.

PHOTONIKZENTRUM, BERLIN
PHOTONICS CENTRE, BERLIN

Sauerbruch Hutton Architects, 1996–1998

Das Innovationszentrum für Photonik liegt in Berlins neuer Wissenschafts- und Technologiestadt im Bezirk Adlershof neben einem aufgelassenen Flugplatz. Der siegreiche Entwurf, den Sauerbruch Hutton Architekten für dieses Forschungszentrum für die Gebiete Optik, Optoelektronik und Lasertechnik vorlegten, umfaßte ursprünglich vier separate, amöbenartige Gebäude. Letztlich entstanden nur zwei Gebäude gemäß diesem Entwurf, während die übrigen zwei von einem anderen Büro in herkömmlicher, rechtwinkliger Manier errichtet wurden. Selbst in dieser reduzierten Form offenbaren sich sofort die reizvollen Möglichkeiten krummliniger Architektur. Das Auge wird behutsam durch einen von scheinbar natürlichen und organischen Rhythmen bestimmten, einladenden Zwischenraum geführt, der durch den Einsatz von lebhafter Farbigkeit noch enorm gewinnt. Beim Photonikzentrum geht es um mehr als ein künstlerisches Objekt in der Landschaft. Das größere der beiden Gebäude ist zwischen der einfachen Verglasung der Außenwand und der doppelt verglasten Innenwand mit einem 700 mm starken Hohlraum ausgerüstet, der im Winter als Wärmepuffer und im Sommer als eine Art Solarkamin dient und so das Jahr über optimale Arbeitsbedingungen gewährleistet. Die farbigen Rouleaus bieten Schutz vor übermäßiger Hitze und vor Lichteinfall in das Gebäude.

»Wir wußten, daß wir Farbe an die Fassaden bringen wollten. Zweck des Gebäudes ist die Erforschung des Lichts im weitesten Sinn, und wir wollten diesen Gedanken auch auf der Außenhaut des Baues zum Ausdruck bringen.« Louisa Hutton

The Photonics Centre is located in Berlin's new City of Science and Technology in the district of Adlershof alongside a disused airfield. The winning scheme by Sauerbruch Hutton for this centre for research into optics, optoelectronics and laser technology, originally comprised four separate amoeba-like buildings. In the event, only two were built in this manner while the remaining two were built in conventional rectilinear mode by another practice. Even on this reduced scale, the exciting possibilities of curvilinear architecture become immediately apparent. The eye is led gently through an inviting interspace of seemingly natural and organic rhythm that is greatly enhanced by the vivid use of colour. There is more to the Photonics Centre than just an artistic object in the landscape. The larger of the two buildings incorporates a 700mm cavity between the single-glazing of the outer wall and the double-glazing of the inner wall that serves both as a thermal buffer zone in winter and as a kind of solar chimney in summer, thereby ensuring optimum working conditions throughout the year. The coloured blinds offer protection against excessive heat and light entering the building.

'We knew we wanted to use colour on the façades, as the theme of the project was research into light and we were keen to bring this idea through to the skin of the buildings.' Louisa Hutton

Industrie Industry

»Es kommt uns fast so vor, als bewegte sich das Gebäude und wäre kein statisches Ding auf dem Gelände; dies betrachten wir als Reaktion auf die Vorgabe, daß wir Gebäude schaffen wollten, die auf diesem annähernd trapezförmigen Gelände beinahe wie Inseln wirken.«
Louisa Hutton

'The buildings seem to us as if they are almost moving and are not static things, in the site – this we see as a response to the condition of wanting to produce buildings as independent islands within a very clear context.' Louisa Hutton

Die beiden ›Amöbenkleckse‹ des Photonikzentrums sind umgeben von den rechtwinkligen Blöcken gradliniger Bauten.

The two 'amoebas' of the Photonics Centre are set between a group of rectilinear buildings from the sixties.

Das Wechselspiel der Farben auf der Außenseite des Gebäudes setzt sich auch im Atrium fort, wo Tages- und Kunstlicht aufeinandertreffen. Die Qualität des Ergebnisses wird erreicht durch die Verwendung eines mineralischen Farbstoffs, der sich mit dem Beton verbindet und so nicht nur etwas auf die Oberfläche Aufgetragenes ist, sondern zum Bestandteil des Bauwerks wird.

The interplay of colour on the outside of the Photonics Centre continues into the atrium, where daylight penetrates the deep mass of the building. The colour is achieved by using a mineral pigment which binds or fuses with the concrete substrate so that the colour becomes part of the structure rather than something merely applied to the surface.

Illusion and reality. At first glance the outside of the Photonics Centre appears to be composed of panels of coloured glass. From the inside, however, the artifice is revealed. The actual colour comes from the dazzling array of blinds. In all, 36 custom-made colours form a kind of loosely arranged spectrum around the building. Since the users of the individual spaces can regulate their own blinds, the general effect is of a work of art in a constant state of flux.

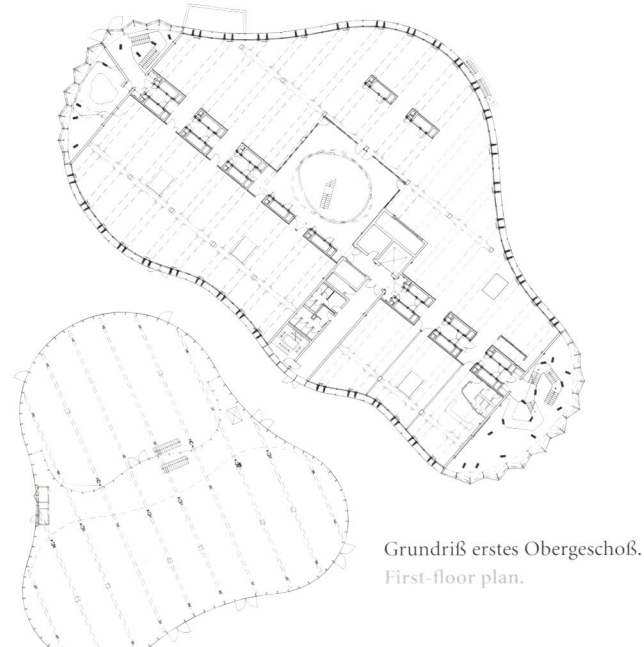

Grundriß erstes Obergeschoß.
First-floor plan.

Illusion und Wirklichkeit. Auf den ersten Blick scheint die Haut des Photonikzentrums aus farbigen Glasplatten zu bestehen. Im Inneren offenbart sich jedoch der Kunstgriff als die gelungene Anordnung farbiger Rouleaus. Insgesamt bilden 36 speziell angefertigte Farben eine Art von frei angeordnetem Spektrum um das Gebäude. Da die Nutzer der einzelnen Räume ihre Rouleaus jeweils individuell einstellen können, entsteht der Eindruck eines in ständigem Wandel befindlichen Kunstwerks.

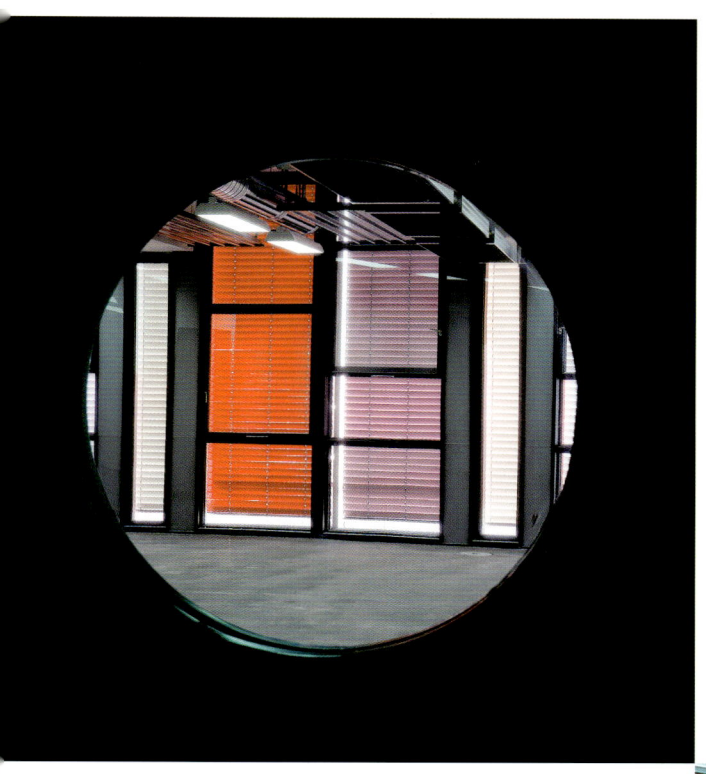

»Es sind sämtlich Räume aus einem Traumland: überlebensgroß, von magischer Farbigkeit und geisterhaft beleuchtet: Das hier mag ein Arbeitsplatz für Menschen sein, aber er vermittelt das ganze surreale Drama einer der Wissenschaft gewidmeten Umgebung.« Isabel Allen, *The Architect's Journal*

'All are dreamland spaces: larger than life, magically coloured and eerily lit: this may be a workplace for people, but it captures all the surreal drama of a landscape devoted to science.' Isabel Allen, *The Architect's Journal*

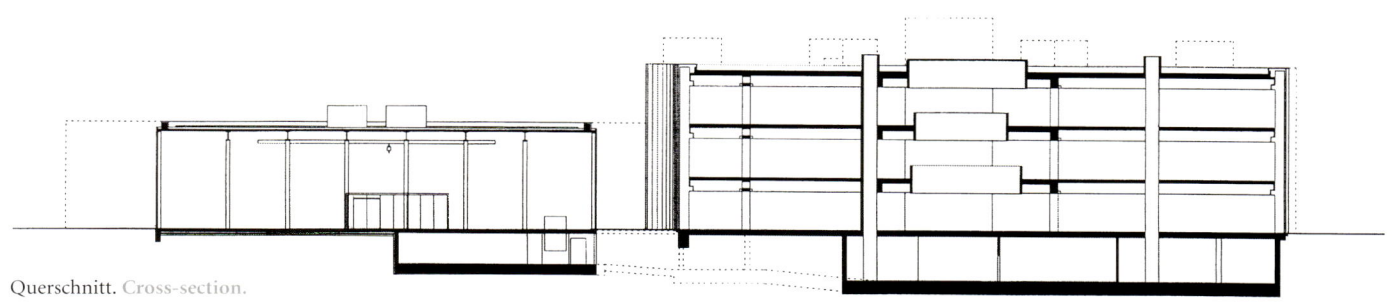

Querschnitt. Cross-section.

BRAUN ZENTRALE, MELSUNGEN
BRAUN HEADQUARTERS, MELSUNGEN

James Stirling, Michael Wilford and Associates in association with Walter Nägeli, 1996–1998

Das Projekt entstand für die Zentrale und Produktionseinrichtungen einer großen deutschen Firma, die medizinische Geräte herstellt. Der Entwurf umfaßt Gebäude für Verwaltung, Forschung, Verteilung, Lagerung und Produktion von Kunststoffteilen sowie eine Kantine und ein mehrgeschossiges Parkdeck. Das Baugelände liegt in landschaftlich schöner Gegend am Zusammenfluß zweier Flüsse in der Nähe von Melsungen. Die beträchtliche Größe der gesamten Anlage nimmt eher Bezug auf andere, von Menschen geschaffene Elemente in der Landschaft wie Brücken oder Viadukte als auf das eher kleinteilige Stadtgefüge von Melsungen selbst. Das Projekt führt vor, wie sich die Erfordernisse einer Fabrik harmonisch mit der Anlage von Parks und Gärten verbinden lassen. Der vordere, dreieckige Teil des Geländes ist als Park mit einem See und begrünten Terrassen angelegt.

The project was designed for the headquarters and production facilities of a large German company manufacturing medical products. The scheme comprises buildings for administration, research, distribution, storage and production of plastic components as well as a canteen and a multi-storey carpark. The site is located in an attractive natural setting at the junction of two rivers near the small town of Melsungen. The considerable size of the overall scheme relates more to other large man-made elements in the landscape such as bridges or viaducts than it does to the relatively small-scale urban layout of Melsungen itself. The project shows how the requirements of a factory can be harmonised with the architecture of parks and gardens. The front area is designed as a triangular park with a lake and landscaped terraces.

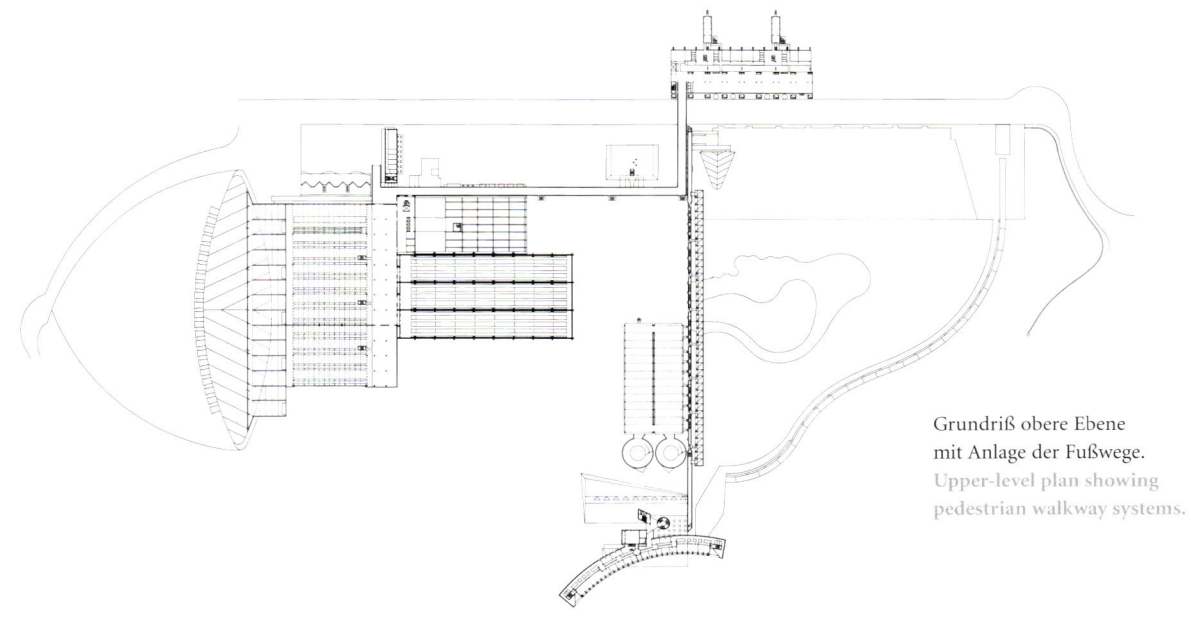

Grundriß obere Ebene mit Anlage der Fußwege.
Upper-level plan showing pedestrian walkway systems.

Industrie Industry

Gebogene Fassade des Verwaltungsgebäudes. Curved façade of administration building.

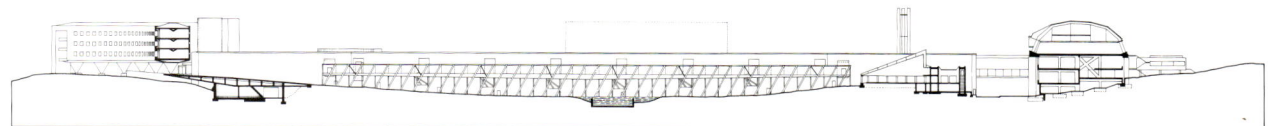

Längsschnitt mit Fußweg. Longitudinal section showing pedestrian walkway.

Eines der auffallendsten Elemente des Entwurfs ist die elegant-abstrakte Geometrie eines elliptischen Gebäudes aus Metall, dem größten auf dem Gelände. Es dient als Zentrum zur Verteilung der Güter; an seiner bogenförmigen Wand können 22 Lastwagen gleichzeitig anfahren.

One of the most striking elements of the design is the elegant abstract geometry of an elliptical metallic building, the largest on the site, which serves as the goods distribution centre. Its curved wall allows 22 trucks to dock simultaneously.

98 : 99

MABEG ZENTRALE, SOEST
MABEG HEADQUARTERS, SOEST

Nicholas Grimshaw & Partners, 1997–1999

Dieser ›Bürokasten‹ stellt die erste Phase eines Gesamtplanes dar, mit dessen Hilfe die wachsende Belegschaft der Firma untergebracht werden soll. Das Gebäude bietet neben Konferenz- und Ausstellungsräumen Platz für Direktion, Qualitätskontrolle, Marketing und Versand. Nach der Vorstellung von Mabeg sollte sich das Gebäude als das Hauptziel für Besucher durch ein bemerkenswertes Erscheinungsbild einprägen. Darüber hinaus sollte der Bau die Firma in einer Reihe von Publikationen und anderen Medien vertreten. Er wurde aus den Materialien Stahl und Beton errichtet; die Fassade ist mit silbrigem Wellaluminium verkleidet. Durchbrochene Metalljalousien, deren Vorderkanten in einem elegant gebogenen Aluminiumprofil auslaufen, halten direkte Sonneneinstrahlung fern. Der ›Bürokasten‹ macht keine Zugeständnisse an seine Umgebung und wurde als kürzlich gelandetes, fremdes Raumschiff beschrieben. In ästhetischer Hinsicht entspricht der Entwurf den bei Mabeg gepflegten Idealen: Präzision, Verfügbarkeit und Innovation; so gesehen verkörpert er die Firma, als deren höchst einprägsame architektonische Visitenkarte er fungiert.

This 'office-box' represents the first stage of a masterplan to accommodate the firm's expanding workforce. The building provides accommodation for management, quality control, marketing and despatch as well as space for meeting and exhibition rooms. As the main focus for visitors, Mabeg insisted that the new building should have a striking appearance and create a lasting impression. In addition, the building would represent the company in a number of publications and other media. The building is of steel and concrete construction. The façade is clad in silvery corrugated aluminium. Perforated metal louvres are used for external sun shading, the front edges of which are shaped in an elegantly curved aluminium profile. The 'office-box' makes no concession to its neighbours, and has been described as a recently landed alien spacecraft. Aesthetically, the design responds to Mabeg's belief in precision, accessibility and innovation. As such, the building represents the physical embodiment of the company, and serves as its highly distinctive architectural visiting card.

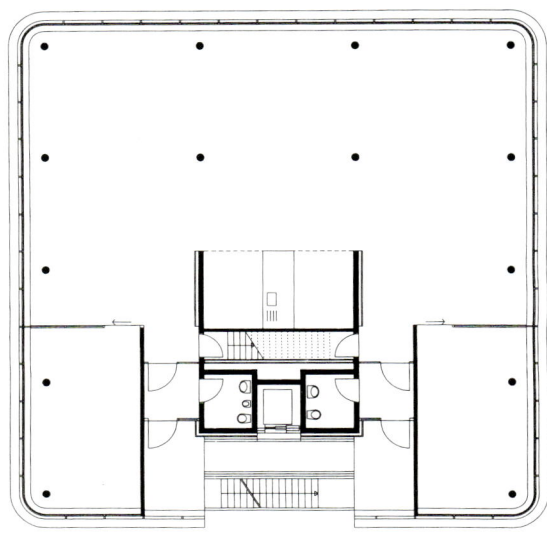

Grundriß Erdgeschoß. First-floor plan.

Die vom Boden abgehobene Bauweise bietet ebenso funktionale wie ästhetische Vorteile, z.B. kann so das darunterliegende Gelände als Parkfläche genutzt werden. Die gerundeten Betonstützen sind sämtlich sichtbar (folgende Seiten) und zeichnen sich im Erdgeschoß mit einer Höhe von 5 m durch besondere Eleganz aus.

The elevated structure offers functional as well as aesthetic advantages. By freeing up the space below, vehicles can park under the building. The rounded concrete supports are all visible (see picture overleaf) and particularly elegant at ground floor level where they are 5m high.

Im Hinblick auf die betriebliche Nutzung kann der neue ›Bürokasten‹ mit seinem demokratischen Werkstattcharakter Mabegs Bedarf an lichtem, offenem Büroraum zufriedenstellen.

In operational terms, the new 'office-box' satisfies Mabeg's need for a light and open-plan environment in a building which has a democratic 'workshop' character.

VITRA FEUERWACHE, WEIL AM RHEIN
VITRA FIRE STATION, WEIL AM RHEIN

Zaha M. Hadid, 1989–1993

Dies ist der Bau, durch den Zaha Hadid bekannt wurde. Vor seiner Entstehung kannte man Zaha Hadid vor allem ihrer visionären Zeichnungen und Gemälde wegen, die allmählich als eigenständige Kunstform betrachtet wurden. Tatsächlich glaubten viele angesichts der expressiven Dynamik in Zaha Hadids Vorstudien nicht, daß danach ein wirkliches Gebäude entstehen könne. Die Ausschreibung für dieses bestimmte Projekt sah den Entwurf einer Feuerwache für das Vitra Möbelwerk vor, die sich auch für eine Vielzahl anderer Nutzungen wie Konferenzen oder Seminare eignen sollte. Rolf Fehlbaum von Vitra sagt, daß er sich zur Arbeit Zaha Hadids stark hingezogen fühlte, »da wir ihre Architekturvision für äußerst dynamisch, gewagt und riskant hielten.« Der Auftraggeber war ferner daran interessiert, daß Zaha Hadid sich in gewohnter Manier mit den vielfältigen Möglichkeiten auseinandersetzte, ein Gebäude zu entwerfen, das mit seiner Umgebung eine Art räumlicher Beziehung eingeht. Der fertige Bau wurde von der Kritik als Rechtfertigung von Zaha Hadids einzigartigem Architekturstil gefeiert, bei dem anscheinend eine fast abstrakt zu nennende Geometrie auf die materielle Realität eines Betonbaues trifft.

This was the building that literally put Zaha Hadid on the map. Until it was built, the architect was mainly known for her visionary drawings and paintings that had come to be regarded virtually as an art form in their own right. Indeed, there were many who when confronted by the swirl and thrust of Zaha Hadid's preliminary project sketches doubted whether a real building could actually be constructed out of them. The brief for this particular project was to design a fire station for the Vitra Furniture Factory that would also be susceptible to a variety of other uses such as conferences or seminars. Rolf Fehlbaum of Vitra says he was strongly drawn to the work of Zaha Hadid, 'because we felt that her architectural vision was very dynamic, daring and also evinced danger.' The client was also keen for Zaha Hadid to explore her habitual preoccupation with the wider possibilities of designing a building that developed a new kind of spatial relationship with its surroundings. The completed project has been hailed by critical opinion as a vindication of Zaha Hadid's unique style of architecture where an almost abstract geometry appears to collide with the physical reality of a concrete structure.

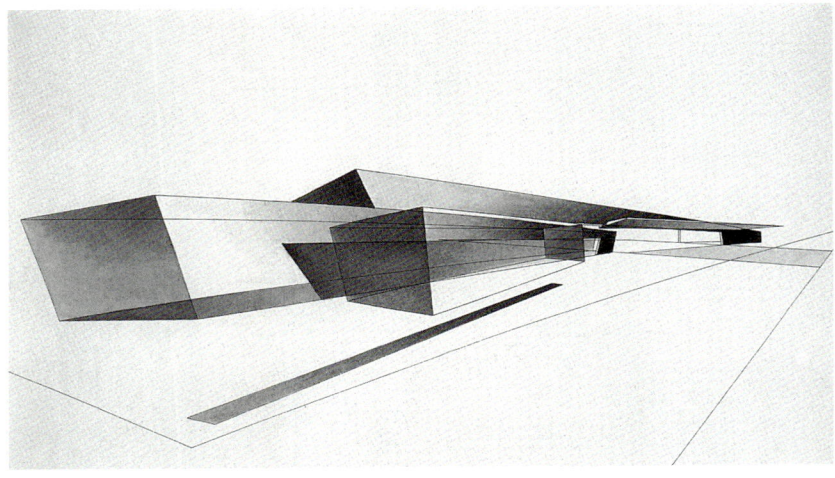

Gemälde/Studie (oben) und fertiger Bau (rechts).
Painting (above) and finished project (right).

»Ich glaube, die Tatsache, daß wir einen sehr guten Bauherren hatten, war auch sehr wichtig. Von Bedeutung ist nicht die Freiheit, sehr viel Geld auszugeben, sondern die Freiheit, architektonische Vorstellungen auszuloten.« Zaha Hadid

'I think the fact that we had a very good client was also very important. The importance lies not in having the freedom of spending a lot of money, but in having the freedom to explore architectural ideas.' Zaha Hadid

»Die Leute haben das immer falsch verstanden, weil die Zeichnungen so explosiv waren. Wir wollten immer jeden Teil des Gebäudes gesondert betrachten. Man glaubte immer, es würde sehr chaotisch, aber unsere Vorstellung war es, die Energie dieses Chaos' in eine Art eingefrorene Momentaufnahme umzuwandeln.« Zaha Hadid

'People always misunderstood because the drawings were so explosive. We always wanted to look at every item of the building separately. People always thought that it would be very chaotic, but it was the idea of how you could extrapolate the energy of this chaos into a kind of frozen moment in time.' Zaha Hadid

Vorläufiges Projektgemälde. Preliminary project painting.

»Das ganze entstand auf Umwegen, weil wir nicht damit anfingen, das Gebäude zu entwerfen. Wir entwarfen den Bau, indem wir uns das ganze Gelände ansahen, seinen Standort festlegten und ihn dann entwarfen.« Zaha Hadid

'It was designed in a roundabout way because we didn't start by designing the building. We designed this building looking at this whole site, then placing it, and then designing it.' Zaha Hadid

»Ich fand auch interessant, wie man etwas schaffen konnte, dem jegliche Detailarbeit fehlt – das heißt, es gibt sehr gute Detailarbeit, es geht nicht um schlechte Details oder darum, wie man Details verstecken kann. Das ist ein weiterer wichtiger Grund, warum Beton ein gutes Material ist, weil man sich sehr früh entscheiden muß, man kann nichts zurechtpfuschen. Es hat eine Präzision, die ich für sehr interessant halte.« Zaha Hadid

'What's also interesting for me is how to achieve something which has an absence of detail – which means that it's very good detail, it doesn't mean bad detail or how you can hide detail. It's another important reason why concrete is a good material because you have to decide very early; you can't fudge it. It has a precision which I think is very interesting.' Zaha Hadid

Industrie Industry

PRESTEL BOOKS ON ARCHITECTURE

Prestel
Munich · London · New York

Prestel Books on Architecture

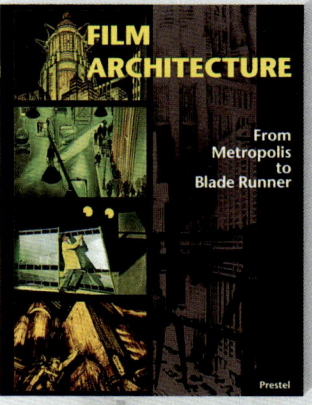

**The Green Skyscraper:
The Basis for Designing
Sustainable Intensive Buildings**

By Ken Yeang

This book presents a general framework for looking at ecological building design, a step-by-step guide to examining the fundamental premises of such an approach, as well as its practical applications to the contemporary skyscraper.

Approx. 296 pp., approx. 112 b/w and 16 color illus.
6 1/2 x 9 in. / 16.5 x 23.5 cm.
ISBN 3-7913-1993-0 Pb.
US$25.95/£15.95/DM48

**The Reichstag: Norman Foster's
Parliament Building**

With a foreword by Norman Foster

A comprehensive overview of Foster's revolutionary design for the lower house of the German parliament, constructed within the shell of the Reichstag building and already world-famous through its imposing glass cupola.

Approx. 120 pp., approx. 80 color and 10 b/w illus.
6 1/2 x 8 1/2 in. / 17 x 22 cm.
ISBN 3-7913-2153-6 Pb.
US$16.95/£9.95/DM19.95

**Film Architecture:
Set Designs from "Metropolis"
to "Blade Runner"**

Edited by Dietrich Neumann

"...a handsome and valuable contribution to this inexplicably neglected field."
World Architecture

"...a fascinating study of movies as the launching pads of avantgarde style."
New York Times

<u>Special Anniversary Edition:</u>
220 pp., 75 color and 219 b/w illus.
9 3/4 x 11 3/4 in. / 24.5 x 30 cm.
ISBN 3-7913-2163-6 Pb.
US$29.95/£19.95/DM 49.80

**Icons of Architecture
The 20th Century**

Edited by Sabine Thiel-Siling

The masterpieces of 20th-century architecture have been compiled in this unique volume, which presents in-depth descriptions, the best in architectural photography, original plans and biographical sketches.

192 pp., 307 color and 215 b/w illus.
9 1/2 x 11 3/4 in. / 24 x 30 cm.
ISBN 3-7913-1949-3 Hardcover
US$29.95/£19.95/DM 49.80

Prestel Munich · London · New York

Front Cover:
Josef Paul Kleihues, Museum of Contemporary Art, Chicago. View of the foyer with a sculpture by James Lee Byars. (*The Monument to Language*, 1955). from the Prestel book *Museums for a New Millennium*. © James Lee Byars: Estate James Lee Byars. Photo: Steve Hall © Hedrich Blessing.

Light Fantastic: The Art and Design of Stage Lighting

By Max Keller

A must for all involved in theater, opera, film, and concert production, this volume documents the fascinating use of stage lighting in a comprehensive way. Technical details, supported by stunning images, make this a unique handbook for all theater buffs.

232 pp., 264 color and 296 b/w illus.
9 1/2 x 12 1/2 in. / 24 x 31 cm.
ISBN 3-7913-2162-5 Hardcover
US$75/£45/DM128

Shaping the Great City: Modern Architecture in Central Europe, 1890–1937

Edited by Eve Blau and Monika Platzer

The city as both the principal site of innovation and experimentation and the generator of a vibrant urban culture during the last decades of the Hapsburg Empire and the years of change in Central Europe that followed it is the focus of this wide-ranging study.

240 pp., 50 color and 272 b/w illus.
9 1/2 x 11 3/4 in. / 24 x 30 cm.
ISBN 3-7913-2151-X Hardcover
US$65/£39.95/DM98

Museums for a New Millennium: Concepts · Projects · Buildings

Edited by Vittorio Magnago Lampugnani and Angeli Sachs

Contemporary museum buildings are often a seismograph of architectural culture. This book introduces 26 museum buildings—designed, still under construction or completed within the last decade, by internationally renowned architects.

Approx. 224 pp., approx. 180 color and 220 b/w illus.
9 3/4 x 11 3/4 in. / 24 x 30 cm.
ISBN 3-7913-2219-2 Hardcover
US$65/£39.95/DM98

The Architecture of von Gerkan, Marg + Partners

Edited by John Zukowsky

Meinhard von Gerkan, Volkwin Marg and their partners are one of the most innovative and prolific architectural offices in Germany. This book presents 50 of the group's finest and most original architectural designs.

272 pp., 311 color and 196 b/w illus.
9 1/2 x 12 1/4 in. / 24.5 x 31 cm.
ISBN 3-7913-1861-6 Pb.
US$49.95/£29.95/DM 78

Prestel Books on Architecture

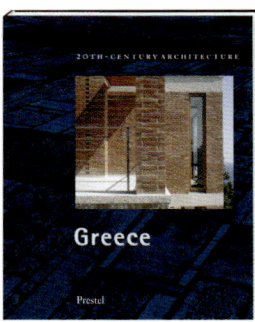

20th-Century Architecture: Greece
Edited by Savas Condaratos and Wilfried Wang

This handsomely illustrated book details how a century's search into the identity and character of the emergent Greek state has manifested itself in the development of Greek architecture.

Approx. 256 pp., 170 color and 420 b/w illus.
9 x 12 1/2 in. / 23 x 32 cm.
ISBN 3-7913-2152-8 Cloth.
US$75/£45/DM128

20th-Century Architecture: Sweden
Edited by Claes Caldenby, Jöran Lindvall, and Wilfried Wang

"Essays chart the political, cultural and sociological changes ... complemented by brief studies of more than eighty architectural highlights." *Building*

400 pp., 295 color and 600 b/w illus.
9 x 12 1/2 in. / 23 x 32 cm.
ISBN 3-7913-1936-1 Cloth.
US$85/£55/DM 148

Architecture in Germany DAM Annual 1999
Edited by Wilfried Wang and Annette Becker, Deutsches Architektur-Museum

At the turn of the millennium, the 1999 yearbook focuses on utopias in design.

Approx. 200 pages, approx. 100 color and 300 b/w illus.
8 x 11 in. / 22 x 28 cm.
ISBN 3-7913-2182-X Pb.
Bilingual edition (German/English)
US$45/£25/DM68

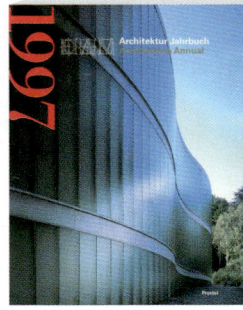

Architecture in Germany DAM Annual 1997
Edited by Wilfried Wang and Annette Becker, Deutsches Architektur-Museum

The 1997 yearbook looks at the challenges being undertaken by architects and planners all over the world and especially in Germany.

200 pp., 98 color and 300 b/w illus. 8 x 11 in. / 22 x 28 cm.
ISBN 3-7913-1849-7 Pb.
Bilingual edition (German/English)
US$45/£25/DM 68

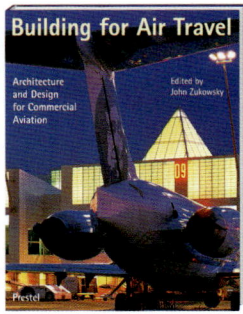

Building for Air Travel: Architecture and Design for Commercial Aviation
Edited by John Zukowsky

"Will be the major source on the subject ... for years to come ... an engrossing work full of wonderfully reproduced, highly evocative pictures."
The Sunday Telegraph Review

256 pp., 103 color, 53 duotone and 216 b/w illus.
9 1/2 x 11 3/4 in. / 24 x 30 cm.
ISBN 3-7913-1684-2 Cloth.
US$65/£39.95/DM 98

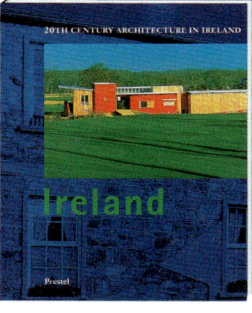

20th-Century Architecture: Ireland
Edited by Annette Becker, John Olley, and Wilfried Wang

Examines the influence of literature and politics on architectural developments.

"An excellent overview of outstanding twentieth-century Irish buildings."
Library Journal

192 pp., 100 color and 360 b/w illus.
9 x 12 1/2 in. / 23 x 32 cm.
ISBN 3-7913-1719-9 Cloth.
US$65/£39.95/DM 98

Ackermann and Partners: Buildings and Projects 1978–1998
Edited by Ingeborg Flagge
English-German edition

This volume demonstrates the clear, simple beauty born of Munich firm Kurt Ackermann and Partners' aesthetic approach to construction and design.

320 pp., 75 color, 295 duotone and 220 b/w illus.
9 1/2 x 11 1/4 in. / 24 x 28.5 cm.
ISBN 3-7913-1935-3 Hb.
US$80/£49.95/DM 148

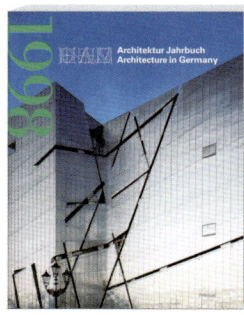

Architecture in Germany DAM Annual 1998
Edited by Wilfried Wang and Annette Becker, Deutsches Architektur-Museum

Architecture in Germany offers an insider's view into what world-renowned architects are building in Germany and what German architects, in turn, are offering the world.

192 pp., 84 color and 262 b/w illus.
8 x 11 in. / 22 x 28 cm.
ISBN 3-7913-2014-9 Pb.
Bilingual edition (German/English)
US$45/£25/DM 68

Boston Architecture 1975–1990
By Naomi Miller, Keith Morgan

"The illustrations are informative, well chosen and beautifully reproduced. The text is clear and readable. This is a book that just about any lover of Boston, at any level of sophistication, can enjoy."
Boston Globe

272 pp., 80 color and 160 b/w illus.
9 1/2 x 11 3/4 in. / 24 x 30 cm.
ISBN 3-7913-1679-6 Pb.
US$29.95/£19.95/DM 49.80

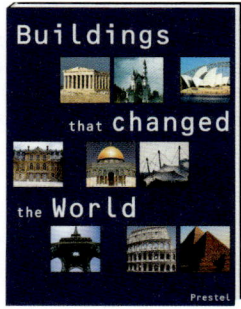

Buildings that Changed the World
By Klaus Reichold and Bernhard Graf

This richly illustrated and informative volume explores the world of architecture in an accessible way, introducing many architectural icons and offering an overview of 4,000 years of architectural history.

192 pp., 425 color illus.
9 3/4 x 11 3/4 in. / 24.5 x 30 cm.
ISBN 3-7913-2150-1 Hardcover
US$29.95/£19.95/DM49.80

Prestel Books on Architecture

Prestel Munich · London · New York

Prestel Books on Architecture

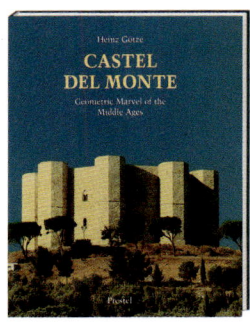

Castel del Monte: Geometric Marvel of the Middle Ages

By Heinz Götze

Castel del Monte's secret lies in the geometric genius of an age long past. This illustrated volume courageously pursues the mystery behind the fortification's formidable walls.

232 pp., 54 color, 35 two-color plans and 200 b/w illus.
8 1/2 x 11 in. / 22 x 28 cm.
ISBN 3-7913-1930-2 Hb.
US$65/£39.95/DM 98

Contemporary British Architects

Essays by Robert Maxwell and Peter Murray

Projects by some of Britain's most famous architects working internationally are presented in this comprehensive survey.

240 pp., 150 color and 140 b/w illus.
9 1/2 x 11 3/4 in. / 24 x 30 cm.
ISBN 3-7913-1825-X Pb.
US$29.95/£19.95/DM 49.80

Hall 8/9 von Gerkan, Marg + Partners

Edited by Volkwin Marg

Text in English and German
The complete absence of central colums and the maximum use of natural daylight are just two of the outstanding features of this single-story hall, which itself could form part of the world exhibition — Expo 2000 — in Hanover.

64 pp., 80 color and 20b/w illus.
9 x 11 3/4 in. / 23 x 30 cm.
ISBN 3-7913-2136-6 Pb.
US$29.95/£19.95/DM 49.80

Hall 26 Expo 2000, Hanover

Designed by the internationally renowned firm of architects Herzog + Partner, Hall 26 is a stunningly futuristic, environment-friendly exhibition hall. With a text in German and English.

64 pp., 80 color and 20 b/w illus.
9 x 11 3/4 in. / 24 x 30 cm.
ISBN 3-7913-1741-5 Pb.
US$29.95/£19.95/DM 49.80

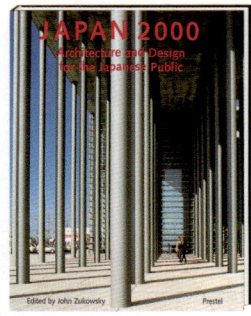

Japan 2000: Architecture and Design for the Japanese Public

Edited by John Zukowsky

"An interesting commentary and critique on the development of architecture and design in Japan from the end of World War II to the present day."   *Building Design*

158 pp., 86 color and 102 b/w illus.
8 1/2 x 11 in. / 22 x 28 cm.
ISBN 3-7913-1906-X Hb.
US$49.95/£35/DM 98

Chicago Architecture and Design 1923–1993: Reconfiguration of an American Metropolis

Edited by John Zukowsky

"This volume is 'the first major study of Chicago's architectural achievements in the 20th century,' and it lives up to its billing."
Library Journal

480 pp., 78 color, 45 duotone, and 510 b/w illus.
8 3/4 x 11 3/4 in. / 22.5 x 30 cm.
ISBN 3-7913-1251-0 Cloth.
US$75/£50/DM 148

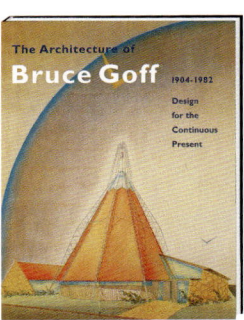

The Architecture of Bruce Goff 1904–1982

Edited by Pauline Saliga and Mary Woolever

This book documents all phases of Goff's long and diverse career, illustrated by dozens of photographs and architectural drawings and including a list of all of Goff's extant buildings.

120 pp., 33 color and 150 b/w illus.
9 x 11 3/4 in. / 23 x 30 cm.
ISBN 3-7913-1453-X Cloth.
US$50/£32.50/DM 78

Hall 13 Expo 2000 Hanover

Edited by Peter Ackermann
With a foreword by Sepp Ackermann

Text in English and German
Designed by the architectural firm Ackermann and Partners, the fair hall has been described as a "structural symbol of simplicity with the quality of the extraordinary."

64 pp., 80 color and 20 b/w illus.
9 x 11 3/4 in. / 23 x 30 cm.
ISBN 3-7913-2018-1 Pb.
US$29.95/£19.95/DM 49.80

Hong Kong Architecture: The Aesthetics of Density

Edited by Vittorio Magnago Lampugnani

"... not only gives an excellent overview of developments in the past ten years, but a sound history of the development of the city."
Building Design

160 pp., 92 color and 209 b/w illus.
9 x 11 3/4 in. / 23 x 30 cm.
ISBN 3-7913-1324-X Cloth.
US$50/£40/DM 98

Daniel Libeskind: Jewish Museum, Berlin

With a foreword by Daniel Libeskind

Scarcely any other contemporary building has been the focus of so much attention and discussion as the Jewish Museum in Berlin.

64 pp., 60 full-color and 20 b/w illus.
8 1/2 x 11 1/2 in. / 23 x 30 cm.
ISBN 3-7913-2075-0 Pb.
US$16.95/£9.95/DM 19.95

Prestel   Munich · London · New York

Prestel Books on Architecture

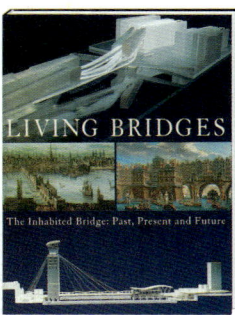

Living Bridges
The Inhabited Bridge: Past, Present and Future

Edited by Peter Murray and Mary Anne Stevens

Examines the contributions inhabited bridges have made to city life from the Middle Ages to the present day.

160 pp., 129 color and 142 b/w illus.
9 3/4 x 12 in. / 24.5 x 30.5 cm.
ISBN 3-7913-1734-2 Cloth.
US$55/£35/DM 78

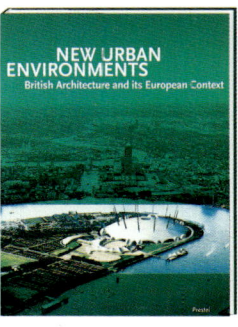

New Urban Environments: British Architecture and its European Context

Edited by Peter Murray and MaryAnne Stevens

"The futuristic designs that will become the monuments of our age."
The Independent on Sunday

192 pp., 187 color and 61 b/w illus.
9 1/2 x 11 3/4 in. / 24 x 30 cm.
ISBN 3-7913-1937-X Hb.
US$65/£39.95/DM 98

radix – matrix: Daniel Libeskind

With an introduction by Kurt Forster and essays by Jacques Derrida, Bernhard Schneider, and Mark C. Taylor

A survey of Libeskind's work, including his most important essays and descriptions of his most recent projects.

176 pp., approx. 65 color and 100 b/w illus.
9 x 11 3/4 in. / 23 x 30 cm.
ISBN 3-7913-1727-X Hb.
US$65/£39.95/DM 98

Sol Power: The Evolution of Solar Architecture

By Sophia and Stefan Behling with a foreword by Norman Foster

"So complete ..., so enthusiastic its illustration of architecture driven by solar power, ... that criticism seems superfluous ... worth every penny."
World Architecture

240 pp., 420 color and 380 b/w illus.
9 1/2 x 12 1/4 in. / 24 x 31 cm.
ISBN 3-7913-1670-2 Cloth.
US$65/£39.95/DM 98

Subway Architecture in Munich

By Christoph Hackelsberger

"Like the system it describes, *Subway Architecture in Munich* is neat, light and airy ... it provides an easy-to-follow technical and componential analysis ... a beautifully illustrated tour of the most architecturally significant stations in the city."
The Times Literary Supplement

144 pp., 52 color and 90 b/w illus.
9 1/2 x 11 1/2 in. / 24.5 x 29 cm.
ISBN 3-7913-1827-6 Cloth.
US$49.95/£29.95/DM 78

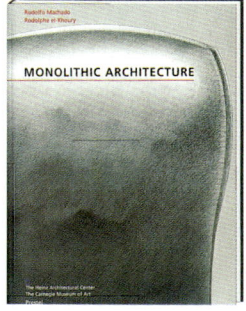

Monolithic Architecture

By Rodolfo Machado and Rodolphe el-Khoury

The first book to document this controversial contemporary phenomenon. This review of provocative, little-known projects by notable architects contributes to the debate about form and formalism in architecture.

173 pp., 30 color and 150 b/w illus.
9 x 11 3/4 in. / 23 x 30 cm.
ISBN 3-7913-1609-5 Cloth.
US$60/£40/DM 98

Paris: Contemporary Architecture

By Andrea Gleiniger, Gerhard Matzig and Sebastian Redecke

"(The) new buildings of merit in Paris since the turn of the century ... in easily accessible form with high quality architectural photography"
FX Magazine

160 pp., 131 color and 131 b/w illus.
9 x 11 3/4 in. / 23 x 30 cm.
ISBN 3-7913-1678-8 Hb.
US$49.95/£35/DM 78

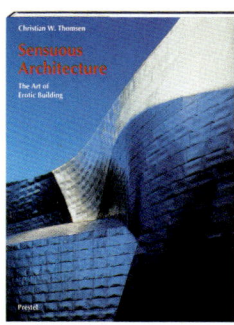

Sensuous Architecture: The Art of Erotic Building

By Christian W. Thomsen and Angela Krewani

"An astonishingly ambitious book."
Building Design

"The first ever examination of this aspect of architecture."
Perspective

184 pp., 205 color and 97 b/w illus.
9 1/2 x 11 3/4 in. / 24 x 30 cm.
ISBN 3-7913-1807-1 Hb.
US$65/£39.95/DM 98

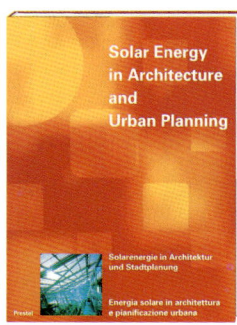

Solar Energy in Architecture and Urban Planning

Edited by Thomas Herzog

"A beautifully bound portfolio of contemporary architectural schemes. ... A magnificent contribution to the continuing debate."
Times Literary Supplement

224 pp., 290 color and 176 b/w illus.
9 1/2 x 12 1/4 in. / 24 x 31 cm.
ISBN 3-7913-1652-4 Cloth.
US$65/£39.95/DM 98

Verbundnetz Gas AG, Leipzig Headquarters Building: Becker Gewers Kühn & Kühn Architects

Text and Concept by Eike Becker

Integrated energy saving technology, natural air circulation, state-of-the-art architectural features have been combined in this award-winning building. Text in English and German

80 pp., full-color and 80 b/w illus.
9 x 11 3/4 in. / 23 x 30 cm.
ISBN 3-7913-2130-7 Pb.
US$29.95/£19.95/DM 49.80

Prestel Munich · London · New York

Prestel Books on Architecture

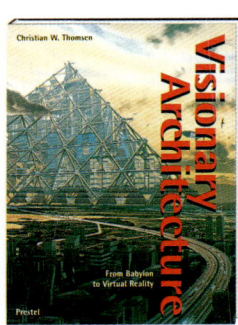

Visionary Architecture: From Babylon to Virtual Reality

By Christian W. Thomsen

Containing a most surprising and rich selection of planned and imaginary architecture, this book spans several millennia, discussing the continuous and fascinating strength of the visionary element in world architecture.

192 pp., 154 color and 126 b/w illus.
9 1/2 x 11 3/4 in. / 24 x 30 cm.
ISBN 3-7913-1425-4 Cloth.
US$60/£40/DM 98

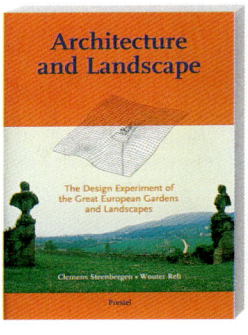

Architecture and Landscape: The Design Experiment of the Great European Gardens and Landscapes

By Clemens Steenbergen and Wouter Reh

An analysis of the various trends in landscape design and architecture in Italy, France and Great Britain throughout the past 500 years.

384 pp., 300 line drawings, 100 photographs and 16 pages of color illus.
6 1/2 x 9 1/4 in. / 16.5 x 23.5 cm.
ISBN 3-7913-1720-2 Pb.
US$ 39.95/24.95/DM 68

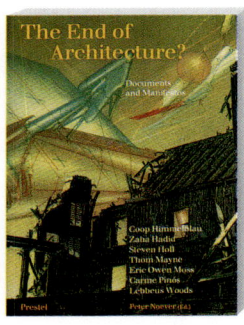

The End of Architecture? Documents and Manifestos

Edited by Peter Noever

Seven internationally renowned architects shatter traditional notions and propose radical solutions for the future of architecture.

136 pp., 63 color and 44 b/w illus.
6 1/2 x 9 1/4 in. / 16.5 x 23.5 cm.
ISBN 3-7913-1263-4 Pb.
US$25.95/£15.95/DM 48

Italian Villas and Gardens

By Paul van der Ree, Gerrit Smienk, and Clemens Steenbergen

"The understated production of this book reinforces its serious intent and its focus on the underlying principles, philosophy, and evolution of the concept of the Italian renaissance villa."
Library Journal

298 pp., 200 line drawings and 50 b/w illus.
6 1/2 x 9 1/2 in. / 16.5 x 23.5 cm.
ISBN 3-7913-1181-6 Pb.
US$29.95/£16.95/DM 48

Projecting Beirut: Episodes in the Construction and Reconstruction of a Modern City

Edited by Peter G. Rowe and Hashim Sarkis

This volume provides criticism and commentaries from specialists directly involved in the rebuilding process — a comprehensive survey of Beirut reborn.

228 pp., 300 illus.
6 1/2 x 9 in. / 16.5 x 22.5 cm.
ISBN 3-7913-1938-8 Pb.
US$35/£19.95/DM 58

Alvar Aalto: Toward a Human Modernism

Edited by Werner Nerdinger

Architectural historians from Finland, Sweden, England, Germany and Switzerland celebrate Aalto's work. Their contributions and findings are presented here in a highly accessible form.

160 pp., monochrome illus.
6 1/2 x 9 1/4 in. / 16.5 x 23.5 cm.
ISBN 3-7913-2049-1 Pb.
US$29.95/£19.95/DM 49.80

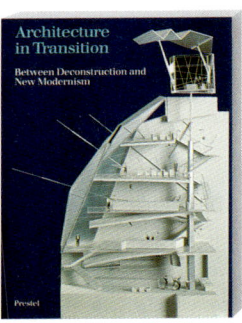

Architecture in Transition: Between Deconstruction and New Modernism

Edited by Peter Noever in cooperation with Regina Haslinger. Epilogue by Philip Johnson

Leading architects present their personal views on the radical trends of deconstruction and new modernism.

160 pp., 100 b/w illus.
6 1/2 x 9 1/4 in. / 16.5 x 23.5 cm.
ISBN 3-7913-1136-0 Pb.
US$25.95/£15.95/DM 48

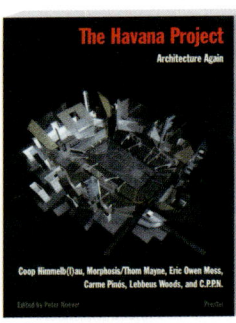

The Havana Project Architecture Again

Edited by Peter Noever

A team of internationally renowned architects examines Havana as a model that epitomizes the problems facing world cities today: slums, a great need for housing and a unique architectural heritage to preserve.

184 pp., 50 color and 50 b/w illus.
6 1/2 x 9 1/4 in. / 16.5 x 23.5 cm.
ISBN 3-7913-1600-1 Pb.
US$ 25.95/£15.95/DM 48.

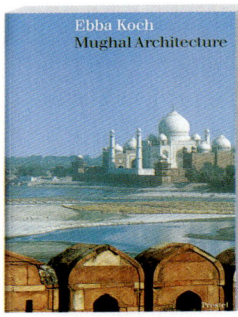

Mughal Architecture

By Ebba Koch

"[This] volume is by far the best available survey of Mughal architecture. It incorporates the latest theories on identifications and chronology, as well as information on hitherto little-known buildings. The text is well written and concise." *India Magazine*

160 pp., 21 color and 164 b/w illus., and 45 plans.
6 1/2 x 9 1/4 in. / 16.5 x 23.5 cm
ISBN 3-7913-1070-4 Pb.
US$25.95/£15.95/DM 39.80

Shaking the Foundations: Japanese Architects in Dialogue

Edited by Christoher Knabe and Joerg Rainer Noennig

In the quest to identify the mind-set and philosophy driving some of the world's foremost Eastern designers, this compilation presents a behind-the-scenes view.

160 pp., 150 b/w illus.
6 1/2 x 9 1/4 in. / 16.5 x 23.5 cm
ISBN 3-7913-2000-9 Pb.
US$29.95/£19.95/DM 49.80

Prestel Munich · London · New York

Icons of Art
The 20th Century

100 of the most important works of art produced this century, each illustrated on a full page and accompanied by a biography.

Edited by Jürgen Tesch and Eckhard Hollmann
Hardcover. ISBN 3-7913-1862-4
US$29.95 £19.95 DM 49.80

Icons of Photography
The 20th Century

90 of this century's best photographers are presented in this richly illustrated volume.

Edited by Peter Stepan
Hardcover. ISBN 3-7913-2001-7
US$29.95 £19.95 DM 49.80

Nude Photography

A homage to the female form with sensuous works by the world's most important photographers.

Edited by Peter-Cornell Richter
Paperback. ISBN 3-7913-1998-1
US$29.95 £19.95 DM 49.80

Africa: The Art of a Continent

"Massive, beautiful, scholarly."
                    Times Literary Supplement

Edited by Tom Phillips. Paperback. ISBN 3-7913-2004-1
US$49.95 £29.95 DM 78   Anniversary Edition

African Masks: The Barbier-Mueller Collection

250 of the finest masks with descriptions of their historical, religious, and symbolic significance.

By I. Hahner-Herzog, M. Kecskési and L. Vajda
Hardcover. ISBN 3-7913-1806-3
US$65 £39.95 DM 98

Keith Haring

A comprehensive compilation of Haring's work showing the full range of his prolific output.

Edited by Germano Celant. Paperback. ISBN 3-7913-1234-0
US$29.95 £19.95 DM 49.80

Fashion in Film

"Gorgeous black-and-white photographs ranging from the early days of the cinema right up to the present …"
                    Cosmopolitan

Edited by Regine and Peter W. Engelmeier
Paperback. ISBN 3-7913-1808-X
US$29.95 £19.95 DM 49.80

The Prestel Art Game

A board game that teaches you about yourself, the other players, and the exciting world of art.

ISBN 3-7913-1945-0
US$39.95 £24.95 DM 78

Paintings that Changed the World:
From Lascaux to Picasso

A richly illustrated volume that tells the story behind the people and events depicted in 90 of the world's greatest works of art.

By Klaus Reichold and Bernhard Graf
Hardcover. ISBN 3-7913-1983-3
US$29.95 £19.95 DM 49.80

Art Forms in Nature:
The Prints of Ernst Haeckel

Extraordinary portrayals of the plant and animal kingdoms — a treat for artists, scientists, and designers.

With contributions by Olaf Breidbach, Irenäus Eibl-Eibesfeld, and Richard Hartmann
Paperback. ISBN 3-7913-1990-6
US$25 £14.95 DM 39.80

BOOKS ON ART, ARCHITECTURE, AND PHOTOGRAPHY

Prestel Head Office:
Prestel Verlag
Mandlstrasse 26
80802 Munich, Germany
Tel: +49 89 3817090
Fax: +49 89 335175
e-mail: sales@prestel.de

Prestel UK:
Prestel Publishing Ltd.
4 Bloomsbury Place
London WC1A 2QA
Tel: +44 (0171) 3235004
Fax: +44 (0171) 6368004
e-mail: sales@prestel-uk.co.uk

Prestel USA and Canada:
Prestel c/o te Neues Publishing Company
16 West 22nd Street, 11th Floor
New York, N.Y. 10010
Tel: (212) 627-9090, Fax: (212) 627-9511
toll-free for orders: 1-800-352-0305
e-mail: tnp@teneues-usa.com

Prestel
Munich · London · New York

Prestel books are available worldwide. Please contact your nearest bookseller or write to one of the above addresses for information concerning your local distributor.

Obgleich die Vitra Feuerwache insgesamt einen Eindruck leichter Eleganz hervorruft, wird nicht der Versuch unternommen, Gewicht und Solidität des Materials, aus dem die einzelnen Bauteile bestehen, zu kaschieren. Die plastischen und konstruktiven Möglichkeiten des Betons werden zur Gänze ausgeschöpft und noch um neue Dimensionen erweitert.

Although the overall effect of the Vitra Fire Station is of lightness and grace, there is no attempt to disguise the real weight and solidity of the material comprising the individual elements. The sculptural as well as the constructional possibilities of concrete are explored to the full and taken into a new realm.

»Es bestand immer der Wunsch nach einem äußerst flexiblen Raum, nach Innenraum und Außenraum und danach, den Charakter von Leichtigkeit beizubehalten. Leichtigkeit, für die es zwei Gründe gibt: Die Leichtigkeit des Gebäudes selbst, aber darüber hinaus berührt es den Boden nahezu nicht.« Zaha Hadid

'There was always this desire to have a highly transformable space, an indoor space and an outdoor space, and to maintain a quality of lightness. The lightness for two reasons: the lightness of the building but also it almost doesn't touch the ground.' Zaha Hadid

Von oben nach unten: Modell und ausgeführtes Projekt.
Model (below) and finished project (bottom).

Erdgebunden und doch zum Himmel schauend: Das aufstrebende Vordach über dem Haupteingang kennzeichnet all die ätherische Eleganz eines startbereiten Überschallflugzeuges. Die Tatsache, daß mit Fertigbeton ein solcher Grad von Leichtigkeit erreicht wurde, stellt einen der Triumphe der Vitra Feuerwache dar.

Earthbound, yet looking to the heavens: the soaring canopy over the main entrance has all the ethereal elegance of a supersonic aircraft poised for take-off. Achieving such a degree of lightness while using the heavy medium of precast concrete represents one of the triumphs of the Vitra Fire Station.

Industrie Industry

STO ZENTRALE, WEIZEN
STO HEADQUARTERS, WEIZEN

Michael Wilford and Partners, 1994–1997

Designed for communications activities, this is the first of the new buildings planned on the valley edge of the company's headquarters in Baden-Württemberg. It comprises three main elements: marketing offices, an oval entrance pavilion and a square base containing training facilities. The building nestles between existing structures and is connected by a footbridge to the first phase of the raised central garden. The office wing glides above the training building, facing the primary approach and forming a dramatic gateway. Its elegant structure heightens the floating sensation and makes the most of the picturesque location. The four floors of offices enjoy spectacular valley views. The building is an exposition of the company's products. The office wing is of reinforced concrete wall, slab and column construction surfaced externally with the Sto insulated stucco system painted white. The walls and terrace of the training centre are clad with the Sto Verotec cladding system utilising square panels of dark grey basalt stone, the voids of which are filled with coloured enamel.

Dieses für kommunikative Aufgaben vorgesehene Gebäude entsteht als erstes in einer Reihe von geplanten Neubauten am Talrand der Firmenzentrale in Baden-Württemberg. Es umfaßt drei Hauptbereiche: Vertriebsbüros, einen ovalen Eingangspavillon und einen rechtwinkligen Sockel mit Ausbildungseinrichtungen. Das Gebäude fügt sich zwischen vorhandene Bauten ein und ist durch eine Fußgängerbrücke mit dem ersten Abschnitt des erhöhten, zentralen Gartens verbunden. Der Bürotrakt mit Blick auf den Hauptzugang gleitet scheinbar über dem Ausbildungszentrum und bildet ein eindrucksvolles Eingangsfanal. Seine elegante Formgebung verstärkt den Eindruck des Gleitens und bringt den malerischen Standort optimal zur Geltung. Aus den vier Büroetagen bieten sich imposante Talblicke. Mit dem Bau stellt die Firma ihre Erzeugnisse zur Schau. Der Bürotrakt besteht aus Stahlbetonwänden in Decken-Stützen-Konstruktion, die mit dem STO Wärmedämm-Verbundsystem mit weißer Endbeschichtung ausgerüstet sind. Wände und Terrasse des Ausbildungszentrums sind mit STO Ventec verkleidet; dabei handelt es sich um eine hinterlüftete Vorhangfassade aus quadratischen, dunkelgrauen Basaltplatten, deren Zwischenräume mit farbigem Email ausgefüllt wurden.

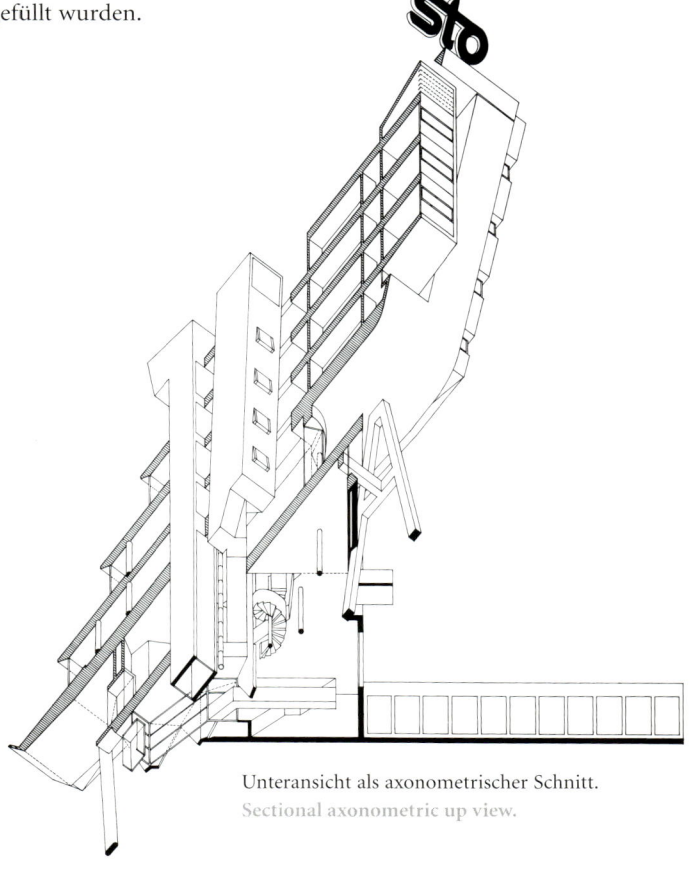

Unteransicht als axonometrischer Schnitt.
Sectional axonometric up view.

Industrie Industry

Der Entwurf eröffnet einige interessante Perspektiven. Das dynamische Äußere findet seine Fortsetzung in der kühnen Innengestaltung. Die abwechslungsreiche Behandlung von Form, Volumen und Farbe sorgt für anregende Entdeckungen. Beim Durchschreiten der verschiedenen Gebäudeteile entsteht ein Gefühl der gespannten Erwartung.

The design opens up some exciting perspectives. The dynamic promise of the external architecture is boldly followed up by the internal arrangements. The varied handling of shape, volume and colour makes for a series of stimulating encounters. A sense of anticipation is generated as one passes through the various parts of the building.

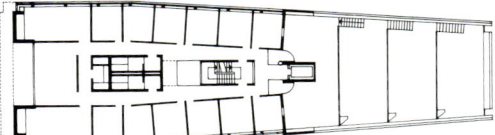

Grundriß viertes Obergeschoß. Fourth-floor plan.

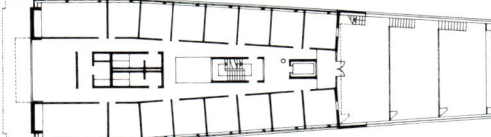

Grundriß drittes Obergeschoß. Third-floor plan.

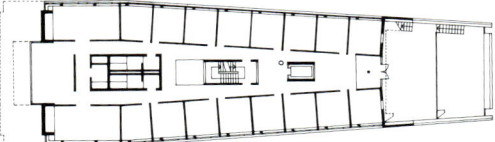

Grundriß zweites Obergeschoß. Second-floor plan.

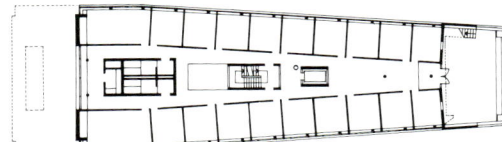

Grundriß erstes Obergeschoß. First-floor plan.

Ebenerdiger Lageplan mit Gartenanlagen. Garden-level plan.

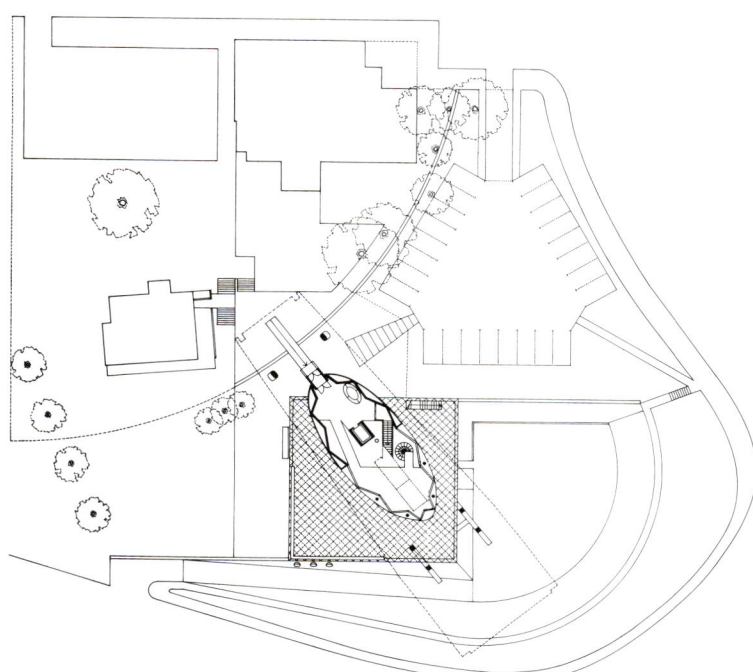

Der sich verbreiternde Grundriß bietet dem zunehmenden Platzbedarf von zentralem Lift, Treppe, Versorgungskern und Konferenzräumen Raum. Der neben der Treppe gelegene offene Schacht läßt Tageslicht ins Innere des Gebäudes einfallen und gestattet Blicke von Ebene zu Ebene.

The tapered plan accommodates the progressive increase in width of the central lift, stair, service core and meeting rooms. The open well adjacent to the stair allows daylight into the centre of the plan and views between levels.

VITRA MÖBELFABRIK, WEIL AM RHEIN
VITRA FURNITURE FACTORY, WEIL AM RHEIN

Nicholas Grimshaw & Partners, 1981

Bei Vitra, einem alteingesessenen, rasch expandierenden Hersteller von Büromöbeln, brannte im Juli 1981 ein Fabrikgebäude ab. Die Versicherung deckte einen sechsmonatigen Produktionsausfall ab, so daß die Aufgabe darin bestand, im Januar 1982 die Produktion wieder aufnehmen zu können. Der Eigentümer von Vitra, Rolf Fehlbaum, brauchte einen Architekten mit Gespür für Industriebauten, der in der Lage sein würde, auf diese Notlage in der kürzestmöglichen Zeit zu reagieren und dabei etwas von bleibendem Wert zu schaffen.

Vitra, a long established and rapidly expanding manufacturer of office furniure, suffered the destruction by fire, in July 1981, of a factory building. Insurance provided cover for six months production loss and the task therefore was a resumption of production by January 1982. Rolf Fehlbaum, the owner of Vitra, needed an architect with a feel for industrial buildings who would be able to respond to the emergency in the shortest possible time and produce something of lasting value.

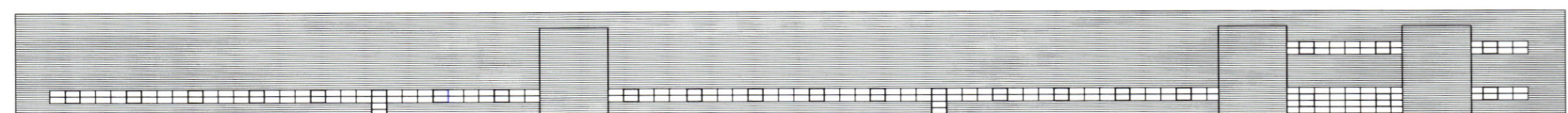

Seitenaufriß. Side elevation.

Industrie Industry

»Anfangs hielten wir eine kabelgestützte Konstruktion für die schnellste Lösung, aber es stellte sich heraus, daß es für Kabel dieser Spannweite eine Lieferfrist von sechs Monaten gab! Deshalb entschieden wir uns für ein sehr gutes Fertigteilsystem, und die Arbeit vor Ort begann innerhalb von drei Wochen. Die Versteifungsplatten und Isolierung entsprachen der Konstruktion, so daß die Einpassung gleichzeitig mit der Verkleidung erfolgen konnte. Wir behielten unsere Verfahrensweise mit den Versorgungstürmen bei, die unabhängig vom Hauptbau entstanden. Der erste Containerlastwagen mit Möbeln verließ die Fabrik genau sechs Monate nach unserem ersten Telefongespräch – 15 000 m² Fabrik waren fertig geworden.« Nick Grimshaw

'At first we thought a cable-supported fabric structure would provide the fastest solution, but it turned out that cables for this span were on six months delivery! We therefore selected a very neat pre-cast structural system and work began on the site within three weeks. The lining panels and insulation followed the structure so that fit-out could proceed in parallel with the cladding. We continued our philosophy of using service towers, which proceeded independently of the main structure. The first container lorry of furniture left the factory exactly six months after our initial phone call – 15,000 m² of factory had been completed.' Nick Grimshaw

Die sanft gewellten Decken im Bürobereich sind die stilistische Antwort auf die winterlichen Schneewehen draußen vor der Fabrik. Der Grundriß offenbart die räumliche Einfachheit dieser ›Instant-Architektur‹.

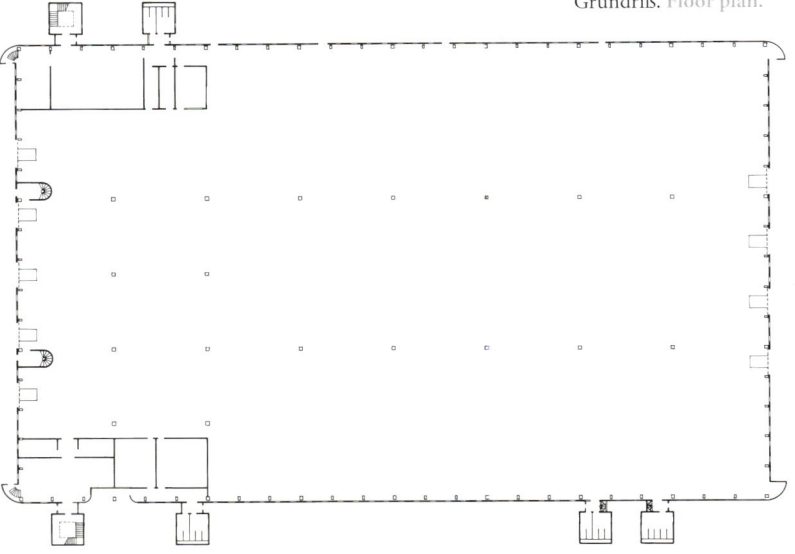

Grundriß. Floor plan.

The gentle undulations of the ceiling in the office area were a stylistic response to the seasonal snow-drifts outside the Vitra factory. The plan reveals the spatial simplicity of this piece of 'instant architecture'.

KREUZFAHRTTERMINAL UND BÜRO-CENTER, FISCHEREIHAFEN HAMBURG
CRUISESHIP TERMINAL AND OFFICES, HAMBURG HARBOUR

Alsop & Störmer, 1990–1993

»Dieses Gebäude gab uns die Gelegenheit, am Wasser zu bauen. Und was für ein Gewässer! Die Elbe ist ein höchst lebendiger Wasserlauf und schafft beständig neue Bilder. Bisweilen wird sie angriffslustig und schwillt bei Flut zu ungewohntem Umfang an. Unser Gebäude bietet von sicherer Warte Aussichten auf diesen mächtigen Fluß.« Will Alsop

'This building gave us the opportunity to build by the water. What a piece of water! The Elbe flows with life and creates new images continuously. Sometimes, it becomes aggressive and floods to new proportions. Our building facilitates views of this mighty river from a safe haven.' Will Alsop

Dieses Projekt für ein neues Kreuzfahrtterminal an der Elbe in Hamburg war als Sieger aus dem vom Planungsdezernat der Stadt Hamburg und der Kreuzfahrtgesellschaft DFDS ausgeschriebenen Wettbewerb hervorgegangen. Die Ausschreibung umfaßte drei Hauptelemente: ein neues Kreuzfahrtterminal mit sämtlichen modernen Einrichtungen, Büroräume für DFDS Seaways sowie einen Gesamtplan für Parken und Abfertigen von Passagierfahrzeugen und Frachtcontainern. Die Unterseite der Serviceebene ist mit poliertem Aluminium verkleidet, das Dach besteht aus einer durchscheinenden Kunststoffmembran. Wände und Dach des um ein Betonskelett errichteten, aufragenden Bürokomplexes sind mit farblos beschichtetem Zink verkleidet. Er ist durch eine verglaste Brücke mit den untenliegenden, von Glaswänden umschlossenen Betriebsanlagen verbunden. Im ursprünglichen, siegreichen Entwurf waren Büro- und Terminalanlagen in einem Gebäude vereint, während das überarbeitete Konzept die beiden Bereiche auf zwei, durch einen schmalen Wasserstreifen getrennte Gebäude verteilt, um das Passieren der Zollkontrollen nach Deutschland hinein sinnfällig zu machen.

This project for a new ferry terminal on the River Elbe in Hamburg was the winner of a competition set by the Planning Department of the City of Hamburg and the ferry company DFDS. The brief contained three main elements: a new ferry terminal providing all the contemporary amenities and office accommodation for DFDS Seaways as well as a comprehensive plan for parking and marshalling of passenger cars and freight containers. The underside of the services platform has a polished aluminium skin, while the roof is a translucent plastic membrane. The concrete-framed raised office building is clad in natural-finish zinc on the walls and roof. It is connected by a glazed bridge to the plant areas beneath which are enclosed by glass walls. In the original winning design the office and terminal space were accommodated within the same building, but the revised scheme has divided the areas into two structures, separated by a strip of water to emphasise the act of passing through customs control into Germany.

Der Hauptbauteil – das Terminal selbst – ist eindrucksvoll geschwungen und nimmt damit die Form von Schiffen und nautischen Bauten auf. Er steht auf hohen Stützen, um bei Sturmfluten Beschädigungen an der Serviceebene vorzubeugen und um am Boden Fahrzeugverkehr zu gestatten.

The main building – the terminal itself – is dramatically curved, echoing the forms of ships and nautical structures. It is raised on legs to prevent damage to the services platform in the event of flooding and to allow vehicle circulation beneath.

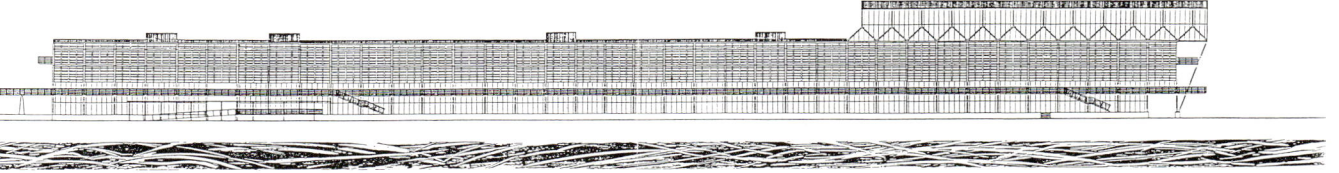

Aufriß der Uferfassade. Waterfront elevation.

Im Terminal wartende Passagiere können durch die geneigte Glasfassade der vorderen Südseite großartige Ausblicke auf die Elbe genießen. Der gesamte Komplex zeichnet sich in Form wie in Funktion durch äußerste Geschmeidigkeit aus – ein, sich über eine Länge von 500 m fortsetzender, schön geschwungener Bau, geeignet, unterschiedlichen Nutzungen Platz zu bieten.

Passengers waiting inside the terminal can enjoy magnificent views out across the River Elbe through the inclined curtain wall glazing of the front south elevation. Both in form and function the entire project is extremely fluid – a beautifully curved design structure repeated over a length of 500m and able to accommodate different uses.

»Jede ›Straße‹ braucht eine Randbegrenzung, und die Elbe macht in dieser Hinsicht keine Ausnahme. Unser Straßenrand bietet eine Abfolge paralleler Ebenen, von denen aus man den Fluß beobachten oder auch vor ihm Zuflucht finden kann.« Will Alsop

'Every street needs an edge definition and in this respect the Elbe is no exception. Our street edge offers a line of parallel platforms from which to both observe and hide from the river.' Will Alsop

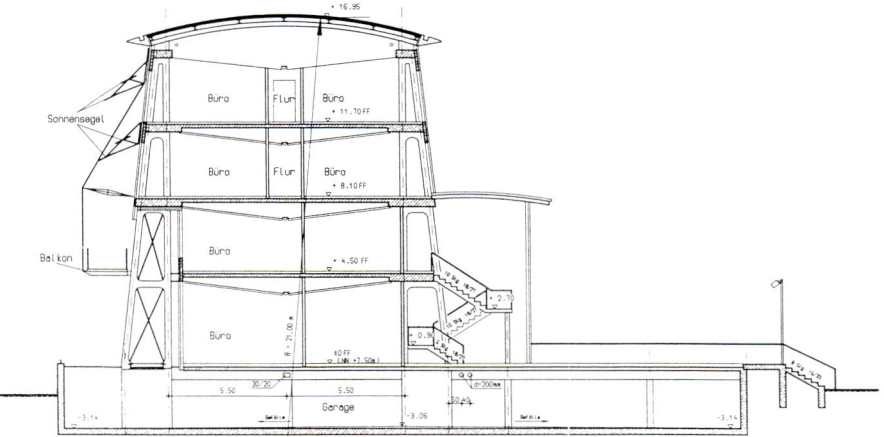

Schnitt durch den Bürokomplex. Section of offices.

Die an Hafenlichter erinnernden Laternen rufen Hamburgs maritimes Erbe ins Gedächtnis.

The lanterns, reminiscent of harbour lights, recall Hamburg's maritime heritage.

LUDWIG-ERHARD-HAUS, BERLIN
LUDWIG ERHARD HOUSE, BERLIN

Nicholas Grimshaw & Partners, 1991–1998

»Es herrschte das starke Gefühl, daß man sehen wollte, was Handel, Industrie und Wirtschaft in Berlin erreichen können. Also ist es ein emblematisches Gebäude; eine freundliche, einladende Art von Gebäude. Nicht ein weiteres Monument. Ich glaube, Berliner mögen Monumente nicht besonders.« Nick Grimshaw

'There was a strong feeling of wanting to look for what trade, industry and commerce could do in Berlin. So it's an emblematic building, a friendly, welcoming kind of building. Not another monument. I think Berliners are very anti-monumental really.' Nick Grimshaw

Die kühne Ausschreibung zu diesem Projekt entsprach der auf die deutsche Wiedervereinigung folgenden Euphorie. Die Berliner Handelskammer wollte ein ›Kommunikationszentrum‹ schaffen, einen Ort, an dem sich sämtliche wichtigen Teilnehmer am Wirtschaftsleben der neuen Hauptstadt treffen oder vertreten sein konnten. Neben Konferenz- und Tagungseinrichtungen sowie Ausstellungsflächen sollte hier auch die Berliner Börse Platz finden. Entsprechend fiel das Projekt weit vielgestaltiger aus als ein herkömmliches Bürogebäude. Das Erdgeschoß ist der Öffentlichkeit sowohl als Schaukasten wie als überdachte Straße zugänglich, die sich über die Gesamtlänge des Gebäudes erstreckt. Die Tatsache, daß auf Erdgeschoßniveau ein ausgedehnter, stützenfreier Raum zur Verfügung stehen sollte, bedingte die neuartige Form des Baues. In der Tat hängt das Gebäude an den charakteristischen Bögen, die dem Ludwig-Erhard-Haus den Spitznamen ›Gürteltier‹ eintrugen. Diese Entwurfslösung, die sich als technische Antwort auf die Ausschreibungsbedingungen organisch ergab, ermöglichte die maximale Ausnutzung des unregelmäßigen Grundstücks, ohne auf einen weiteren Hochhausblock zurückgreifen zu müssen. Dank der Flexibilität des Erdgeschosses werden für die Eigentümer des Ludwig-Erhard-Hauses künftig ohne größere bauliche Veränderungen eine Vielzahl von Nutzungen in Frage kommen. Hier handelt es sich in der Tat um ein Bauwerk für das neue Millennium.

The brief for this project was a bold one, forged in the euphoria following German reunification. The Berlin Chamber of Commerce set out to create a 'Communication Centre', a place where all the principal players in the economic life of the new capital could either meet or be represented. In addition to housing the Berlin Stock Exchange, there were to be conference and catering facilities as well as exhibition spaces. Accordingly, the project is much more varied than a conventional office building. The ground floor is accessible to the public both as a showcase and as a covered street that runs the length of the building. Providing an extensive column-free space at ground level constitutes the practical reason behind the novel shape of the structure. The building actually hangs from the distinctive arches that have earned the Ludwig Erhard House its 'armadillo' nickname. This design solution, which emerged organically as a technical response to the brief, has made possible the maximisation of the irregular shape of the site without recourse to erecting yet another high-rise block. The flexibility of the ground floor will also enable the owners of the Ludwig Erhard House to envisage a multiplicity of uses in the future without incurring major structural alterations. This is quite literally a building designed for the new millennium.

Handel und Verwaltung Commerce and Administration

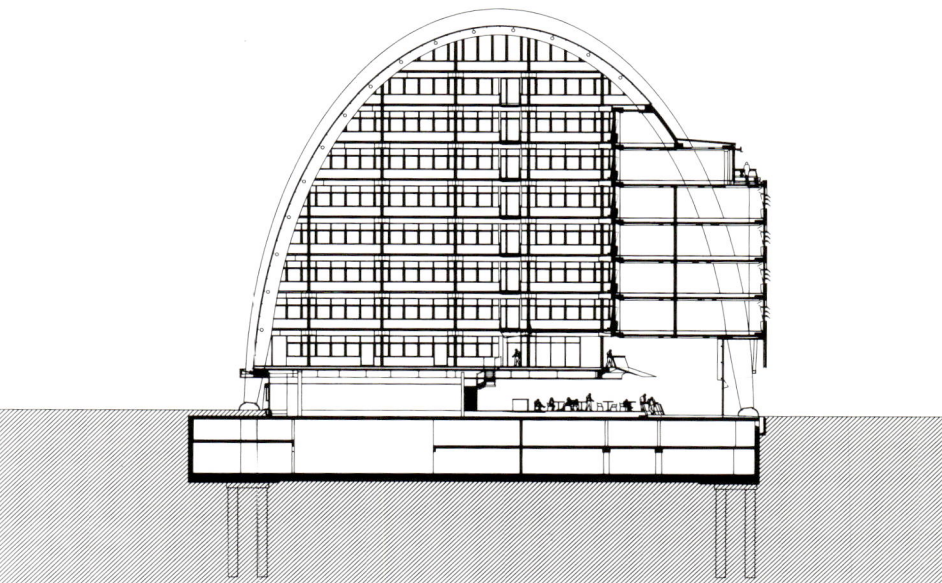

Dem Ludwig-Erhard-Haus gelingt es, die traditionelle Straßenführung zu respektieren und mittels der organischen Form der Bögen, die sozusagen das Skelett des Gebäudes bilden, seiner Individualität Ausdruck zu geben.

The Ludwig Erhard House manages to respect the traditional street line while expressing its individuality through the organic shape of the arches that form the ribcage of the building.

Querschnitt. Cross-section.

Das Gerüst des Ludwig-Erhard-Hauses bilden 15 elliptische Stahlbögen von abgestufter Spannweite, deren Auflagerungen auf einer Seite aufgereiht sind, auf der anderen einen sanft geschwungener. Umriß bilden. Der Gedanke der sichtbaren Konstruktion ist außerdem in zahlreichen kleinen Details im gesamten Gebäude präsent.

At the core of the Ludwig Erhard House stand 15 elliptical steel arches, of progressively different spans, with the bearings along one side lined up in a row, and those of the other describing a gently curving profile. The idea of naked engineering also manifests itself in many small details throughout the building.

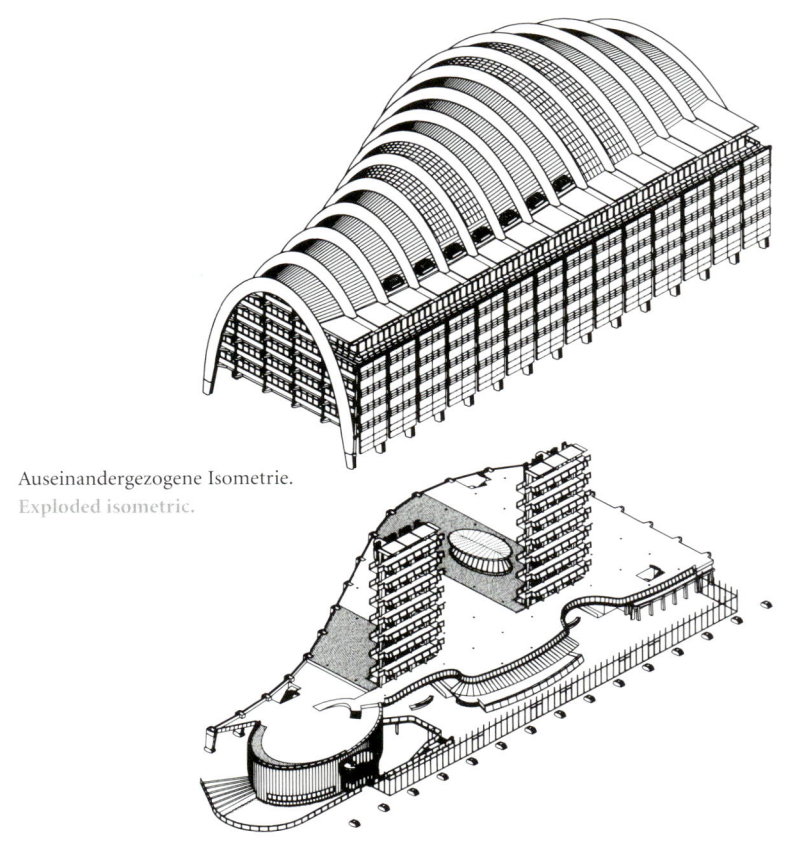

Auseinandergezogene Isometrie.
Exploded isometric.

Handel und Verwaltung Commerce and Administration

Die Bogenkonstruktion ergab im Inneren einige reizvolle Räume. Große Innenhöfe dienen außerdem auch als Klimapuffer. Für den Gesamtplan wurde eine räumliche Choreographie konzipiert, dank derer sich beim Durchschreiten des Gebäudes immer neue faszinierende Ausblicke eröffnen.

The arch construction has created some exciting internal spaces. Large atria also serve as climatic buffer zones. The over-all plan has been spatially choreographed in order to open up dramatic views as one passes from one part of the building to another.

Die Aufzüge ähneln kleinen Raumkapseln, die den Besucher aus der Enge der Börse hinaus in die relative Offenheit der Innenhöfe und schließlich zu atemberaubenden Blicken auf die Berliner Skyline befördern, die sich durch das obenliegende Glasdach bieten. Der Hersteller der Aufzüge bestand auf Kunststoffgehäusen für die Fahrkabinen; das Wunschmaterial des Architekten war jedoch Aluminium, und schließlich fand sich eine kleine, auf die Restaurierung von Oldtimern spezialisierte Firma in England, die die Arbeiten ausführte. Des weiteren zeichnen sich die Fahrstühle durch ihre Holzverkleidung aus, die ein in jede Kabine eigens eingebautes Sprinklersystem erforderlich machte.

The lifts resemble miniature space capsules that take the visitor from the confinement of the Stock Exchange out into the relative openness of the atria and finally to some sensational views of the Berlin skyline through the glazing at the very top. The lift manufacturer insisted that the housing of the cars had to be done in plastic, but the architect wanted aluminium and eventually found a small company in England that specialised in restoring vintage cars to do the job. Another unique feature of the lifts is their wooden panelling which necessitated an inbuilt sprinkler system being installed in each.

Im Zentrum des Gebäudes liegt das ovale Parkett der Berliner Börse. Es erhält Tageslicht durch die obenliegende Öffnung zu einem Atrium. Der Grundriß läßt die geschickte Nutzung eines schwierigen Grundstücks erkennen.

In the core of the building lies the oval dealing room of the Berlin Stock Exchange. It derives natural light through a skylight opening to an atrium. The plan reveals the clever use of an awkward site.

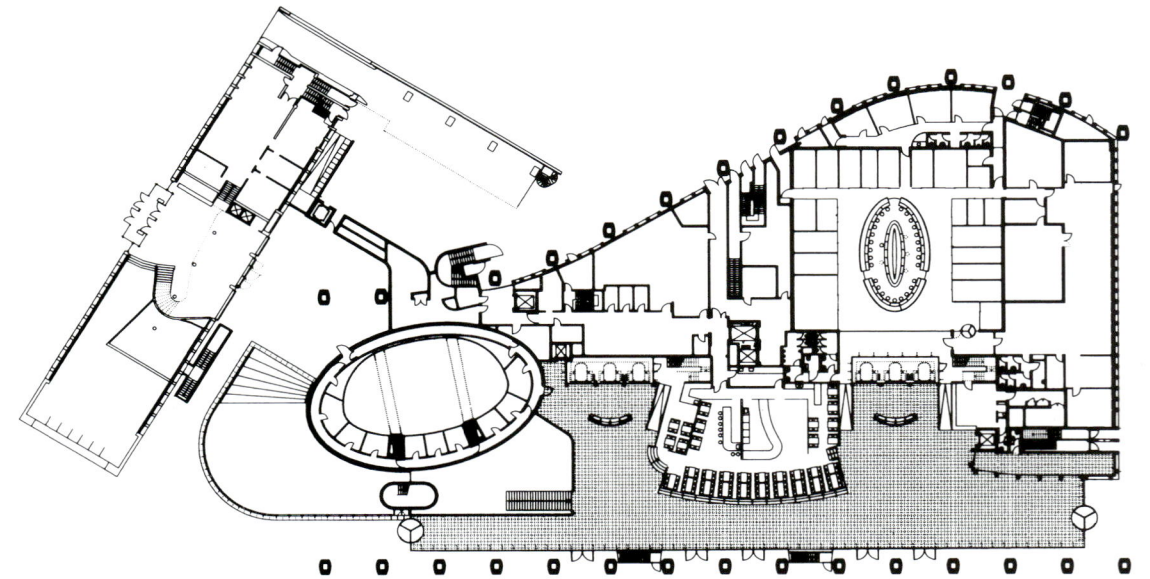

Grundriß Erdgeschoß. Ground-floor plan.

Handel und Verwaltung Commerce and Administration

»Falls jetzt die Börse auszieht oder sich ganz auf elektronischen Handel verlegt, besteht die Möglichkeit, das ganze Geschoß erneut umzuwidmen. Es ist eher so eine philosophische Einstellung meinerseits, daß ich finde, das Erdgeschoß eines Gebäudes sollte die Möglichkeit bieten, im Laufe der Jahre anders genutzt zu werden; auf diese Weise hat der Bau viel länger Bestand, und in der Regel sind es das Erdgeschoß oder die unteren Ebenen, die man verändern möchte.« Nick Grimshaw

'Now, if the Stock Exchange moves out or goes electronic, then it leaves the possibility of replanning that whole area once again. It's rather a philosophical thing with me that I feel the ground floors of buildings ought to be able to be re-used over the years because it gives the buildings a much longer life and on the whole it's the ground floor or the lower levels you want to change.' Nick Grimshaw

KAISTRASSE, DÜSSELDORF
KAISTRASSE, DÜSSELDORF

David Chipperfield Architects, 1994–1997

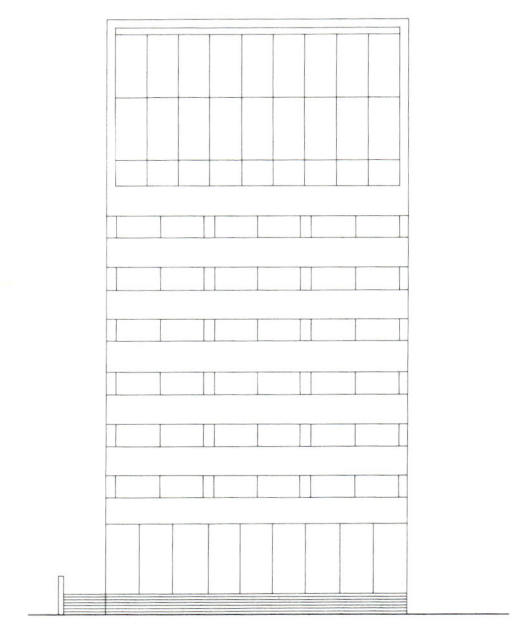

Aufriß von Café und Terrasse. Café/terrace elevation.

Das Gebäude ergänzt eine Gruppe neuer oder auch renovierter Bauten im Hafengebiet von Düsseldorf. Bestimmend für das Quartier sind solide Industriebauten von schlichter Form und aus dauerhaften Materialien. Viele der Industriebauten im Sanierungsgebiet wurden abgerissen und durch geschickt gestaltete, moderne, mit den neuesten, technischen Materialien verkleidete Bürogebäude ersetzt. Dieses Projekt versucht, dieser Schablone zu entgehen. Es war der Wunsch des Auftraggebers, daß dieses Gebäude und die zugeordneten Räume für das Gebiet die Funktion eines Zentrums übernehmen sollen. Der Bau besteht aus zwei miteinander verzahnten Elementen, ein *in situ* gegossener Betonblock, der über einem mit schwarzer Graphitfarbe gestrichenen Stahlrahmen steht. Der Beton erfüllt die strengen Wärmeschutzverordnungen, indem er im Gebäudeinneren dämmend wirkt und sämtliche Innenwände und Böden von der Außenhaut isoliert. Er wurde mit einer strukturierten Oberfläche versehen. Schlichtheit und Unmittelbarkeit der Materialien nehmen Bezug auf den starken ästhetischen Kontext des Hafengeländes und vermeiden bewußt die normalerweise von Fassaden neuer Bürokomplexe erwartete, technische Raffinesse.

The building contributes to a group of new and renovated buildings in the port area of Düsseldorf. The area is dominated by strong industrial buildings of simple form and robust materials. Many of the industrial buildings in the reconstruction area have been taken down and replaced by modern offices, cleverly designed and clad in the latest technical materials. The project attempts to avoid this formula. It is the desire of the clients that this building and its associated spaces should form a focal centre for the area. The building is composed of two interlocking elements, an *in-situ* concrete mass sitting over a steel frame painted in black graphite. The concrete deals with stringent thermal regulations by insulating on the inside of the building and isolating all internal walls and floors from the external skin. It is finished in a textured surface. The simplicity and directness of the materials refer to the strong aesthetic context of the harbour site and purposely avoid the technical sophistication normally demanded by the façade systems of office developments.

Das für ›kreative Bewohner‹ wie Bildhauer und Maler intendierte Kaistraßenprojekt wurde als Abfolge doppelstöckiger Lofts mit Mezzaningeschossen konzipiert; dadurch entsteht auf den nach Norden und Süden zu gelegenen Fassaden jeweils eine ›Ordnung‹. Das obenliegende Loft zeigt nach Westen und schließt den Gebäudekörper ab.

The Kaistraße project, intended for occupation by 'creative tenants' such as sculptors and painters, is conceived as a series of double-height lofts with mezzanine floors, establishing a grand order on the north and south façades. The top loft faces west and terminates the mass of the building.

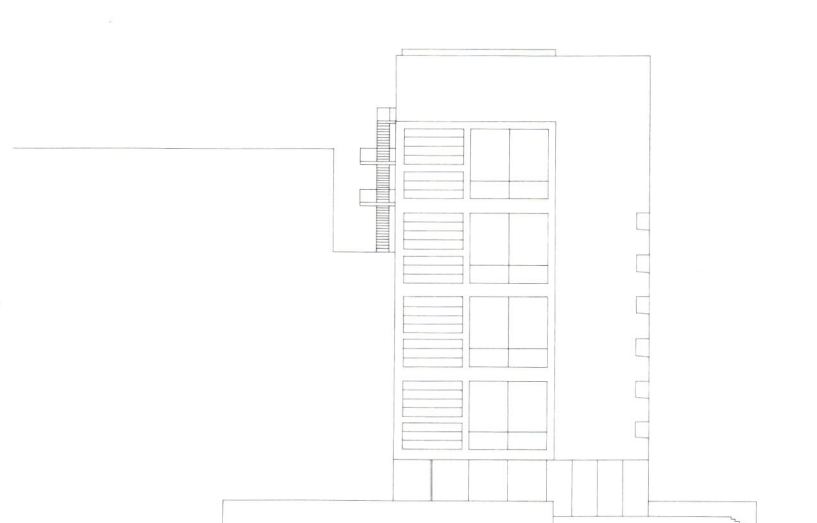

Aufriß der dem Fluß zugewandten Seite. Riverside elevation.

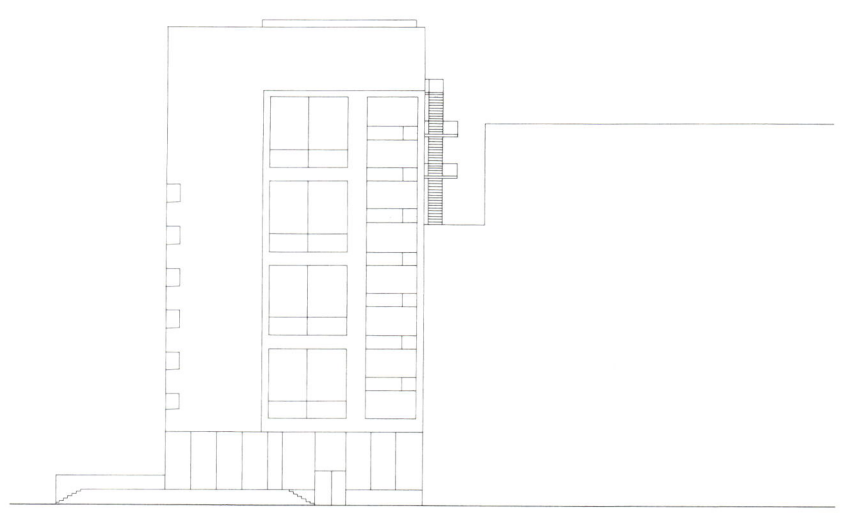

Aufriß der an der Kaistraße gelegenen Seite. Kaistraße elevation.

Handel und Verwaltung Commerce and Administration

Große Fenster eröffnen Panoramablicke über die Hafenanlagen von Düsseldorf. Diese gerahmten Ausblicke begründen eine starke Beziehung zwischen Innen- und Außenraum.

Large windows open up panoramic views across the waters of the Düsseldorf docks. These framed vistas establish a powerful relationship between the internal and external spaces.

BÜROGEBÄUDE DAIMLER CHRYSLER, POTSDAMER PLATZ, BERLIN
DAIMLER CHRYSLER OFFICES, POTSDAMER PLATZ, BERLIN

Richard Rogers Partnership, 1993–1999

Der Aufriß der Südseite verdeutlicht, wie es dem Architekten gelang, innerhalb der engen Begrenzungen eines traditionellen Berliner Straßenkarrees mit der vorgeschriebenen, festliegenden Dachhöhe zu arbeiten.

The southerly elevation shows how the architect managed to work within the tight urban constraints of a traditional square Berlin block with a fixed roof level as laid down by the planners.

Diese beiden als B4 und B6 bekannten Bürogebäude ergänzen sich zu einem Paar, das mit Blick auf den Park auf angrenzenden Grundstücken an der Linkstraße steht. Im Gegensatz zum benachbarten Wohngebäude B8, auch ein Entwurf der Richard Rogers Partnership, präsentieren die Bürobauten der Außenwelt ihre deutlich geschäftsmäßigeren Fassaden. Für die 29 000 m² Fläche in den oberen Geschossen wurden die neuesten Erkenntnisse der Niedrigenergieversorgung angewendet. Die Büros sind so konzipiert, daß sie zur Gänze natürlich belüftet werden und die kostenneutrale nächtliche Abkühlung sowie über Tag die Sonneneinstrahlung nutzen. Wesentliche Merkmale des Gebäudes sind eine direkte Folge des umweltgerechten Entwurfs. So schlägt sich die fortschrittliche Bautechnik beispielsweise in der komplexen Aufreihung von Platten nieder, die jeweils so angeordnet wurden, daß es den unterschiedlichen Anteilen von Licht, Schatten, Hitze, Kälte und Wind entspricht, denen die verschiedenen Teile der Fassade ausgesetzt sind. Bei diesen beiden prägnanten Bauten verschmelzen sämtliche verschiedenen Elemente erfolgreich zu einer innovativen Kombination von High-tech-Stil und Funktionalität.

These two office buildings known as B4 and B6 form a complementary pair situated on adjacent sites looking across Linkstraße to the park. By contrast to the neighbouring residential building B8, which was also designed by the Richard Rogers Partnership, the office blocks present their noticeably more business-like façades to the outside world. The 29,000m² of accommodation located in the upper storeys incorporate the very latest in low-energy know-how. The offices were designed to be fully naturally ventilated and to make use of night-time free cooling and day-time solar radiation. Some significant features of the architecture are a direct result of the environmental design. For example, the advanced building technology is expressed through a complex array of panels arranged according to the varying amounts of light, shade, heat, cold and wind to which each part of the façade is exposed. In these two striking and distinguished buildings all the various elements come effectively together to create an innovative fusion of high-tech style and function.

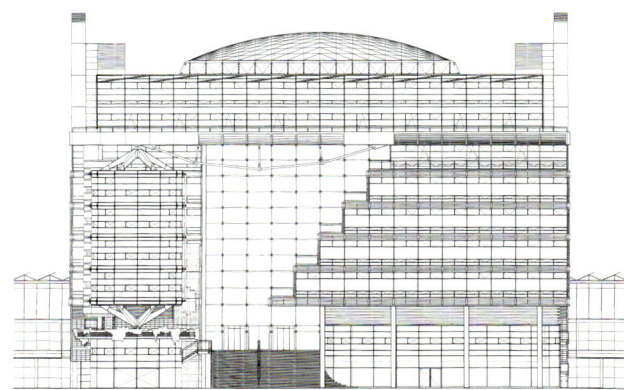

Handel und Verwaltung Commerce and Administration

Das Atrium wird vollständig mit Außenluft belüftet. Zur Optimierung von Raumklima und Luftzirkulation wurden hochkomplizierte Computersimulationen durchgeführt. Ebenso trägt die Sonnenbestrahlung zur Beheizung bei und reduziert so den Energieverbrauch im Winter. Die natürliche Belüftung gewährleistet das ganze Jahr hindurch ein angenehmes Raumklima im Eingangsbereich und in den an das Atrium angrenzenden Büroräumen.

The atrium is fully naturally ventilated. Highly sophisticated computer simulations were conducted in order to optimise the thermal conditions and airflow. Solar radiation contributes to the heating and thereby reduces energy consumption in the winter. The natural ventilation ensures that a comfortable climate prevails in the entrance area and offices adjacent to the atrium throughout the year.

Der Architekt schuf ein äußerst vielfältiges, reizvolles Gebäude, dessen große Außentreppe als prägnantes Merkmal ins Auge fällt. Die einzelnen Elemente vereinen sich zu einer attraktiven Straßenfassade.

The architect has introduced a high degree of stylistic variety and interest. The grand external staircase forms a bold design feature. The individual elements combine to present an exciting façade to the street.

Der runde Turm umfaßt eine Reihe von Konferenzräumen, von denen sich Panoramablicke über den Park und die Stadt, ebenso wie Aussichten auf andere Gebäudeteile bieten.

The circular tower contains a series of meeting rooms that enjoy panoramic views over the park and the city as well as opening up some intriguing views onto other parts of the building.

Handel und Verwaltung Commerce and Administration

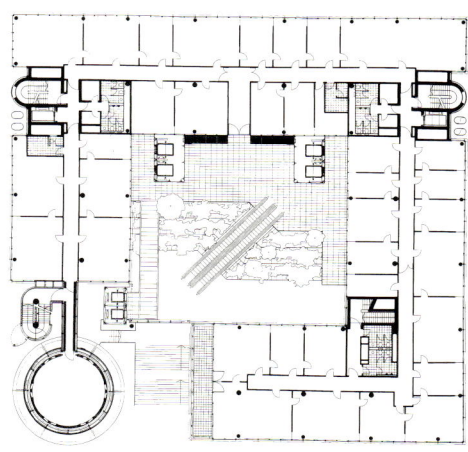

Grundriß zweites Obergeschoß.
Second-floor plan.

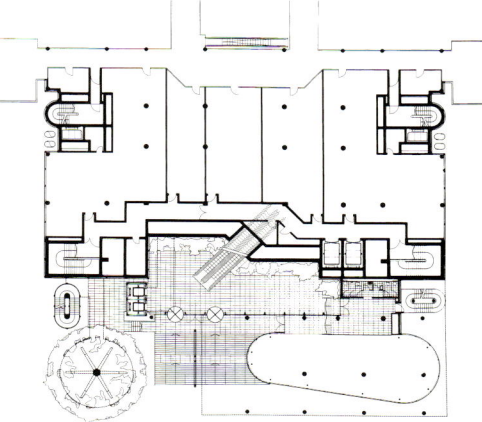

Grundriß erstes Obergeschoß.
First-floor plan.

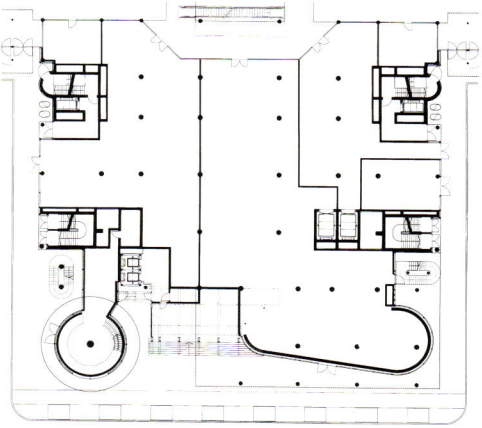

Grundriß Erdgeschoß.
Ground-floor plan.

COMMERZBANK, FRANKFURT
COMMERZBANK, FRANKFURT

Foster and Partners, 1991–1997

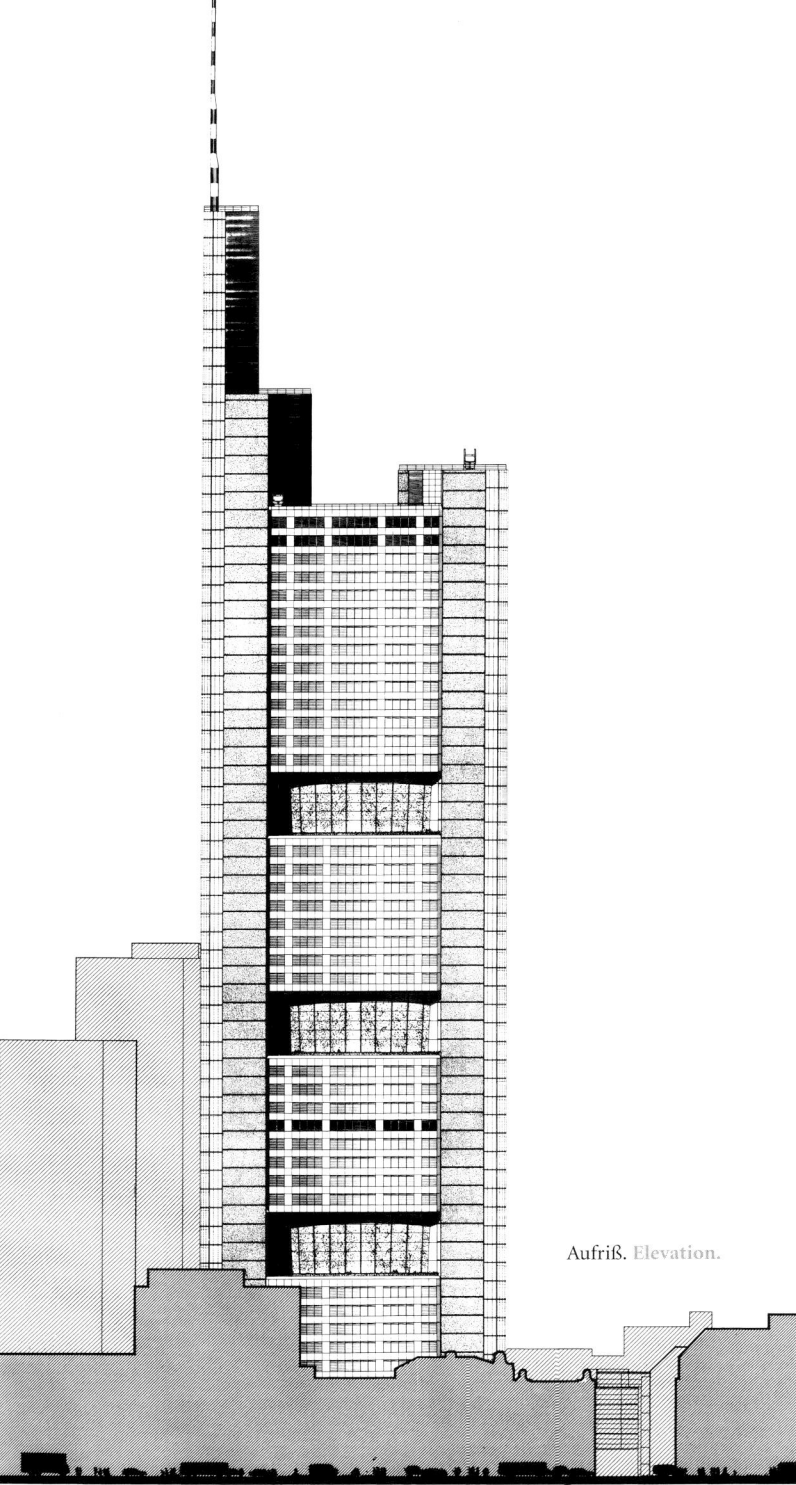

Aufriß. Elevation.

Der aus dem Wettbewerb für die Zentrale der Commerzbank siegreich hervorgegangene Entwurf bot die willkommene Gelegenheit, ein sowohl symbolisch wie funktional ›grünes‹ Gebäude zu konzipieren. Als solches kann es für sich in Anspruch nehmen, das weltweit erste ökologische Hochhaus zu sein, eine Leistung, die in enger Zusammenarbeit von Auftraggeber, Stadtplanern und Architekten entstand. Der Turm hat die Form eines Dreiecks, das sich aus drei ›Blättern‹ und einem zentralen ›Stamm‹ zusammensetzt. Die Blätter entsprechen den Büroetagen, der Stamm einem großzügigen, zentralen Atrium, das als natürlicher Belüftungsschacht fungiert. Aufzüge, Treppen und Versorgungseinrichtungen wurden an den drei Ecken zu Gruppen zusammengefaßt, die die zu kleinen, dorfähnlichen Strukturen gruppierten Büros und Gärten ergänzen. Paarweise angeordnete, vertikale Masten tragen acht Geschosse umfassende Vierendeelträger, die ihrerseits freitragende Büroebenen abstützen. Somit bleiben nicht nur die Büroetagen stützenfrei, sondern dank der Vierendeelträger kommen auch die Gärten ohne derartige Elemente aus. Der gut 300 m hohe, 53geschossige Turm erhebt sich neben dem bestehenden Commerzbank-Gebäude aus dem Zentrum des Stadtkarrees. Durch Umbau und Renovierung der Blockrandbebauung konnte der Maßstab des Viertels auf Straßenniveau erhalten werden. Der Turm der Commerzbank gilt derzeit als Europas höchstes Gebäude.

The competition-winning scheme for the headquarters of the Commerzbank provided a welcome opportunity to design a building which is symbolically and functionally 'green'. As such, it may claim to be the world's first ecological highrise tower, an achievement that resulted from a close co-operation between client, city planners and architects. The form of the tower is triangular, made up from three 'petals' and a central 'stem'. The petals are the office floors, the stem a great central atrium which provides a natural ventilation chimney. Lifts, staircases and services are placed in the three corners in groups designed to reinforce the village-like clusters of offices and gardens. Pairs of vertical masts, enclosing the corner cores, support eight-storey vierendeel beams, which in turn support clear span office floors. Thus, not only are there no columns within the offices, but the vierendeels also enable the gardens to be totally free of structure. The fifty-three-storey tower, just over 300m high, rises from the centre of the city block alongside the existing Commerzbank building. By rebuilding and restoring the perimeter edge buildings, the scale of the neighbourhood has been preserved at street level. The Commerzbank tower currently ranks as the tallest building in Europe.

Handel und Verwaltung Commerce and Administration

Aus der Frankfurter Innenstadt dem Bug eines großen Ozeandampfers gleich aufsteigend, macht die Zentrale der Commerzbank ihre eindrucksvolle Präsenz geltend. Norman Foster war nicht mit der Absicht, Europas höchstes Gebäude zu errichten, ans Werk gegangen. Die endgültige Höhe ergab sich als direkte Folge der gewünschten Büroflächen, die sich nur so im Rahmen der von den Planern erlaubten, äußerst beschränkten Grundfläche unterbringen ließen. Der Bankenturm gehört heute zu Frankfurts prägnantesten Bauwerken.

The Commerzbank HQ exerts an imposing presence, emerging from the inner city of Frankfurt like the bow of a great ocean liner. Apparently, Norman Foster did not set out to design Europe's tallest building. The final height was arrived at as a direct consequence of accommodating the required floorspace within the restricted footprint permitted by the planners. The building is now one of Frankfurt's most recognisable symbols.

Die Dreieckform der Commerzbank ist am Grundriß und den Ausblicken auf die Gärten aus den Büros und entlang der Flure gut erkennbar. Die künstliche Beleuchtung stellt sich auf die natürliche Helligkeit ein. Ausgeklügelte Steuerungsmechanismen ermöglichen es dem Einzelnen, im jeweils eigenen Bereich das gewünschte Raumklima zu bestimmen. Bis auf die Räume der Vorstandsmitglieder sind sämtliche Büros mit Glaswänden ausgestattet.

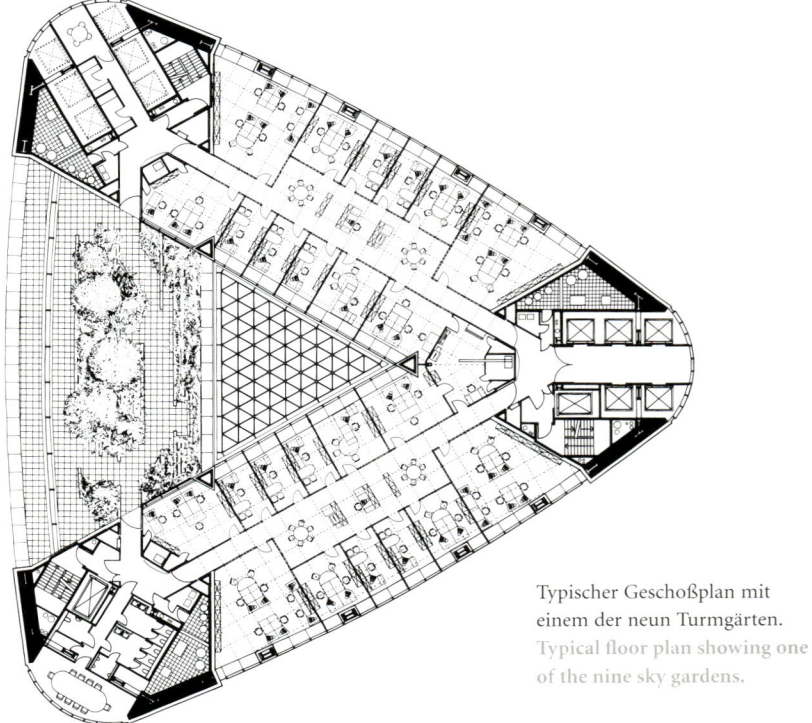

Typischer Geschoßplan mit einem der neun Turmgärten.
Typical floor plan showing one of the nine sky gardens.

The triangular form of the Commerzbank is readily apparent from the plan as well as in the garden views from the offices and along the corridors. Artificial lighting adjusts to natural luminosity. Sophisticated controls allow individuals to programme the precise environmental conditions within their own spaces. All offices have glass walls except for those of the board members.

Handel und Verwaltung Commerce and Administration

Einem modernen Pendant der Hängenden Gärten von Babylon gleich umziehen die neun, sich jeweils über vier Geschosse erstreckenden Turmgärten der Commerzbank spiralförmig den dreieckigen Grundriß. Der Blick aus einem typischen Bürofenster (rechts) gestattet dem Benutzer, über den Garten hinweg zu anderen Büros und darüberhinaus zur Stadt zu schauen.

Like a modern equivalent of the Hanging Gardens of Babylon, the nine sky gardens of the Commerzbank, each four storeys high, spiral around the triangular plan form. The views from a typical office window (right) allow the occupant to look across the garden to other offices and the city beyond.

Skizze von Norman Foster.
Sketch by Norman Foster.

Im Erdgeschoß befindet sich ein belebter Bereich mit Cafés und Restaurants, in dem sich Bankangestellte und Passanten wie auf einer traditionellen Piazza treffen und verweilen können.

At ground-floor level there is an animated area with cafés and restaurants where bank workers and the general public can meet and mingle as if on a traditional piazza.

Schnitt, der das Verhältnis von Büros und Gärten zeigt.
Section showing offices in relation to gardens.

GLASHALLE
NEUE LEIPZIGER MESSE, LEIPZIG
GLASS HALL, NEW LEIPZIG TRADE FAIR, LEIPZIG

Architects von Gerkan, Marg und Partner in cooperation with Ian Ritchie Architects, 1993–1996

Volkwin Marg vom Büro von Gerkan, Marg und Partner gewann im April 1992 den Wettbewerb für die neue Leipziger Messe. Aufgrund der Notwendigkeit, in kürzester Zeit eine Baugenehmigung und die Produktionsreife für eine Stahl-Glas-Konstruktion zu erreichen, bot Volkwin Marg Ian Ritchie die Kooperation an. So wurden Ian Ritchie Architects von gmp mit dem gemeinsamen Design-Engineering für die Konstruktion der Eingangshalle und der Verbindungsbrücken beauftragt. Aus dieser beispiellosen Zusammenarbeit eines deutschen und eines britischen Architekturbüros entstand ein phantastisches Bauwerk. Ian Ritchies fachmännisches Können im Umgang mit Glaskonstruktionen vereint Technik und Architektur in spektakulärer Weise. Die Ausgangsidee der deutschen Architekten, das großartige, majestätische Gewölbe des Leipziger Hauptbahnhofs nachzuempfinden, wurde höchst erfolgreich verwirklicht. Mit Ritchies Hilfe wurde die imposante Stahl-Glas-Konstruktion zur modernen Ikone der Stadt. Abgesehen von der technischen Leistung kommt dem Projekt, im Rahmen der nach der Wiedervereinigung in Angriff genommenen wirtschaftlichen Sanierung des ehemaligen Ostdeutschland, enorme symbolische Bedeutung zu.

Volkwin Marg of the practice von Gerkan, Marg und Partner won the competition for the new Leipzig Trade Fair in April 1992. Because of the urgent need to get authorization for and speedy production of a steel and glass construction, Volkwin Marg invited Ian Ritchie to collaborate. Thus Ian Ritchie Architects were commissioned by gmp to carry out design engineering for the construction of the entrance hall and the link bridges. What emerged from this unique collaboration between German and British architectural firms is a stunning creation. Ian Ritchie's expertise with glass construction brings engineering and architecture together in spectacular fashion. The original vision of the German architects to emulate the majestic great vault of Leipzig's main railway station has been triumphantly realised. With Ritchie's help the imposing structure of steel and glass has become a modern icon for the city. Apart from its technological achievement, the project also has huge symbolic significance for the economic regeneration of the former East Germany following re-unification.

»Die Glashalle ist der erste und letzte Eindruck, den jemand vom Messegelände mitnimmt.«
Josef Rahmen, Geschäftsführer, Leipziger Messe

'The Glass Hall is the first and last impression that one takes away from the Trade Fair.'
Josef Rahmen, Manager, Leipziger Messe

Handel und Verwaltung Commerce and Administration

Die Kooperation von Volkwin Marg und Ian Ritchie brachte eine technische Innovation und eine architektonische Sensation nach Leipzig, die an die Kristallpaläste des 19. Jahrhunderts anknüpft.

The collaboration between Volkwin Marg and Ian Ritchie brought technical innovation and an architectonic sensation to Leipzig, that recalled the glass constructions of the nineteenth century.

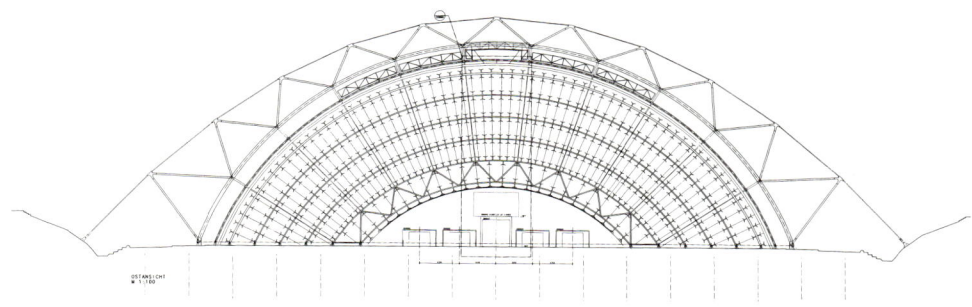

Aufriß der Westseite. West elevation.

Innenansicht. Interior view.

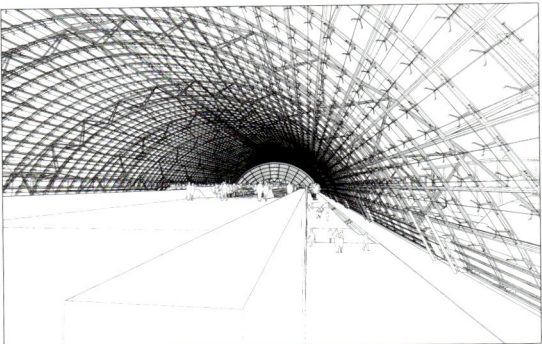

Dank des gläsernen Tonnengewölbes entsteht ein gewaltiger Innenraum. Bei einer maximalen Höhe von 30 m überspannt es eine Breite von 80 m, eine Länge von 244 m, eine Fläche von 20 000 m² sowie ein Raumvolumen von 350 000 m³; diese Maße tragen dem Bau den Titel des ›größten Glaspalastes der Welt‹ ein.

An enormous internal space is created by the barrel-vault of glass. Spanning a width of 80m, a length of 244m and with a maximum height of 30m, it covers a surface area of 20,000m², that is a volume of 350,000m³, which earns it the title of 'the biggest glass palace in the world'.

Handel und Verwaltung Commerce and Administration

»Wenn man Leuten die Leipziger Glashalle zeigt, muß man die Architektur nicht erklären. Sie leuchtet jedem unmittelbar ein.« Henning Rambow, ehemaliger Mitarbeiter von Ian Ritchie Architects.

'The nice thing about the Leipzig Glashalle is that when you show it to people, you don't have to explain the architecture. It's apparent to everyone.' Henning Rambow (former associate of Ian Ritchie Architects).

Handel und Verwaltung Commerce and Administration

Auseinandergezogene Isometrie.
Exploded isometric.

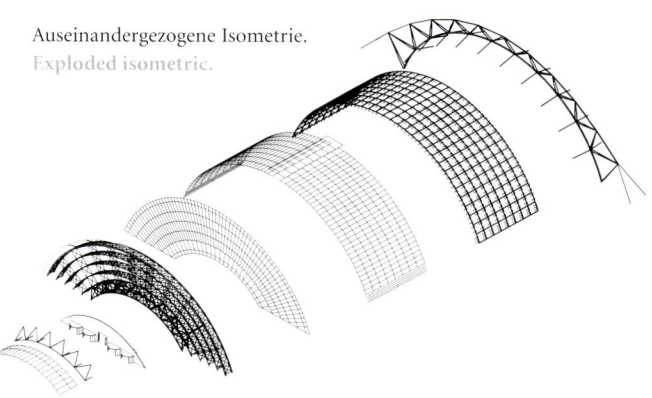

Das Geniale der Konstruktion besteht darin, daß die Glasscheiben als innere Hülle an der außenliegenden Konstruktion des Stahlgewölbes aufgehängt sind. Die allgemein als ›Froschfinger‹ bekannten Elemente befestigen das Glas an der Konstruktion. Man entwickelte ein neuartiges Silikonverbundsystem, um zwischen den einzelnen Platten flexible, wasserdichte Verbindungen zu gewährleisten.

The ingenuity of the construction lies in hanging the glass panels as an inner shell from the external arrangement of the steel vault. The castings, popularly known as frog fingers, secure the glass to the structure. A novel silicone bonding system was developed to form flexible, watertight joints between the individual panels.

GSW HAUPTVERWALTUNG, BERLIN
GSW HEADQUARTERS, BERLIN

Sauerbruch Hutton Architects, 1991–1999

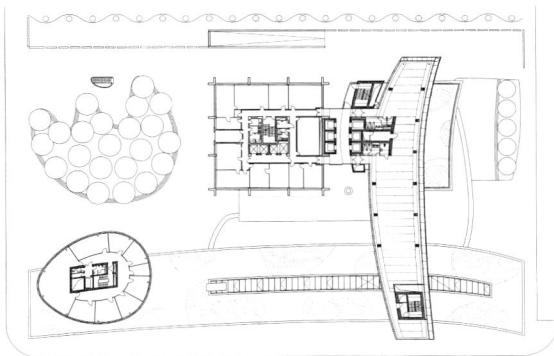

Der typische Lageplan zeigt deutlich, wie die neuen Baukörper den vorhandenen Hochhausblock umgeben und so das mit einem quadratischen Gebäude bestandene rechteckige Grundstück durch gebogene Elemente beleben.

The typical floor plan clearly shows how the modern elements are grouped around the original block in order to integrate the set-back existing building into a new composition, taking account of the structure of the historic city.

Der Auftrag für die Zentrale der ›Gemeinnützige Siedlungs- und Wohnungsbaugesellschaft‹, GSW, am Check Point Charlie sah vor, ein Gebäude, das im Jahre 1961, kurz vor dem Bau der Berliner Mauer, errichtet worden war, um 20 000 m² Bürofläche zu erweitern. Die Architekten erwogen die verschiedenen Möglichkeiten einer flachen Bebauung, um das gesamte Gelände auszunutzen. Schließlich entschloß man sich jedoch, auf die in dieser Gegend vorhandenen Hochhausblocks, die sich im geteilten Berlin zu beiden Seiten des Niemandslands gegenübergestanden hatten, mit einem Prozeß ›retrospektiver Integration‹ zu antworten. Die Anlage wird von einem schlanken, bogenförmigen Scheibenhochhaus beherrscht, das mit dem vorhandenen Turm verbunden ist. Im Verein mit einem kleinen, runden Gebäude bildet ein langgestreckter Flachbau die reizvolle Straßenfront. Diese verschiedenen Elemente vereinen sich in der fertigen Anlage zu einem bemerkenswerten Gebäudekomplex. Die Architekturstile der 50er und 90er Jahre bestehen in einer Weise nebeneinander, die die jüngste Stadtgeschichte dieses Teils von Berlin respektiert und zugleich für die Zukunft ein markantes, neues Wahrzeichen schafft.

The commission for the GSW headquarters near Checkpoint Charlie involved adding 20,000m² of office space to an existing building that had been completed in 1961 just before the Berlin Wall was erected. The architects studied the various options of a low-rise development to cover the entire site. However, they finally decided to respond by a process of 'retrospective integration' to the existing pattern of high-rise blocks in this area that had grown up facing one another across the former no-man's land of a divided Berlin. Dominating the scheme is a slim, curved slab of a tower that links with the original block. An attractive streetfront is provided by a long, low structure extending to a small circular building. In the finished project these different elements come together to create an exciting conglomeration of buildings. The architectural styles of the 1950s and the 1990s co-exist in a way that respects the recent urban history of this part of Berlin while creating a striking new landmark for the future.

Altes und Neues stehen harmonisch nebeneinander. Der eleganten Verbindung bogenförmiger und gradliniger Formen gelingt es, das sanierte 50er-Jahre-Hochhaus als positives Element in die Gesamtanlage zu integrieren. Diese Ansicht verdeutlicht den positiven Beitrag der GSW-Zentrale zur urbanen Struktur dieses Viertels.

The old and the new stand harmoniously alongside one another. The elegant fusion of curvilinear and rectilinear shapes successfully integrates the refurbished 1950s block as a positive element in the overall scheme. This view clearly illustrates the positive contribution of the GSW HQ to the urban fabric of the neighbourhood.

Der Rundbau im Vordergrund fungiert als ungewöhnlicher Blickfang und optische Brücke zu den dahinterstehenden, höheren Bauten.

The small 'pillbox' building situated in the foreground functions as a novel kind of eye-catcher that provides a visual stepping-stone leading up to the taller structures behind.

Die roten Rouleaus des Turms werden von den einzelnen Nutzern der Büros bedient und sorgen so, gleichsam wie ein dynamisches Stadtgemälde, für das ständig wechselnde Erscheinungsbild der Außenhaut. Die natürliche Belüftung des Hochhauses wurde ökologischen Richtlinien entsprechend konzipiert; Frischluft zirkuliert dabei im Inneren der ein Meter tiefen, doppelschaligen Konvektionsfassade. Zwischen den zwei Glasschichten entsteht ein Sog, der verbrauchte Luft quer durch das Gebäude aus den Büros zieht.

The blinds of the tower, in varying shades of red, are controlled by the individual occupants of the offices so that the west façade changes constantly like a dynamic urban painting. The natural ventilation of the high-rise has been conceived along ecological lines with fresh air circulating inside a 1m-deep flue that acts like a thermal jacket.

Perspektivische Zeichnung: GSW-Zentrale im Verhältnis zu den anderen Bauten.
Perspective drawing shows GSW in relation to other blocks.

»Wir sahen einen langgestreckten, niedrigen Bauteil mit Läden und Restaurants vor, um den Straßenpassanten wieder das Gefühl städtischen Lebens zu vermitteln.« Louisa Hutton

'We included a long, low building with shops and restaurants to give back city life to people walking along the street.' Louisa Hutton

AGIPLAN ZENTRALSTELLE, MÜHLHEIM
AGIPLAN HEADQUARTERS, MÜHLHEIM

Foster and Partners, 1992–1996

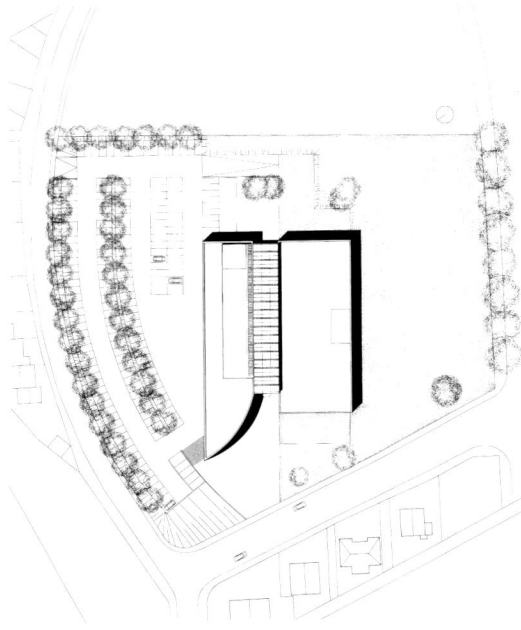

Lageplan. Site plan.

Die Erweiterung der Agiplan Zentralstelle in Mühlheim ist eines von mehreren Projekten, die Foster and Partners derzeit im Ruhrgebiet betreuen; die Region ist bestrebt, marode Industrieareale neu zu beleben und neue Architektur in vorhandene, bauliche Strukturen zu integrieren. Die Aufgabe bestand darin, ein bestehendes, vom Firmengründer entworfenes, relativ modernes Gebäude aus den siebziger Jahren durch neuen Büroraum zu erweitern; zwischen den beiden Gebäudeteilen entstünde so ein zentraler Bereich, der für Angestellte und Öffentlichkeit zum Dreh- und Angelpunkt der Firma werden sollte. Der 5200 m² umfassende Anbau verhilft Agiplan durch seine ausschwingende, gebogene Fassade zu einem dynamischen öffentlichen Erscheinungsbild sowie zu einem neuen Eingang. Das Gebäude vereint sämtliche, zuvor in der ganzen Region verstreuten Abteilungen von Agiplan unter einem Dach. Es gibt darin Großraum- und Einzelbüros, eine Galerie sowie eine Bibliothek mit Atrium, in dem wechselnde Ausstellungen Platz finden, eine Cafeteria für die Belegschaft und einen Empfangsbereich. Planungsraster und Geschoßhöhen des neuen Gebäudes entsprechen denen des alten. Der Neubau wird über seine Peripherie mit Frischluft versorgt; die Abluft wird energiesparend über das Atrium extrahiert. Durch den Gebrauch von Sonnenschutzverglasung und Doppelfenstern mit im Zwischenraum integrierten Jalousien werden die Folgen von Sonneneinstrahlung wie Blendung und Überhitzung minimiert. An der Nordseite verhilft die transparente Wärmeisolierung den dahinterliegenden Einraumbüros zu bestmöglichem Tageslicht.

The new addition to the Agiplan headquarters in Mülheim is one of several projects by Foster and Partners in the Ruhr which seek to revitalise depressed industrial areas and integrate new architecture into the older building fabric. The challenge was how to extend an existing relatively modern 1970s building, designed by Agiplan's founder, and to create new office areas with a central space between the two wings which could become the heart and focus of the company for both staff and the public. The 5,200m² addition has a sweeping curved façade, which gives Agiplan a dynamic public face and a new entrance. The building brings together under one roof all the firm's departments previously scattered around the region. It provides flexible and cellular offices, a gallery and library plus an atrium accommodating temporary exhibitions, a staff cafeteria and reception area. The planning grid and floor heights of the new building match those of the old. The building is naturally ventilated along its perimeter. Return air is extracted via the atrium space, which helps to reduce energy consumption. Solar glare and gain are minimised with the use of sun protection glazing and double glazed panels with integral louvres in the cavity. On the north façade, transparent thermal insulation maximises daylight into the cellular offices behind.

Die genaue Grenzlinie zwischen Alt und Neu ist auf dem Grundriß erkennbar. Die Transparenz des verglasten Zwischenstücks erlaubt interessante Einblicke in Büros und öffentliche Räume. Das Atrium ist mit Eichenparkett, die Büroetagen mit leuchtend blauem Teppichboden ausgestattet.

The precise demarcation between old and new is visible on the plan. The transparency of the glazed structure permits interesting views into the offices and public spaces. The atrium has an oak parquet floor, while the office areas have a vibrant blue carpet.

Grundriß erstes Obergeschoß. First-floor plan.

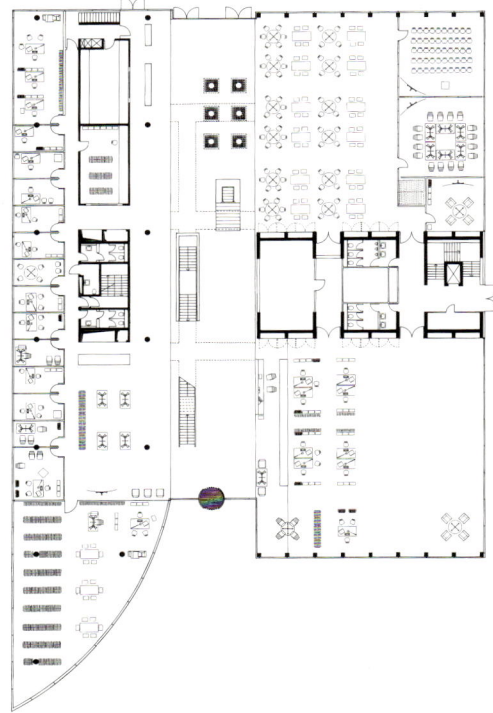

Handel und Verwaltung Commerce and Administration

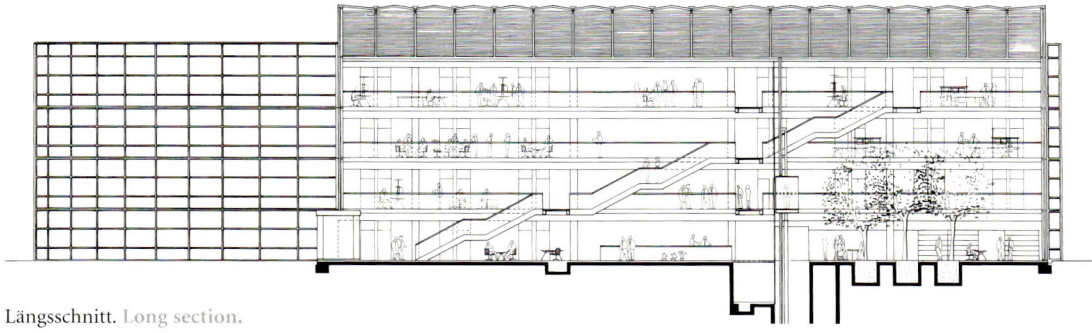
Längsschnitt. Long section.

Ein imposantes, 18 m hohes Atrium verbindet den alten und neuen Gebäudeteil auf allen oberen Stockwerken durch Laufstege sowie durch eine den ganzen Raum durchziehende, eindrucksvolle Treppe. Das Glasdach läßt Tageslicht in die benachbarten Büros fallen. Die jetzt atriumseitige Fassade des alten Flügels wurde komplett entfernt und durch eine gläserne Balustrade ersetzt, die der des neuen Anbaus gleicht.

A dramatic 18m-high atrium links the old and the new wings with walkways on each of the upper floors and a striking staircase cascading down from top to bottom. The glazed roof allows daylight to penetrate the adjacent offices. The façade of the old wing, now on the atrium side, has been entirely removed and replaced by a glass balustrade mirroring that of the new addition.

ABBILDUNGSNACHWEIS
PHOTOGRAPHIC ACKNOWLEDGEMENTS

DANKSAGUNG
ACKNOWLEDGEMENTS

r: rechts right / l: links left / t: oben top / b: unten bottom / m: Mitte middle

2, Dennis Gilbert; 6, 7, Peter Cook; 10, b r, from: The Building News, 187, II, p. 169, in: *Das Englische Vorbild*, Munich: Prestel, 1974; 11, t l, AKG London; 12, t r, AKG London; 13, t, Michael Jenner; 13, b, SMPK, Nationalgalerie, Berlin; 14, t, AKG London; 15, t, AKG London; 16, t, Michael Jenner; 16, b, Michael Jenner; 17, t, Michael Jenner; 18, t l, Marlies Hentrup; 18, t r, Richard Bryant; 19, t, Dennis Gilbert; 20, b, British Embassy, Berlin; 21, b, Dennis Gilbert; 22, b, Aleksander M. Perkovic; 23, t, Deutsche Bundespost; 24, t, Valerie Bennett/Arcaid; 24, b, David Chipperfield Architects, 25, b, Dan Stevens; 25, b, Steve Double; 26, b, Udo Hesse; 27, Roderick Coyne; 27, t, Rudi Meisel; 31, Richard Bryant; 32, t, Foster and Partners; 32, m, Richard Davies; 32, b, Richard Davies; 33, t, Nigel Young; 33, b, Dennis Gilbert; 34, t, Dennis Gilbert; 34, m, Sir Norman Foster; 34, b, Dennis Gilbert; 35, Nigel Young; 36, Dennis Gilbert; 37, Nigel Young; 38, Foster and Partners; 39, Dennis Gilbert; 40, t, Dennis Gilbert; 40, m, Dennis Gilbert; 40, b, Dennis Gilbert; 41, t, Dennis Gilbert; 41, m, Nigel Young; 41, b, Dennis Gilbert; 42, t, Richard Bryant; 42, b, James Stirling, Michael Wilford & Assoc.; 43, Richard Bryant/Arcaid; 44, l, Alastair Hunter; 44, r, Richard Bryant; 45, t, Richard Bryant; 45, m, Richard Bryant; 45, b, Richard Bryant; 45, l m, James Stirling, Michael Wilford & Assoc.; 46, Richard Bryant; 47, Richard Bryant; 48, James Stirling, Michael Wilford & Assoc.; 49, Richard Bryant; 50, l, Richard Bryant; 50, r, James Stirling, Michael Wilford & Assoc.; 51, Richard Bryant; 52, l, Christian Richters; 52 r, Zaha M. Hadid; 53, t, Helene Binet; 53, b, Zaha M. Hadid; 54, t, Helene Binet; 54, b l, Zaha M. Hadid; 54, b r, Zaha M. Hadid; 55, t, Helene Binet; 55, b, Zaha M. Hadid; 56, Helene Binet; 57, t l, Helene Binet; 57, t r, Christian Richters; 57, m, Christian Richters; 57, b, Christian Richters; 58, l, Richard Bryant; 58, r, James Stirling, Michael Wilford & Assoc.; 59, t, Richard Bryant; 59, b, Richard Bryant; 60, Richard Bryant; 61, James Stirling, Michael Wilford & Assoc.; 62, Richard Bryant; 63, Richard Bryant; 64, Roderick Coyne; 65, t, Roderick Coyne; 65, m r, Alsop & Störmer; 65, b l, Roderick Coyne; 66, l, Roderick Coyne; 66, r, Roderick Coyne; 67, Roderick Coyne; 68, t, Peter Cook; 68, b, Peter Cook; 69, t, Peter Cook; 69, b, Peter Cook; 70, t, Peter Cook; 70, b l, Peter Cook; 70, b r, Peter Cook; 71, Peter Cook; 72, Peter Cook; 73, t, Peter Cook; 73, b, Peter Cook; 74, l, Peter Cook; 74, r, Peter Cook; 75, Peter Cook; 76, t, Laurie Abbott, Richard Rogers Partnership; 76, b, Richard Rogers Partnership; 77, Katsuhisa Kida; 78, t, Katsuhisa Kida; 78, b l, Katsuhisa Kida; 78, b r, Katsuhisa Kida; 79, Katsuhisa Kida; 80, t, Katsuhisa Kida; 81, t, Katsuhisa Kida; 81, b, Laurie Abbott, Richard Rogers Partnership, 82, Foster and Partners; 83, t, Dennis Gilbert; 83, b, Foster and Partners; 84, t l, Foster and Partners; 84, b l, Dennis Gilbert; 84/85, Dennis Gilbert; 86, t, Stefan Müller; 86, b, David Chipperfield Architects; 87, t, Stefan Müller; 87, b, Stefan Müller; 88, t l, Stefan Müller; 88, m r, Stefan Müller; 88, b, David Chipperfield Architects; 89, t r, Stefan Müller; 89, m l, Stefan Müller; 89, b r, David Chipperfield Architects; 90, Bitter + Bredt Fotografie, Berlin; 91, Bitter + Bredt Fotografie, Berlin; 91, Sauerbruch Hutton Architects; 92/93, Bitter + Bredt Fotografie, Berlin; 94, t, Sauerbruch Hutton Architects; 94, b, Bitter + Bredt Fotografie, Berlin; 95, t, Bitter + Bredt Fotografie, Berlin; 95, m, Bitter + Bredt Fotografie, Berlin; 95, b, Sauerbruch Hutton Architects; 96, l, Richard Bryant; 96, b, James Stirling, Michael Wilford & Assoc.; 97, Richard Bryant; 98, t, Richard Bryant; 98, b, Richard Bryant ; 99, t, James Stirling, Michael Wilford & Assoc.; 99, b, Richard Bryant; 100, t, Werner Huthmacher; 100, b, Nicholas Grimshaw & Partners; 101, Werner Huthmacher; 102/3, Werner Huthmacher; 104, l, Zaha M. Hadid; 104, r, Christian Richters; 105, t, Zaha M. Hadid; 105, b, Christian Richters; 106, t, Christian Richters; 106, b, Helene Binet; 107, l, Helene Binet; 107, r, Helene Binet; 108, t l, Christian Richters; 108, m r, Zaha M. Hadid; 108, b l, Christian Richters; 109, Christian Richters; 110, t, Richard Bryant; 110, b, Michael Wilford; 111, Richard Bryant; 112, t, Michael Wilford & Partners; 112, b l, Richard Bryant; 112, b r, Richard Bryant; 113, t, Michael Wilford & Partners; 113, b l, Richard Bryant; 113, b r, Richard Bryant; 114, t, Reid & Peck; 114, b, Nicholas Grimshaw & Partners; 115, l, Reid & Peck; 115, r, Reid & Peck; 116, l, Nicholas Grimshaw & Partners; 116/17, Reid & Peck; 118, Roderick Coyne; 119, t, Roderick Coyne; 119, b, Alsop & Störmer; 120/121, Roderick Coyne; 121, t r, Alsop & Störmer; 121, b r, Roderick Coyne; 122, © Willebrand; 123, t, © Willebrand; 123, b, Nicholas Grimshaw & Partners; 124, t r, © Willebrand; 124, b r, Nicholas Grimshaw & Partners; 124, b l, © Willebrand; 125, t, © Willebrand; 125, b, © Willebrand; 126, © Willebrand; 127, © Willebrand; 128, t, © Willebrand; 128, b, Nicholas Grimshaw & Partners; 129, l, © Willebrand; 129, r, © Willebrand; 130, b l, Julia Oppermann; 130, t r, David Chipperfield Architects; 131, Julia Oppermann; 132, t l, Julia Oppermann; 132, t r, Julia Oppermann; 132, b, David Chipperfield Architects; 133, t r, Julia Oppermann; 133, b l, Julia Oppermann; 134, l, Katsuhisa Kida; 134, r, Richard Rogers Partnership; 135, James Morris; 136, Katsuhisa Kida; 137, Katsuhisa Kida; 138, t, Katsuhisa Kida; 138, b, Katsuhisa Kida; 139, l, James Morris; 139, r, Richard Rogers Partnership; 140, Foster and Partners; 141, l, Ian Lambot; 141, t r, Ian Lambot; 141, b r, Ian Lambot; 142, t l, Ian Lambot; 142, m l, Ian Lambot; 142, b l, Ian Lambot; 142, r, Foster and Partners; 143, Ian Lambot; 144, t, Sir Norman Foster; 144, b, Ian Lambot; 145, t l, Nigel Young; 145, b l, Foster and Partners; 145, t r, Nigel Young; 145, m r, Nigel Young; 145, b r, Ian Lambot; 146, Jocelyne Van den Bossche; 147, t, Jocelyne Van den Bossche; 147, b, Ian Ritchie Architects; 148, t, Ian Ritchie Architects; 148, b, Jocelyne Van den Bossche; 149, Jocelyne Van den Bossche; 150, Jocelyne Van den Bossche; 151, t r, Jocelyne Van den Bossche; 151, m, Ian Ritchie Architects; 151, b, Jocelyne Van den Bossche; 152, Sauerbruch Hutton Architects; 153, t, Bitter + Bredt Fotografie, Berlin; 153, b, Bitter + Bredt Fotografie, Berlin; 154, Bitter + Bredt Fotografie, Berlin; 155, l, Sauerbruch Hutton Architects; 155, r, Annette Kisling 156, Foster and Partners; 157, t l, Klaus Ravenstein; 157, b l, Nigel Young; 157, b r, Foster and Partners; 158, Nigel Young; 159, t, Nigel Young; 159, b, Foster and Partners

Diese Publikation wurde durch die freundliche Zusammenarbeit mit den folgenden Architekturbüros ermöglicht:
This book has been made possible through the kind co-operation of the architects whose names head the practices of:
Alsop & Störmer
David Chipperfield Architects
Foster and Partners
Nicholas Grimshaw & Partners
Zaha M. Hadid
Ian Ritchie Architects
Richard Rogers Partnership
Sauerbruch Hutton Architects
Michael Wilford and Partners

Unser Dank gilt ferner:
The following individuals also helped in a variety of ways:
Lawrence Abbott, Isabel Allen, James Allen, Marta Badia-Martin, Christian Bahr, Florian Beigel, Kate Bennett, Mark Braun, Christian Brensing, Rainer Büchel, Frank Burbach, Eric Cain, Eric Callway, Donnathea Campbell, Roger Dawe, Jo Dawes, Thomas Deuble, Wolfgang Dobler, Keith Dobson, Markus Dochantschi, Peter Dupont, Stefan Gerstner, Romaine Govett, David Grieve, Sue Hargreaves, Isabelle Hartmann, Jackie Hawkins, Anthony Hoyte, Rebecca Hudson, Birgit Ihlau, Achim Jaeger, David Jenkins, Derek Jones, James Leatham, Kate Lee, Michael Lommertz, Fred London, Malcolm McGregor, Gillian McInnes, Roomana Mahmud, Corinna Mehldau, Alp Mehmet, Eddie Miles, Julia Moran, Beth Morgan, Sophie Murphy, Margit Naundorf, Jane Oldfield, Laura Parker, Bill and Mona Paton, Alicia Pau, Richard Paul, Kerstin Piontek, Uwe Rainer Prim, Josef Rahmen, Henning Rambow, Elke Ritt, Fionnula Russell, Helle Schimitzek, Neven Sidor, Lucien Smith, Michael Smith, James Soane, Michael Stiff, Karin Storz, Ivonne Strachwitz, John Thompson, Georg Thurn, Trevor Todd, Robert Torday, Elizabeth Walker, Roswitha Wenzl, Stephen Whittle, Ania Wilder-Mintzer, Tim Williams, Tina Wilson, Mike Wood, Nicole Woodman, Ute Wüest von Vellberg, Juan Lucas Young.

Herzlich gedankt sei auch all den Photographen, die im Abbildungsnachweis einzeln erwähnt sind.
The important contribution of all the photographers listed in the photographic acknowledgements is gratefully received.

Unser Dank gilt natürlich auch den Mitarbeitern der British Library, des RIBA und des Deutschen Historischen Institutes.
Thanks are also due to the staff at the British Library, RIBA and German Historical Institute.